From Parents to Partners

From Parents to Partners

Building a *Family-Centered* Early Childhood Program

Janis Keyser

 Redleaf Press
www.redleafpress.org

 naeyc

Published by Redleaf Press
a division of Resources for Child Caring
10 Yorkton Court
St. Paul, MN 55117
Visit us online at www.redleafpress.org.

National Association for the
Education of Young Children
1313 L Street NW, Suite 500
Washington, DC 20005
NAEYC order number 2004

First edition 2006
Cover photographs by Bonnie Aldridge and Janis Keyser.
Interior typeset in Centaur MT
Interior photos by Bonnie Aldridge and Janis Keyser.
Printed in the United States of America
13 12 11 10 09 08 07 06   1 2 3 4 5 6 7 8

Redleaf Press books are available at a special discount when purchased in bulk for special premiums and sales promotions. Contact the sales manager at 800-423-8309 for details.

Library of Congress Cataloging-in-Publication Data

Keyser, Janis.
    From parents to partners : building a family-centered early childhood program / Janis Keyser.
      p. cm.
    Includes index.
    ISBN-13: 978-1-929610-88-4
    ISBN-10: 1-929610-88-2
  1. Early childhood education--Parent participation. I. Title.
    LB1139.35.P37K49 2006
    372.21--dc22
                                                            2006014094

Printed on acid-free paper.

This book is dedicated to the teachers and parents in my classes who have so generously shared their insights, perspectives, challenges, frustrations, successes, and stories.

Contents

From Parents to Partners

Acknowledgments

My son told me a few years ago, "You know, Mom? Gratefulness is a gift to the person who holds it." In this case I am a deeply gifted individual. I am grateful to the families I have known over my years of teaching for persisting with me even when I wasn't listening well and for sharing their knowledge and vulnerability with me and each other.

I want to thank the teachers who offered their expertise for this book: Arlae Gomez, who taught me about truly supporting families at pick-up time; Bonnie Aldridge, who has never met a parent or child she didn't love; Eddie Jobe, for his enthusiasm and dedication; Jill Golsh, for her delight in children's discovery; Lupe Cortes, for her optimism and support of parents and students; Luz Marina Cardona, for her unwavering commitment to honoring family culture and language; Mayo Cruz, for the way he honors the truth; Nancy Spangler, who lives family-centered care every day in her classroom; Vicki Neville Coffis, for her insightful sense of humor; Amy Rather, who deeply respects children and families; Bethany Kientzel, who truly partners with families; Claudia Vestal for her model and her mentorship of family child care providers; Kathy Newman, who really understands the family network; Margarita Castro, for her ability to understand family expertise; and Tricia Pastor, for bringing family partnership into after-school care.

Thank you to the children and families from Cabrillo College Children's Center. Thanks to Leslie Cheung and Jo-Ann Panzardi for their parent perspectives on the partnership. My admiration goes out to the administrative staff of the children's center for their respect and nurturing of families from the beginning: Gloria Valencia, Raneta Schreiner, Arriba Alston-Williams, and Christina Lee.

I am grateful to my colleagues in the Early Childhood Education Department at Cabrillo College for providing a community that nurtures and inspires teachers, as well as students and children, to grow: Julie Edwards for infusing respect for families into every aspect of our curriculum and work; Nancy K. Brown for the heart she brings to our work; Ofelia Garcia for creatively building bridges for families and students; Michelle de la Selva Patterson Chao for insisting that we walk the talk; Eric Hoffman for creatively partnering with families in the classroom; Lenore Kenny for her commitment to justice; Consuelo Espinosa for gently guiding and supporting us to reach our shared vision.

I am continually inspired and encouraged by people and organizations in our profession: Janet Gonzalez-Mena, Peter Mangione, Ron Lally, the Program for Infant/Toddler Caregivers, Mary Smithberger, Rebeca Valdivia, the Family Partnership Institute, and the FPI training team.

Thanks to the students in my Working with Families classes who continuously provide ideas, examples, and insight.

My deep gratitude goes to Bonnie Aldridge for her wonderful photos of children, families, and teachers.

Thanks to Laura Davis, who has taught me so much about writing and contributed her insight to this book.

I am grateful to Cabrillo College, the Board of Trustees, and the Sabbatical Review Board for supporting the sabbatical to write this book.

I am especially grateful to my children, Lee, Calvin, and Maya, who continually help me understand what it is to be a parent, provide listening and insight, nurture my optimism, and remind me about a parent's ability to keep growing. I am forever grateful to their dad, Leon, who taught me that every human being is precious.

Thanks to Jake, Leny, and Juli, who have generously shared their TV room with my office, and to Pete, who keeps my home fires burning and my eyes open to the natural world.

I am grateful to Beth Wallace, my editor, for providing the spark and carefully nurturing the flame of this book. Her vision, intelligence, guidance, and support have been invaluable to me.

Introduction

I remember the unbridled enthusiasm I brought to my first preschool teaching job more than thirty years ago. I was so excited to be working with children, and I was intent on saving the world through my work. I began to get a little discouraged when Christopher's dad didn't want him wearing a dress in the fantasy area and when Araceli's grandmother brought her to school dressed for a party every day. Soon parents became my project. How could I convince them that they should be more like me? Now I can't even imagine what my conversations with those parents sounded like. I probably owe each of them an apology, but more than that, I owe them my gratitude for sticking with me and helping me learn about the strength, wisdom, experience, love, and investment each of them brought to parenting.

Most teachers are drawn to the profession because of their love for children and their skill in working with them, but almost all of us have discovered that working with children's families is as much a part of our jobs as working with children. For most of us, this discovery has come in stages. The first stage of the developmental path many teachers have taken can be labeled "Save the child." Most of us have had the experience of knowing one or more children we wanted to take home with us. "If I could just save this child from her parents, her life would be much better." After our imaginary houses were filled with numerous children, we discovered the need to come up with a new paradigm. The second developmental stage is "Save the parents." If we can't rescue all the children from their parents, we can at least teach the parents everything we know about good child development practice so they can care for their children the same way we do. While this kind of thinking has some merit, it fails to acknowledge the gifts, resources, goals, and culture that all parents hold for their children. The final developmental stage in this theory is "Partnership with families." This is where we acknowledge that both teachers and parents have the knowledge, expertise, experience, and resources that are needed for the best education, care, and support for every child (Gonzalez-Mena and Eyer 2004).

When I heard Ellen Galinsky talk about family-centered care in a keynote address several years ago, I finally had the words to describe what I had been discovering since my early days working with children and families. Families—not just children—are in the center of care, and as children's primary teachers and advocates, families are essential partners in the care and education of their children.

Our work with families evolves as we explore the implications of family-centered care. Our language has been changing as well. It is challenging to find language that includes and describes all families, genders, cultures, and abilities. In this book the term "family" is often used instead of "parent." This is an attempt to include *all* of the significant people who care for the child: aunts, uncles, grandparents, foster parents, older siblings, neighbors, adoptive parents, friends, and parents. The term "family" can be confusing in some contexts because it includes young siblings and others who might not need to be consulted or involved in events, such as an individual conference with the teacher. In these situations "parent" is used. When it is used, it refers to any and all people who are taking a primary care role with a child (outside of the child care setting). The terms "parent" and "family" are thus used somewhat interchangeably in the book.

Similarly, this book is intended for any person who cares for children in a professional way: teachers, family home child care providers, in-home child care providers, friends, neighbors, and relatives. Whenever the term "teacher" or "provider" is used, it refers to any of these people. The terms "school," "classroom," "child development program," and "program" are also used interchangeably and refer to any setting where child care and education are taking place.

The Reflection and Exercise boxes throughout the book are intended to help you connect with and understand the information in the book and apply it to your own thinking, practice, and experience. They are not formal exercises that you need to do exactly as they are written. Use and adapt them so that they will work for you. I encourage you to take some time with them because they are intended to make the book an interactive, hands-on learning experience, which we all know is the best way to learn. Enjoy!

REFERENCES

Gonzalez-Mena, Janet, and Dianne Widmeyer Eyer. 2004. *Infants, toddlers, and caregivers: A curriculum of respectful, responsive care and education*. 6th edition. New York: McGraw-Hill.

The Importance of Family-Teacher Partnerships

"It's all about relationships!" you might hear as you walk by a group of teachers attending a training workshop. This slogan should be the cheer for the early childhood profession, because it truly is the cornerstone of what we do well in our field. Early childhood teachers understand that creating relationships with children is essential to their practice. Teachers learn how to develop trust and attachment in their relationships with infants. With toddlers they create connections that promote children's budding sense of autonomy. Teachers form relationships with preschoolers that encourage children's initiative. From strong, trusting, responsive relationships between children and adults come cognitive development and literacy, social, and emotional development, as well as language and physical development. The critical nature of children's relationships with adults in their early development is highlighted by theorists such as Erik Erikson, who told us that the first human emotional milestone is the infant's trust and attachment to a caregiver (Erikson 1963), and Lev Vygotsky, who showed us how important social interactions are to children's developing thinking skills (Kearsley n.d.).

What is less obvious to the early education profession is the importance of another relationship in the lives of young children. The relationships that occur among the important adults in a child's life are as important as the relationships between a child and those adults. Children's emotional safety and sense of well-being are deeply affected by the adult relationships surrounding them. Children are also taking an intensive observation course on relationships: they learn how to communicate, express caring, solve problems, and work together from watching the adults around them. This course includes all the significant adults in a child's life, not just family members, and their relationships with one another. The relationships between a teacher and a child's family members have tremendous potential for affecting the life of a young child. Another early childhood theorist, Urie Bronfenbrenner, sheds light on this in his model of human ecology (Bronfenbrenner 1990). Bronfenbrenner says that people don't develop all on their own but that their development is affected by all the different systems they are a part of (such as their family, their school or educational program, their church, and so on) and also by the way those systems interact with one another. For this reason Bronfenbrenner sees the interactions between home and school as very important in the child's development. He advocates for building bridges between home and school that include "ongoing patterns of exchange of information, two-way communication, mutual accommodation, and mutual trust" (Bronfenbrenner 1990). What are children learning from the relationships they see between their early childhood caregivers and teachers, and their important family members?

Most of us remember the feelings we had watching our parents or other family members laugh, love, or argue together. For example, one teacher, Angelica, remembers fondly the times her parents sang together after all the children were in bed. "I would lie there listening to them sing, and I had the warmest, safest feeling." Another teacher, Chris, remembers the arguments his mother and grandmother had. "There would be a few short, sharp words, and then the air would be icy. You could feel the anger, but there weren't words for it. I felt scared as a child, but I didn't know what to say or who to turn to because my most important people weren't talking about it." When we read about these memories, it's easy to see how the interactions between these important family members affected the children involved, helping them feel either safe and comfortable or afraid and confused. What do you suppose the children learned about how to express love or anger? They possibly learned that love is expressed through doing things together, or that anger should only be expressed "nonverbally."

Here's another example: one parent, Tamara, remembers an encounter between her father and her kindergarten teacher. "My father walked me to school on my first day of kindergarten. When we got to the school, he went up to the teacher to introduce us. The teacher smiled at him and said, "Hello, Mr. Mendoza." I had never heard my father called 'Mr.' My father beamed, and I immediately fell in love with my teacher." Why do you think this interaction was so powerful for the child involved? What did the child learn about respectful relationships between adults? What did she learn about who was welcome at

her school? How do you think this relationship between her teacher and her family affected her learning? This example shows us how very important the relationships between teachers and parents are in the lives and success of children, and illustrates Bronfenbrenner's point. Where are we in the early childhood field in developing these sturdy bridges between home and school?

THE TEACHER'S PERSPECTIVE

While a few teachers are accomplished and experienced in building strong relationships with families, many teachers struggle with this essential task. Some feel competent working with children but lack the same confidence and experience working with adults; some are motivated to develop relationships with families but aren't sure where to begin; many have begun the process of building relationships and have come up against what feels like a dead end. Let's listen to some teachers.

"I have always wanted to work with children. It's the adults that are hard for me."

"I love working with children. They are so much more natural than grown-ups."

"I would love to have a meaningful relationship with each of the families in my program, but where would I get the time?"

"If I could just work with children and ignore their parents, I would have the perfect job."

"I know parents mean well, but they often just get in the way when I'm taking care of their kids."

"When I'm with the children, I know what I'm doing. When I'm with the parents, I feel tongue-tied."

"It's hard when the parents hang around in the classroom. I just want them to go, so I can teach."

"It seems like parents either ignore me or criticize what I am doing with their kids."

"I finally decided to post the parents' names by their children's cubby, so I could at least greet them by name in the morning."

"I love every other part of my job, but I'm terrified of the parent conferences and parent meetings."

These statements represent the feelings of many teachers, especially those who have been attracted to teaching by their interest in and love for children, not their desire to work with adults. Building relationships with children is different than building relationships with adults. Many excellent teachers struggle with even the simplest day-to-day communications with parents, and most of us have experienced the challenge of negotiating differing opinions, miscommunication, and misunderstandings with parents about the care and education of children.

REFLECTING ON YOUR FEELINGS ABOUT WORKING WITH FAMILIES

Use these questions to explore your feelings about working with families, and discuss your thoughts with coworkers or fellow students:

What are your feelings about working with families?

What do you enjoy about it, and what is hard?

What do you consider your strengths in working with families?

What do you hope to learn that will help you feel more comfortable and be more effective in working with families?

THE PARENT'S PERSPECTIVE

Like teachers, families have a range of feelings about their relationships with their children's teachers. Some families don't even consider that there could be a place for them at school; some would like to have a relationship with teachers but are uncertain about how to do it; some families have clear ideas of how they would like to be involved but perceive roadblocks in communication; and some are actively frustrated with their interactions with teachers. Here is what some parents have said about their connections with their children's teachers:

"I have so many questions for the teachers, but they seem so busy with the children, I don't feel like I should interrupt."

"There is one teacher that I can talk to about my child, but when she isn't there, I don't get any information."

"I often have information I want to tell the teacher about my child's needs or health or about what is happening in our family, but I can't figure out a good time to talk to him."

"I love spending time with my child in the program. I learn so much from watching the teachers and seeing what my child plays with and who her friends are, but I wonder if I'm in the way, if the teachers just want the school to be for the kids."

"I'm curious about what my child does there all day, but when I ask him, he says, 'Nothing,' and I never hear from the teachers."

"Sometimes I feel embarrassed when I'm in the classroom and my child is acting up. The teacher always seems to know what to say, and I'm afraid to open my mouth and sound stupid."

"I'd like to do a special activity with the kids, but I don't know how the school feels about parents in the classroom."

"I'd like to know more about the school, like their policies and what they are teaching the children, but I don't know who to ask."

"I told the morning teacher that my child needed to be taken to the toilet, but she didn't tell the afternoon teacher, so my child had an accident in the afternoon. I was really frustrated."

BUILDING BRIDGES: DO WE REALLY NEED THEM?

Sara Lawrence-Lightfoot writes, "There is no more complex and tender geography than the borderlands between families and schools" (2003). Is it really necessary for teachers to have good relationships with parents? What if teachers decide not to tread on the tender geography of family partnerships? Can't they just focus their energies on the children in their care and let parents worry about what happens at home? In fact, this is the way many good teachers have been doing it for years. But as we can see in the preceding examples, children, parents, and teachers all suffer when we fail to cross the borderlands and build the essential link between teachers and families. Children miss out on consistency of care and education and on the opportunity to see the people from two parts of their lives come together cooperatively for their benefit. Families don't experience the teacher's respect and support for their important role in the education of their children. These parents also miss the opportunity to partner with and learn from their children's teachers. Teachers who don't have ongoing mutually respectful relationships with families lose a crucial chance to learn about the children in their care. They miss the potential resources and information families can offer to help teachers do the best job possible. This missing knowledge and resources make their jobs more difficult and less rewarding. On the other hand, the benefits of family-teacher partnerships for children, teachers, and families make the learning, uncertainty, and challenges of building and nurturing those partnerships well worth the effort.

FROM RELATIONSHIP TO PARTNERSHIP

Partnerships are a unique kind of relationship. They are different from some of the relationships that currently exist between teachers and parents. A partnership is a relationship between equals; each person in a partnership is equally valued for his or her knowledge and contribution to the relationship. This doesn't mean that both partners bring exactly the same thing to the partnership. It means that each is respected for his or her unique contribution. In a partnership people are interested in understanding the other person's perspective, engaging in two-way communication, consulting with each other on important decisions, and respecting and working through differences of opinion. People in partnership often discover that working through these differences increases the trust in the relationship; they find that they are enriched by the experience of working toward shared visions and goals.

Most of us have "partnered" with families in one way or another. On one end of the continuum partnership may include teachers making simple requests of families like "Who can bring a piñata, make phone calls, wash the nap sheets, or fix the slide?" On this end of the continuum the teacher and program staff make most of the decisions, and parents are just responsible for choosing whether they can do a certain task. On the other end of the continuum families create and design the program, hire the teachers, and consult on all decisions—large and small—that affect the program. Between these points, along the continuum, are many ways for both families and teachers to use their initiative, share resources, and collaborate with each other. When families and teachers truly team up, it can provide benefits for everyone: children, parents, teachers, and the program. Partnerships provide teachers and families an ally, a listening ear, acknowledgment for their important work, and information to help them do a better job. At first it is easy to see how this kind of partnership can benefit children. What is less obvious is how it benefits parents and even teachers. Ultimately, it benefits the program and the larger community as well because it is the basis for larger networks of support. Are you interested yet? Read on for more information about those benefits.

> ### REFLECTING ON WHAT YOU KNOW ABOUT THE BENEFITS OF FAMILY-TEACHER PARTNERSHIPS
>
> Think of ways a family-teacher partnership might benefit children, parents, and caregivers. Make a separate list for each group. Share your lists with your coworkers or your fellow students, and compare it to the lists here. Did you come up with ideas that aren't included on this list? Discuss.

How Do Children Benefit?

What do children learn from the teacher-parent relationship? What do children learn if the relationships between their teachers and parents are supportive, respectful, nurturing, and communicative? The benefits for children of partnerships between home and school fall into the two main categories we discussed at the beginning of the chapter:

◆ Children's emotional environment is conducive to learning.
◆ Children's own social development is modeled on healthy relationships.

Children learn about themselves and take cues for their own behavior from the relationships around them. Young children experience the relationships around them from an egocentric perspective; they assume that everything they see and hear is about them. They don't differentiate between what the world thinks about their family and what the world thinks about them. They naturally see themselves as an extension of their parents and family. When their parents are honored, as in Tamara's story above, they feel honored. Watching their parents interact with the teacher communicates to the child whether the teacher is a

person the child can feel safe with. The more comfortable the parent feels with the teacher, the more permission the child will have to develop a trusting relationship with the teacher. As we have learned from Erikson, a trusting relationship with the teacher and a safe emotional environment are essential for children to develop and learn.

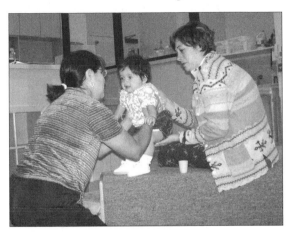

One of the most important developmental tasks of young children is to develop social relationships with other people. Through watching adults in relationship with one another, children see social, communication, and problem-solving skills modeled. This is how they learn how to be with other people, both peers their own age and other adults. Watching the adult relationships around them, children see what to expect in their own relationships. Through watching adult relationships, children can learn effective or ineffective communication skills; they can learn that differences of opinion can be talked about and resolved, unsuccessfully argued about, or ignored; they learn the nuances of what respect or disrespect looks like in relationships with other people.

Children learn from all aspects of the adult relationships around them—not just from spoken words but from the body language, tones of voice, and facial expressions of the adults involved.

They pay attention to the tone of a conversation as much as they do to the words. They watch how far apart people stand when they are talking. They watch how a person's face looks when they are in conversation. They might not have words to describe it, but they know exactly how much respect and appreciation exists in all the significant relationships around them. When teachers develop respectful, caring relationships with children's families, children notice and benefit.

How Do Families Benefit?

Families are also beneficiaries when teachers and parents engage in effective relationships. They benefit through having information, resources and referrals, acknowledgment, support, listening, empathy, and someone to share the tender and tough moments. Family also benefit because, through this partnership, they can leave their child in care with a feeling of security and confidence.

◆ Through their interactions with teachers, parents have access to information about child development and teaching strategies.

I was so worried that my two-year-old was going to grow up to be a criminal. He was always taking other kids' toys. He didn't care about the toy he had. He just wanted the one the other kid had. But his teacher kept explaining to me that he was just trying to play with the other kids. We discussed and tried out some helpful ways to respond to him, and, sure enough, he is now the kid everyone wants to play with.

◆ Families can receive acknowledgment for the important yet sometimes invisible work they do as children's first teachers.

I always talk to my daughter. When we go on a walk or to the store or on the bus, we are continually talking. We talk about what we see, we ask questions, and we tell stories. When her teacher saw us one day having a conversation in the garden at school, she told me that I was helping my daughter learn a wonderful vocabulary, which *would help her learn to read. I felt so proud that I was helping my child learn. I thought only teachers did that.*

◆ Parents have a sounding board, support, and referrals to resources when they feel challenged.

"When my four-year-old was still in diapers, I was desperate. I asked her teacher for help. He listened to all my concerns, strategies, and observations. Then he gave me some articles and the name of a pediatrician who had helped several children with toileting. He also asked if I would like another parent who had gone through this to call me. It felt so good for him to listen to my story, and I was so relieved that there were resources out there I could use.

◆ Parents can share their child's joys and accomplishments as well as struggles and sorrows with teachers who care deeply about their children.

When my child took her first step, I called my mother. Then I immediately thought, "I need to call her teacher."

◆ Finally, parents who have a trusting and respectful relationship with their child's teacher can leave their child in care with a feeling of confidence and security.

When he is with Bethany, I feel totally confident that he will be well taken care of. I know Bethany as a person. She cares about him like I do!

Partnerships with teachers offer families unique resources and give support that most families don't find elsewhere. These essential, readily and regularly available relationships help break the isolation some parents feel, by offering them a true partner in the care and education of their child.

How Do Teachers Benefit?

It seems obvious that children and families benefit from increased partnerships between parents and teachers. This alone might make it the right thing to do, but in a profession in which teachers are almost always underpaid and overextended, it can be hard to take on a new challenge if it seems that it benefits everyone else. The good news is that children and families aren't the only ones who benefit from successful teacher-family relationships. A teacher's quality of life increases significantly when school-home bridges are built. Here are some of the benefits for teachers:

◆ Partnerships with families provide opportunities for parents to learn about, acknowledge, and appreciate the significant work teachers do with children. Often the work of teachers is "invisible," just like the work parents do with children.

I started simply at pick-up time telling the parents some short observation about their child's day. They were so responsive. Suddenly, I felt like I was getting some appreciation for the hard work I do all day.

◆ When parents share their knowledge of their children and family, teachers can understand children and families better. This understanding helps teachers develop a program and curriculum that better meets the needs of each child, and gives teachers a wonderful sense of job satisfaction.

When I started making an effort to speak to every parent at drop-off and pick-up time every day, I felt so much more comfortable. I no longer dreaded seeing parents, and I realized that parents were giving information to me about their child and family that I had no idea about. I feel like I know these children so much better, having had this opportunity to talk with their parents, and this information has changed my curriculum and the way I interact with these children. I can see right away the difference it makes for children. I love my job!

◆ Successful communication with families helps teachers feel more effective and confident.

I knew I should be communicating with parents, but it is so hard for me to talk to adults, so I started with a daily "news flash board." Every day I listed several activities we did that day. Parents started coming up to me, asking me about the activities and thanking me for the information! It was a great way for me to start communication with them.

◆ Many teachers experience the satisfaction of children's increased trust in them as communication increases with families.

Ever since I started talking to Yvette's grandmother, I've noticed that Yvette really seeks me out when she needs help. I think she appreciates the bond she sees developing between me and her grandmother.

◆ Facing the challenges in our relationships with parents helps deepen our connection and trust with them. When teachers solve difficult issues with families, they are less afraid and find it easier and more enjoyable to interact with those families.

I have good relationships with most of the parents in my program, but there are a few who either avoid me or are "needy" all the time. I decided to approach my "difficult" parents and ask each of them for a suggestion of how we could improve our communication. I was amazed at the simple, specific suggestions that most gave me. Even the ones who said, "I don't know" have been more responsive since I asked the question. I find myself looking forward to our check-ins now.

◆ Families can provide crucial resources to the program through their ideas, expertise, materials, volunteer energy, and community connections.

The other day I was trying to put together a camping curriculum, and I just mentioned in passing to a parent that I was looking for small tents. She said she had a couple I could use, and then she got so excited about the curriculum that she offered to bring in some camping pictures and equipment we could use. She even called another parent to ask if they had some old flashlights to donate. I keep forgetting what incredible resources families are to our program. Somehow, I always think I have to do everything myself.

As these teachers' stories show, when they began to enter into partnerships with families, their jobs became easier. The interactions they had found to be intimidating weren't so scary anymore. They experienced more support from families for their program and for their teaching, and they felt more connections to families and children. It was easier for them to do good work with children, and that made them enjoy their jobs more. These are the benefits for teachers of creating partnerships with families.

REFLECTING ON WHAT YOU KNOW ABOUT BUILDING PARTNERSHIPS

Write down your thoughts about these questions, or discuss them with coworkers or fellow students:

In what ways are you already partnering with families?

In what ways would you like to further build partnerships with families?

Do you have questions, worries, or concerns about building partnerships with families?

It is clear that children, teachers, and families all benefit from strong school-home relationships. What can teachers do to create these kinds of bonds? Remember that people in the early childhood field are skilled at relationship building. We know how to successfully engage with children, and we are also experienced at facilitating children's relationships with each other. As different as adult relationships are, they are based on the same solid set of skills you already use every day with children: using two-way communication, listening, observing, nurturing, teaching, learning, empathizing, learning about the other person's

perspective and experience, imagining the other person's healthy intention, communicating one's own needs, working toward a balance of needs, setting positive limits, using redirection, offering choices, brainstorming, and negotiating solutions to problems. You can adapt and apply these skills to building effective relationships with the families of the children in your care. This book will help you.

FAMILY-CENTERED CARE: THE KEY TO PARTNERSHIPS

The goal in creating relationships with families is to build respectful and mutual partnerships. Partnerships enrich both teachers' and families' relationships with children and bring together their mutual expertise for the benefit of the child. Family-centered care provides the base upon which partnerships can thrive. As the name implies, in family-centered care, relationships with families are acknowledged as central to good care and education for young children. Five characteristics of family-centered programs make them different from other early childhood programs.

In family-centered early childhood programs, teachers and families

- recognize and respect one another's knowledge and expertise
- share information through two-way communication
- share power and decision making
- acknowledge and respect diversity
- create networks of support.

Recognizing and Respecting One Another's Knowledge and Expertise

Families and teachers care deeply for children. Families are children's first, primary, and most enduring teachers and advocates. Teachers are dedicated to providing the best care and education they can for each child. Families and teachers bring their own vision, hopes, knowledge, and resources to their relationships with children and with one another. In family-centered care parents and teachers share mutual respect and truly value the expertise, experience, skills, and perspective that each person brings to the partnership.

Sharing Information through Two-Way Communication

Two-way communication is a cornerstone of family-centered care. It is a key factor in turning a relationship into a partnership. In every partnership each participant brings resources, knowledge, and values. In the family-teacher partnership families know things about their children that teachers don't know but that are essential for teachers to learn in order to provide children the best care possible. Teachers have education and experience in child development and working with children that families don't necessarily have and that can be helpful to families in understanding and teaching their children. Two-way communication supports the partnership by providing essential information to both people and also by conveying mutual respect.

Sharing Power and Decision Making

In order for the partnership between families and teachers to work effectively, both members of the team need to understand the essential role that families as well as teachers play in making decisions about children's education. This idea can be challenging for teachers who worry that if families are empowered in this way, teachers will lose their authority, philosophy, or program. Some teachers have experienced families as demanding or critical or have felt that families had "way too much" power, but sharing power and decision making doesn't mean that families make all the decisions. Instead, it means that families are empowered to be significant partners with teachers and programs in making the best educational

and care decisions for their children.

Families don't always naturally see themselves as their children's primary teachers. Because parenting has historically been an "invisible" job, neither parents nor the surrounding community routinely notices all of the teaching, guiding, nurturing, and advocating families do for children. In addition, child development research, expert opinion, and subsequent consumer pressure to buy all of the newest products to maximize a child's potential can make families feel ill-equipped in their role as children's primary teachers, mentors, and guides. While teachers are not responsible for a parent's sense of empowerment, they are positioned wonderfully to help facilitate parents' understanding of the important role they play in their children's lives. Teachers can listen to parents' challenges, support parents' efforts, acknowledge parents' competence on a daily basis, and invite families to share decisions about their children's care and education.

Acknowledging and Respecting Diversity

The children and families and staff members in early childhood programs belong to many different cultures, ethnicities, family structures, and socioeconomic classes. They may speak languages other than English and have a variety of physical abilities and gender roles. In family-centered care each child and family is acknowledged, appreciated, and included. Acknowledging diversity involves learning about each child, family, and teacher. Respecting diversity means being able to honor ways of being and doing things that are different from one's own, even practices that may feel wrong when we first come into contact with them. Learning to respect diversity and include all families is a worthwhile journey that includes self-reflection and self-knowledge as well as learning about others. This journey exposes us to a variety of viewpoints, ideas, and ways of life. It opens doors to new relationships and ways of thinking. When families and teachers feel known and respected for who they are, they can create trusting and authentic partnerships with each other.

Creating Networks of Support

A network is a system of connections and relationships in a group of people that provides help, information, and support to each of its members. In a child care setting a network includes family members as well as teachers, staff and administrators, and the surrounding community. Networks broaden the pool of assets and connections in a child care setting and provide families a wide range of resources. Contemporary families face many challenges in raising healthy children. They may need a variety of services and information, including counseling, job training and referral, social services, transportation, parenting and child development information, housing referrals, addiction services, respite care, crisis support, education, child care, and others. Most teachers want to be helpful to families and can also feel overwhelmed in the face of families' needs.

Sometimes teachers feel as if it is their job to provide all the help that everyone needs. Teachers enter the education profession because they genuinely like to help people, and teaching and caring for young children are some of the best ways to truly serve humankind. However, when teachers expect themselves to meet all of the needs of children and families, they may begin to feel inadequate. Interestingly, our drive to "do it all" may inadvertently prevent other people from experiencing the joy and feeling of accomplishment that comes from being the "helper." Teachers have a unique opportunity to be a resource to the people in their child care programs: they can provide direct help, and they can also help families make connections so that the families can give and take support through a larger network of resources. Embracing a network model takes the burden off one person to be the resource for everyone. In addition, the network model gives many people the gratifying feeling of being a resource to others.

Authentic, respectful, and mutual partnerships between teachers and families hold the potential to transform the care and education of young children, the support systems available for families, the working conditions and job satisfaction of teachers, and the health of our communities. In this book we will examine the importance of strong teacher-family partnerships in the lives of children, families, and teachers; we will look at both the benefits and the challenges of building teacher-family partnerships; and we will explore how to weave the five characteristics of family-centered care through each aspect of a child development program to create and nurture those partnerships.

REFERENCES

Bronfenbrenner, Urie. 1990. Discovering what families do. In *Rebuilding the nest: A new commitment to the American family*. Edited by David Blankenhorn, Steven Bayme, Jean Bethke Elshtain. Milwaukee: Family Service America. Information found on http://www.montana.edu/www4h/process.html.

Erikson, Erik H. 1963. *Childhood and society*. New York: Norton.

Kearsley, Greg. n.d. Social development theory (L. Vygotsky). http://tip.psychology.org/vygotsky.html.

Lawrence-Lightfoot, Sara. 2003. *The essential conversation: What parents and teachers can learn from each other*. New York: Ballantine Books.

Five Principles of Family-Centered Care

Over the past twenty years, the field of child development has undergone an evolution of thinking about families. We have come to the idea of family-centered care. This model was originally developed in the fields of medicine and special education. Family-centered care is based on these assumptions:

- All people are basically good.
- All people have strengths.
- All people have different but equally important skills, abilities, and knowledge.
- All people need support and encouragement.
- All families have hopes, dreams, and wishes for their children.
- Families are resourceful, but all families do not have equal access to resources.
- Families should be assisted in ways that help them maintain their dignity and hope.
- Families should be equal partners in the relationship with service providers.

  (Iowa's Early ACCESS and Iowa SCRIPT)

These assumptions can help us gain a deeper understanding of the principles of family-centered care in our programs. What teachers believe about parents and families will affect the success of the partnership. Without these assumptions many teachers find themselves "at odds" with parents, believing that parents are working against them or are ignorant. When teachers assume that parents are good, strong, skillful, resourceful, and equal, it is easier to provide support and encouragement in ways that allow families to maintain their dignity and hope. When conflicts arise, teachers are much more hopeful and confident about a resolution when they believe that families are good and have strength. When teachers understand that families have hopes and dreams for their children, it is natural that families would be included in any educational goal setting that happens. Once a teacher has this "strengths-based" perspective on families, it is natural to implement family-centered care.

CHANGING ASSUMPTIONS ABOUT FAMILIES

Think about a family you feel uncomfortable with or challenged by. Look at each assumption in the list above, and think about this family. If it is difficult to apply all of the assumptions to this family, start with one or two. How does your perception of this family change using these assumptions? Discuss this with a coworker or another student.

Parent Education and Parent Involvement

How is family-centered care different from parent education and parent involvement? The early childhood profession started with a focus on children and grew to include parent education. Historically, parent education has been defined as a one-way process with an assumption that teachers know better than parents about what children need. It presumes that what parents need most is information from a child development or parenting expert. Parent education includes events such as parent meetings with an educational focus; parent libraries with books, articles, and handouts; parent conferences; and parent trainings.

While parent education can be a very important component of family-centered care, by itself it doesn't encourage parent input or include parent expertise. Alone, it doesn't promote equal partnership. Parent education as part of family-centered care includes the perspective that families have expertise, skills, resources, and hopes for their children, and it encourages parents to partner with teachers to decide on topics, find guest speakers, plan trainings, participate on panels, share their expertise with other families, and actively participate in goal setting and in parent conferences.

From parent education the profession expanded to include parent involvement, which has been described as "letting parents work on our turf with our rules." Like parent education, this kind of parent involvement has consisted of primarily teacher- and program-directed activities in which parents and families are fairly passive participants. Examples include assigning parents jobs to do for the school and having parents cut out shapes for activities curriculums, make phone calls, or wash the cot sheets. Often parents are glad to do these kinds of tasks to support the school, and while this is a clear attempt at working together with parents, this definition of parent involvement still does not include mutual, reciprocal partnerships (Galinsky and Weissbourd 1992). Parent involvement that is part of family-centered care includes parent initiative in planning and deciding on ways to be involved. In family-centered care teachers and families participate together more equally, cooperatively, and inclusively.

Family-Centered Care Principles

Family-centered care is a holistic approach to working with children and their families. The specific principles of family-centered care can be implemented in many different ways. Family-centered care principles can be used in an after-school program, a parent cooperative (or "co-op"), a parent/infant/toddler play group, Head Start, a family child care home, center-based care, or another child development program. Partnerships with families might include parents acting as teachers in the classroom, or it might involve co-planning parent meetings with a representative group of family members. Two-way communication might occur in an interactive journal shared by teacher and family, or it might be accomplished with e-mail or on the floor of the classroom while children are playing nearby. Family-centered care programs can look very different from each other. The defining characteristic in a family-centered care program is that all five principles will be in place. Remember those from the first chapter? In family-centered care, families and teachers build partnerships by

- recognizing and respecting one another's knowledge and expertise
- sharing information through two-way communication
- sharing power and decision making
- acknowledging and respecting diversity
- creating networks of support.

Looking in depth at the five principles of family-centered care, you will discover the many ways in which each principle is integrally related to all of the others. Acknowledging diversity is crucial for respecting the knowledge and expertise of families. Two-way communication is essential for sharing power and decision making, and it is a primary step in building networks. The more familiar you become with the principles, the clearer the interrelationships will be. In this chapter, we'll look at the five principles of family-centered care in depth.

RECOGNIZING AND RESPECTING ONE ANOTHER'S KNOWLEDGE AND EXPERTISE

Families and teachers each bring unique expertise and experience to the partnership. Recognizing and respecting the knowledge of each person is essential to building an effective partnership. Parents have funds of knowledge about their individual children and family over time and in many different circumstances (Moll et al. 1992; González et al. 1995). Parents teach children language, skills, values, and ideas. Parents advocate for their children's safety, rights, and education. Families choose educational settings for their children. Some families are aware of the importance of their role in their child's growth and development, while others are not. Teachers have education and training in child development, as well as experience in working with children in groups. A teacher-family partnership is only effective when parents as well as teachers feel competent, confident, and respected. In this kind of a relationship, families experience empowerment, a sense of self-confidence, and clarity about the validity of their role. Empowerment here does not mean that parents have power over others; instead it refers to their own growing sense of confidence and effectiveness in their job as parents.

PARENT EXPERTISE

What do families know about their children? Make a list of all the information that a family might know about their child. How much of this information do your families share with you? Look at the list in the section on "Parent Knowledge and Expertise," and compare it with your list.

Parent Knowledge and Expertise

Often, neither teachers nor families recognize all the expertise that families bring to a partnership. Some families come to your program with a strong sense of empowerment in place, accompanied by the knowledge of the important role they play in their children's education. Other parents, because of their own personal, family, or cultural background, may not feel as confident as parents or as ready to be equal partners with teachers. Some of these parents may feel they lack knowledge about children in the face of caregiver knowledge and expertise. Other parents may feel intimidated because of their own childhood experiences with teachers and schools. Still other parents may believe it is disrespectful to tell the teacher how to do his or her job.

There are other challenges to parents feeling empowered. Parents are more aware and educated about children than ever before, yet they are also more vulnerable than ever before. As research increasingly shows the importance of children's development in the first few years (including before they are born), parents are faced with a more complex job. Not only are they responsible for keeping their children safe and happy, they are also responsible for brain development and the social, emotional, physical, and language development of their children. Today, parents must make many more decisions than previous generations of parents had to make. They have to decide about medical care and immunizations, about what educational products to buy, about finding the best child care. With this increased responsibility many parents experience diminishing confidence in their parenting skills.

Simply acknowledging all the information family members have about their child and their family can help to make the partnership more equal. Families know the child's and the family's history, and families affect the child's future through their hopes, plans, and goals. They know family and cultural beliefs and practices as well as the child's temperament, characteristics, and habits. Families know the members of the child's immediate and extended families, including the relationship the child has with each family member. Here is a look at some of the specific information families know.

The child's history, including

- how the child came into the family
- the child's health history
- significant events in the child's life
- significant people and relationships in the child's life.

Their hopes for their child, including

- the family's plans, goals, and dreams for the child's future.

The child's culture and family practices, including

- parenting styles
- beliefs about teaching, learning, and discipline
- values, beliefs, and expectations related to children
- practices around caregiving: eating, dressing, bathing, health, sleeping
- practices around transitions: hellos and good-byes, separations

- significant events and practices related to those events
- family's and child's style of communication
- the name(s) of the child's culture(s).

The child's temperament, characteristics, and habits, including

- the child's unique style of communication
- the child's likes and dislikes
- how the child responds to different experiences
- things that help the child feel comfortable
- things that make the child uneasy, stressed
- the child's way of expressing her or his feelings
- the child's eating, sleeping, self-comforting, and toileting habits.

The child's family and extended family structure, including

- who the members of the child's family are, where they live, how often the child sees them, and the nature of the child's relationship with them.

By truly acknowledging the experience, information, hopes, and beliefs of families, teachers can learn from, listen to, and partner successfully with families. The growth of a teacher's respect for family expertise is a natural catalyst for family empowerment.

Supporting Parent Confidence and Empowerment

While teachers are not responsible for a family's sense of empowerment, they can help create a context in which it can grow. Iowa's Early ACCESS program has identified some roles providers can play in supporting a family's clarity about the importance of their parenting and a family's confidence and effectiveness in making decisions. These providers are skilled in the use of helping practices and understand they are not "rescuers" of families. They can

- help families to feel hopeful
- assist families to identify and successfully use their abilities and capabilities
- assist families to make their own choices and decisions
- actively support family decisions
- suspend their judgments of families
- assist families to envision and plan for the future
- assist families in becoming interdependent with communities of informal and formal support
- credit families for successful outcomes.

It can be challenging to develop these effective helping practices without "rescuing" or "doing it" for families. It is hard to determine professional boundaries with families and easy to step over the line. Remember what you know about working with children: children learn better and feel more confident when they do it for themselves. This is true for people of all ages. When a child can't climb up a ladder, we offer listening, encouragement, information, and alternatives, but we let the child take the initiative to climb the ladder. When a parent is frustrated about her child's eating, we can offer listening, encouragement, information, and alternatives, but we let the parent figure out how and when she wants to proceed. Even when it seems easier to "just do it" for someone, it is always more instructive and empowering when the person we are trying to help can do it for herself.

Helping parents to become empowered is a lifelong gift to them and their families. Parents are teachers and advocates for their children in hundreds of ways. Many families who come to understand their important role as their young child's teacher and advocate go on to provide leadership in their families and in their children's schools and communities for many years.

SUPPORTING PARENT CONFIDENCE AND EMPOWERMENT

In the preceding section, look at the list of ways teachers can support parents' confidence and ability to make effective decisions for their children. Think about all the things you have done with families in the past month. Are there examples of ways you have supported parent empowerment? Looking at the list, can you think of any new ways you could support family confidence and empowerment? Discuss with coworkers or fellow students.

Teacher Knowledge and Expertise

Effective family-teacher partnerships need the expertise of both parent and teacher. Often, however, teachers' knowledge is taken for granted and not identified, acknowledged, or appreciated. Like families, teachers bring significant expertise into the family-teacher partnership. Most teachers have experience as well as education and training. Experience has given them the opportunity to see many different children over time and informs them about the wide continuum of children's behavior and temperament. Education and training about child development and teaching practices through classes, workshops, conferences, and professional meetings give teachers information about the ages and stages of childhood, curriculum development, child observation, and assessment. While parents know the most about their individual children, teachers know the most about children in general.

TEACHER EXPERTISE

As a teacher, what kind of knowledge and information do you have about children? Think about your training, education, and experience. What have you learned? Share your list with coworkers or fellow students.

Here are some examples of what teachers know about children.

Teachers know:

child development

- the stages of development children normally go through, including physical, social/emotional, cognitive, creative, and language development
- what to expect of children at different ages
- the reasons for children's challenging behavior and effective ways to respond to that behavior based on their experience with many different children
- the variety of temperaments one might see in a group of children and ways of working with differing temperaments.

how to work with children in groups

- what to expect of children in groups and how to manage children's behavior in a group setting, including mealtimes, group times, naptime, hellos and good-byes, transitions, and open-choice play
- how to design learning environments for groups of children
- how to help children learn to communicate and solve problems with others
- how to assess children's development and needs and how to design curriculum and activities that will help children grow.

SHARING INFORMATION THROUGH TWO-WAY COMMUNICATION

Communication builds partnership through the sharing of information, and, equally important, through the trust, understanding, and sense of connectedness that develop when people have a chance to really listen to and speak with one another. True listening gives the speaker a chance to reflect on his or her own thoughts and experiences and gives the listener the opportunity to more deeply know the speaker.

Information sharing in a child development program has often traditionally been "one way," from teachers and program to families. Child development programs have access to many different information resources that can be helpful to families in understanding their children and learning new ways to nurture and educate them. Parent education is an important service. However, in family-centered care, information needs to be available to both families and teachers. Two-way communication gives teachers the opportunity to learn from families, just as families can learn from teachers.

Two-way communication can happen in all interactions with families. Transforming existing systems so that information can pass back and forth between teachers and families can be an exciting and challenging task for teachers and programs. Most programs already have some existing channels for receiving information from families, including daily check-ins and child information forms. Achieving two-way dialogue successfully in every form of communication needs support on several levels. It requires both people with communication skills and systems that create time and space for that communication to happen. For example, teachers need training in two-way communication strategies so that they will have the skills to communicate. They also need logistical support: time in their schedules, a place to meet, or a computer to write a newsletter, for example. This requires administrative support, such as paid time for interactive family conferences, meetings, and home visits or adequate classroom staffing so that informal conversation can happen regularly with families.

What ways of inviting families to share information with you ended up on your list? Information forms? Daily check-ins? Home visits? Parent con-

TWO-WAY COMMUNICATION

List all of the ways you can receive information (both in written form and orally) from families. Is there information about children and families that you would like to have but are not receiving right now? What kind of information would you like to have? Can you think of ways to create more two-way communication with families?

ferences? Parent meetings? Bulletin boards? Interactive journals? Newsletters? Informal notes? E-mail? Phone calls? Throughout this book you will find many ideas developed by teachers and programs. These ideas are meant to encourage you to discover how best to open up two-way communication with families in your program.

SHARING POWER AND DECISION MAKING

What does it mean to share power and decision making? It might mean that a teacher and parent decide together when a child should start weaning from the pacifier or how to help a child who has become afraid of the neighborhood garbage truck. Shared power and decision making might mean that several parents sit on an advisory board that makes policy and personnel decisions for the school. Shared decision making means different

things in different programs, but in all cases the emphasis should be on "shared." This means that certain decisions are made with input from both families and teachers.

For example, I experienced a surprising example of shared power and decision making when I accompanied my son on his first day in college. I eagerly attended the parent orientation speeches before classes began and was surprised and impressed when the president of the college said, "When your son or daughter leaves this college, I expect that he or she will be changed in a significant way. I expect, also, that our institution will be changed in a significant way from having had your child and family in our college."

Some teachers feel intimidated by the concept of parent empowerment and of shared decision making. Shared decision making may be worrisome if you have visions of parents taking over the classroom and demanding special treatment for their children. These fears are based on the assumption that parents will be making all the decisions for your programs without input from you. Shared decision making does not mean that families are solely responsible for programmatic decisions or that teachers are solely responsible for family decisions. A lot of shared decision making between families and teachers is ultimately either the family's or the teacher's responsibility.

For example, when Toby's dad was making plans to take Toby on his first airplane trip, he consulted with Toby's teacher for any ideas she had that might help. When Toby's nap routine started changing in the program, Toby's teacher consulted with his dad about sleep and family routines at home. Toby's dad made the final decisions about his trip, and Toby's teacher made the final decisions about his nap routine at school, but both partners were better prepared to make their decisions because of the input of the other. There are also some decisions that will be decided by consensus. One key in shared decision making is defining who is ultimately responsible for the decision or whether it will be a consensus decision.

If you feel concerned about parent empowerment, it is important to remember that people who feel powerless are more likely to be critical and demanding, needing to have everything go their way. They are less likely to see others' perspectives. On the other hand, parents and teachers who feel genuinely competent and resourceful are much better at "sharing the care," listening to others' ideas, and becoming mutual advocates for children.

Shared decision making can be used to develop goals for children, to decide when a child should start toilet learning at school, or to help a child through the separation transition. It can be used for curriculum and policy development, for the development of the parent program, for fund-raising and community outreach. Lots of shared decision making occurs easily between families and teachers without anyone really noticing—for example, deciding on pick-up times, food and napping routines, school-home communication systems. A family wants to bring a piñata full of candy, and the program negotiates with them to fill it with little toys instead. A teacher plans to serve peanut butter sandwiches, and a parent informs her that his child has a peanut allergy; they decide that he should have a cheese sandwich instead. This is shared decision making.

When needs, ideas, and beliefs conflict, shared decisions are more challenging. For instance, a parent doesn't want his child to nap, and school policy is that all children participate in rest time; a grandparent doesn't want her granddaughter to play in the sandbox, and school practice is that children can choose their activity areas. These kinds of shared decisions take creativity, listening, and negotiation. (See chapter 6 for more information to help you negotiate these difficult situations.) Shared decision making relies on the expertise of both families and teachers, and it requires two-way communication, clarity on both

sides about who is ultimately responsible, and a mutual desire to provide the best care and education for a child.

ACKNOWLEDGING AND RESPECTING DIVERSITY

As child education and care professionals we are asked to do some of the most important and immediate work around diversity issues. Every child we care for is a member of a family, ethnic group, socioeconomic class, and culture (usually several cultures). As they grow, children define themselves by how people respond to them, their families, and their cultures. They watch to see how their language, family structure, socioeconomic class, and physical abilities are treated and represented in the world. When a child hears her language spoken only in her home and watches people turn away from her grandfather when he speaks, she quickly learns that her own language is not valued. When a child listens to all the songs about families with dads and moms and his family is made up of two moms and him, he assumes that his family isn't really a family. When a child can't find a book about a dad who is in jail like hers, she wonders if her dad can really be a dad. When a teacher admires a child's home because it has wheels and can move, a child feels excited about where he lives. When a child does a finger play with the teacher about her uncle and grandmother, she feels honored for who her family is.

Truly acknowledging and respecting the diversity that exists in our contemporary communities offers teachers and families, as well as children, a rich and unique opportunity. Exploring, acknowledging, and embracing diversity are essential to building true partnerships with each family in the program. Because of historical and contemporary oppression in our society based on our differences, many of these differences have become loaded issues. Rather than understanding that the divisions and inequality of power surrounding the differences create the problems, many of us see the differences themselves as the problems.

Society, the early childhood profession, and we as individuals are evolving in our thinking about diversity. We have moved through tolerance ("I don't understand the difference, it scares me a little, but I'm going to try to put up with it") and ignoring differences ("All children and families are exactly alike"). We are now moving toward the realization that diversity offers valuable ways to look at things, deeper ways to understand our humanity, and new resources. We are coming to the acceptance that we can't know ahead of time all the variety of ways of thinking and doing things we might encounter, but that we can embrace the opportunity to learn about different perspectives, beliefs, and practices.

Culture

Every aspect of how parents and teachers care for, educate, and think about young children is embedded with cultural perspectives and beliefs. How we respond when a child cries, how we decide it is time for a child to eat, what we define as healthy and as sick, what we believe are appropriate clothes to wear, how we express love, what we expect to do for children and what we expect them to do on their own are examples of the millions of ways that culture affects who we are as people, parents, and teachers. Further, particularly if we haven't had much chance to meet people outside of our own culture, each of us believes that our way of doing things is the only way of doing things—hence the best way.

The first time we bump up against a different way of thinking about and caring for children, we experience shock. We may feel that our way (what we have known and believed all our lives) is being threatened. We often feel that the "other way" of doing things doesn't make any sense or is wrong. A teacher may feel critical of a family who lets their child walk around the house while eating, who carries their child all the time, or who wants to toilet train their infant. A parent might feel

critical of a teacher who doesn't hug children, who refuses to use a child's nickname, or who sends their child home because of a runny nose. People sometimes feel a sense of personal attack when someone does something differently from the way they would. Most often, we don't understand the context of the other way of thinking.

Barbara, a toddler teacher, recalls an experience she had with Monte's family.

I couldn't believe how overprotective Monte's family was. He had to have his shirt on all the time. He couldn't play with water. His mom was terrified of him being wet. She wanted him in mittens and a hat outside even when it was sixty-five degrees. After I got to know his mother a little more, she told me that she had been to the emergency room with Monte when he was a baby with pneumonia and that she was worried that he would get sick again. She believed that keeping him warm and dry at all times was the best thing we could do to keep him healthy. In my family, kids get wet and dirty all the time. We love to take walks in the rain. But, in talking with Monte's mom, I could see that she had a different belief.

This example not only shows a different cultural belief about keeping children healthy but also demonstrates the way a significant event might bring out a different response from a parent. That response can be influenced by the parent's cultural knowledge.

Another confusing thing is that you can't always "see" culture. Many of us have learned to believe that we can know a person's culture by looking at him. However, culture is not the same as "ethnicity." You are born with ethnicity, or a genetic combination of your birth family members. You learn culture from the family you live in and from your community. Culture defines codes of behavior and ways of perceiving things that you learn from the people around you as you grow up.

One challenge in acknowledging a family's

home culture may come from the family members themselves. Some families have come to believe that they will be more successful in this country by ignoring their culture and language. Marina tells a story about a Tibetan family in her preschool class:

When I first met Yeshe, Nima, and their daughter, Sonam, I asked them about their family, culture, and language. They made it clear to me that they wanted their daughter to only speak English in our program. I told them that I also wanted their daughter to learn English but that I wanted her to feel comfortable and her family to feel acknowledged here, as well. They reluctantly agreed to teach me some words in Tibetan. I went searching for things from the Tibetan culture that I could include in the classroom. I found a children's book that I liked and I showed it to Nima. She looked through it and discovered a song engraved in a rock in a picture in the book, and she started singing it. I asked her if she would teach it to us, and she did. It became a favorite song for children in circle time. I also downloaded some Tibetan music and played it in the classroom. I didn't get any response from Sonam. I asked Yeshe about it, and he said that it isn't the kind of Tibetan music that his family listens to. I think the most significant thing that happened with that family is when Yeshe came to me at the end of the year and said, "Thank you for reminding me that I am Tibetan."

Family Structure

Most of us carry around a picture in our minds of what a good or perfect family looks like. The pictures we carry affect how we think about the families we encounter. In some way, every family we meet gets compared to the "norm" we hold. For many of us, this means we don't even feel good about our own families, and we may be conveying messages to the children and families in our care that their families aren't measuring up, either.

REFLECTING ON WHAT WE BELIEVE ABOUT FAMILY

Close your eyes, and come up with a picture of "family." Take a few minutes to create your picture as fully as you can. Open your eyes. How does your picture of "family" compare with the family you grew up in? How does it compare with the families you are working with? How does it compare with the family you are in now? Was your picture of family a single type of family or a broader definition of many different ways families can look and act? Does your definition of family need any work so that it can include all the different kinds of families you know? Write down your thoughts, and/or share them with coworkers or fellow students.

After doing this exercise, Sue, a teacher for thirty years, said this about her image of "family":

The ideal family that I carried in my mind for years even had a white picket fence in the front yard. In my ideal family the mom stayed home and the dad went to work every day. I discovered that this picture interfered with my feeling successful about my own family and most of the families I knew. In my family the mom went to work every day and the dad stayed home to take care of the kids. Over time, watching my own and other families, I came to realize that the success of families is not in the picket fence, where they live, or even who the members are and what their roles are. My ideal began to focus more on how the family provided care and nurturing for its members.

Sue's story describes a shift in thinking about family as structure—who is in the family and what the family looks like—to family as function—how the family and the relationships in it work to provide the care, nurturing, and support its members need. Gloria Steinem summarized this idea when she wrote of family, "It's not form that matters, it's content" (Gandhi 2000).

CREATING NETWORKS OF SUPPORT

There are several ways to think about networks of support and resources. Parents are natural resources for one another. They share many of the same questions, needs, dilemmas, and successes. A parent who is two weeks ahead of another family in figuring out sleep issues may be the perfect resource for the other sleep-deprived family. Networking can start with building upon and using families' informal community support systems before relying solely on professional, formal services (Iowa's Early ACCESS and Iowa SCRIPT 2004).

Often this family-to-family networking happens spontaneously, as in this example. Pui is a parent who had spent countless hours researching and learning about the special education system in order to get the services she needed for her child. When she learned that another parent, Leticia, was trying to find help for her son with autism, Pui called, ordered, and paid for a special education rights handbook in Spanish. Pui met with Leticia, talked to her about resources, and reminded her of her rights. Pui reports that Leticia received everything she requested for her son.

Many families have family, friend, and community networks in place that support their health and well-being. Families have implemented many kinds of formal and informal networks with each other, including child care co-ops and exchanges; dinner delivery for new or sick parents; play groups; car pools; parent support and discussion groups; moms', dads', or parents' nights out; and group camping trips.

Teachers can assist families to identify what resources their informal support networks can provide to meet specific needs and concerns. Teachers can also play a key role by facilitating contacts between families and their communities in order to build informal networks.

Another network of support exists between parents and teachers. Parents can provide teachers, programs, and other families with all kinds of resources, such as ideas, creative thinking, cultural information, language skills, time and energy, and community resources and connections. In exchange, teachers can offer referrals, information, and assistance to connect families to other resources. The surrounding community is also part of a network of support for families. Agencies, groups, resources, activities, businesses, and classes in the community can provide education and support to families if they know where to look and how to access them.

Facilitating, nurturing, and helping to create networks of support are important roles for child care professionals. These networks offer families and programs the ongoing, comprehensive resources needed for them to thrive. In addition, networks offer all participants the opportunity to be a resource to others, to be a significant contributor to the community, and to discover the gift of reciprocity.

A simple example of this happened in Beth Ann's family child care program. Beth Ann works to set up an environment in which parents can meet, connect, share experiences, and build relationships. She is especially watchful at pick-up and drop-off times when parents are at her home together. She recalled,

I always try to notice if two parents are talking together so I can watch their kids and give them the time to talk. One morning I noticed Lynn and Sheila off to one side talking. Sheila was crying. At pick-up time that day, Lynn showed up with a bouquet of flowers. She asked me to make sure that Sheila got them. This is just a small example of how I see the parents in my program building lifetime connections to each other.

Networks broaden two-way communication into multi-way communication. They allow for more people and resources to enter the partnership and expand the support system.

NETWORKS OF SUPPORT

What networks are currently in place in your program? community resources for families? family-to-family networks? family-teacher networks? Are there networks you would like to help create in your program? Discuss with coworkers or fellow students.

OBSTACLES TO FAMILY-CENTERED CARE

As beneficial as family-centered care is for children, families, and teachers, there are several possible obstacles to fully implementing it. If you can identify and understand these obstacles, it is easier to address and overcome them. It's important to understand that these obstacles are not anyone's "fault" but are the products of people's experience and context. Acknowledging this fact will help to increase everyone's empathy for the other people involved and move both parents and teachers beyond blame of themselves or one another.

Obstacles for Families

Contemporary families experience multiple stressors that interfere with their feelings of success and ability to be partners with their children's teachers. Many families feel stressed about money, time, sleep, housing, transportation, balancing work and family, and parenting decisions. If you were to ask each of the families in your program about their week, how many of them would answer that they got everything done they wanted to, got enough sleep, had enough time with their kids, had enough money for all their expenses, and felt confident about all the parenting decisions they made? Families feel the pressure to do more for their kids with less time.

More parents work outside the home than in past generations. The job market has increasingly opened up to women. The economy of our country depends on the work of both women and men. The financial health of many families depends on the income of two working people, both because the cost of raising families is at an all-time high and because people's basic standards of living have risen. The outcomes for families from these trends include more children in child care, a significant number of parents feeling ambivalent or guilty about being away from their children because of their need or choice to work, many families experiencing a shortage of time for their children and for household tasks, and many families facing financial stress. Because of these realities, the following kinds of feelings may emerge for families in relationship to child care:

◆ Protective feelings

"How can I keep my child safe if I'm not the one caring for her?"

"Is this teacher too young?"

"Can this teacher care for my child if she is not a parent herself?"

◆ Guilt

"I'm not a good parent if I don't do all of the care for my child."

◆ Gate keeping

"Only I can care adequately for my child."

"If someone else cares well for her, does that mean I'm not doing a good enough job?"

◆ Resentment and jealousy

"The teacher gets her all day when she is happy, and I get her at night when she is tired and cranky."

"He eats for his teacher, but he doesn't eat for me."

◆ Frustration

"I'm always in such a hurry. There is so much to do after I pick her up that I don't even have time to talk to her teacher."

Aside from these questions and feelings, many parents bring their own experiences and assumptions to their children's first school experience. Parents may feel intimidated by the teacher, just as they did in third grade by their own teacher. Parents may feel stupid in front of the teacher and respond by trying to prove that they are smarter or know better or by staying quiet. Parents may have learned to be deferential to the teacher out of respect and not feel able to express their own ideas, beliefs, and expertise related to their children. Others may have a vision of teachers as older and therefore "mature" and be surprised or uneasy about a teacher who is young. Some parents may feel so protective and concerned about their own children that it is difficult for them to see that the teacher has responsibility for other children and the classroom as well.

REFLECTING ON OBSTACLES FOR TEACHERS IN BUILDING FAMILY-CENTERED CARE

What are the obstacles you face in building family-centered care? Remember that these obstacles don't mean you are a bad or unskilled teacher. Obstacles may include things you haven't learned yet, lack of resources to deal with multiple families' needs, and lack of goals or systems in your program to foster partnerships. Remember, also, that recognizing the obstacles is the first step toward overcoming them. Make a list of obstacles, and ask a coworker to make his or her own list. Share and discuss your lists, and compare them to the lists on the next page.

How are these feelings and stresses manifested in the teacher-family relationship? Parents may ignore or avoid teachers. They may be critical or judgmental of the teachers and the program. Parents who are feeling guilty may attempt to micromanage their child's care, giving teachers highly detailed instructions. Parents may remain in the classroom, unable to leave their child, or they might dash in and out of the classroom without talking to anyone. Parents may ask tons of questions or be overly talkative. Understanding the contexts of families and parents can help teachers figure out and respond to the sources of many of these behaviors. (For more on understanding and responding to challenging parent behavior, see chapter 6.)

Obstacles for Teachers

The child care and education profession has a solid corps of talented, dedicated, invested teachers who are working for the benefit of children and families. However, many challenges affect the ability of these professionals to implement family-centered care.

Teachers of young children are expected to have broader and more complex skills than ever before. Not only are they supposed to provide excellent care and education to children who are facing multiple stressors, they are expected to be culturally and linguistically competent to teach children from many different languages and cultures. Teachers are expected to build effective partnerships with and provide referrals and services to families under stress. Teachers need to be literate in all of the latest developments in their field including current licensing requirements and documentation, evaluation, and assessment criteria from their oversight and licensing agencies. Further, teachers are expected to develop and maintain highly professional relationships with all of the program staff. Unbelievably, many teachers are supposed to do this with little or no paid planning, preparation, or professional development time. Further, wages in most of the field put child care and education professionals at risk for not being able to provide for their own families.

Challenges for teachers in building partnerships may include

- lack of experience and/or training on building family-centered care

◆ no time available for two-way communication, getting to know families, or partnership building

◆ no comfortable, accessible, private space available for meeting with parents

◆ not enough coverage in the classroom for daily check-ins with families

◆ communication barriers, including language differences, and lack of training in effective communication skills

◆ lack of experience or training in working in a culturally diverse program.

Further, many teachers experience feelings or personal issues such as the following in working with families—often related to social inequities, stereotypes, and oppression:

◆ unappreciated for their expertise and the hard work they do

◆ inadequate when talking with parents because they are not parents themselves

◆ less comfortable and experienced working with adults than with children

◆ critical of parents' perceived lack of child development knowledge

◆ lack of respect from the family because the teacher is younger than the parents

◆ less valued than the parents of the children they care for because of classism. (Many teachers do not make enough money to afford to have their children in the child care programs they provide for others.)

How might these feelings manifest in the teacher-family relationship? Teachers' feelings may show up as criticism or judgment of parents and families, avoidance of contact with families, resentment of parents and families, or complaints about families. If teachers understand the sources of these behaviors, it can be easier to learn to overcome them.

In order to think about this in more depth, try to imagine yourself in the following scenarios. Spend a few moments thinking about each one, and perhaps writing down your thoughts.

Scenario I: You are a child, and your two favorite people in the whole world don't like each other very much. They don't say it, but you can tell. When they are together, their conversations are short, sometimes they are irritated with each other, and sometimes they don't even speak to each other. How do you feel?

Scenario 2 : You are a parent, and this is the first time you have brought your child to school or child care. You were afraid of most of your own teachers. You never felt smart or competent in school. How do you feel this first day bringing your child to school?

Scenario 3: You are a teacher. You love working with children. In fact, you became a teacher because you are much more comfortable with children than you are with adults. You know that children come with parents attached, but part of you wishes parents would just leave them at the door so you can do your work with the children in peace. When parents come in, you don't quite know what to say to them. They seem to have a lot of demands about their children; some don't even seem to trust you. Sometimes they seem critical; sometimes they ignore you. How do you feel?

PROBLEM SOLVING THE OBSTACLES TO BUILDING FAMILY-CENTERED CARE

Given the potential obstacles to building family-centered care and your insights from the scenarios above, what are some of the possible solutions or supports that you can envision? Think about specific things you can do immediately in your role as a teacher or administrator, and think also about longer-term programmatic changes that could address some of these obstacles. Discuss with coworkers or fellow students.

All of these feelings for children, parents, and teachers are natural, given their experiences. Working together to understand our own experiences and those of others will help us identify the sources of discomfort in our relationships and communicate with each other in ways that build our relationships, our trust, and our mutual support.

SUPPORTS FOR FAMILY-CENTERED CARE

While obstacles to family-centered care exist, we also have many strategies and solutions to address them and to build support for a new way of working with families. Some are readily accessible—the kinds of things you can do when you go to work on Monday morning. Others will take more planning, collaboration, and long-term implementation to put into practice.

Strategies for Immediate Implementation

Here are ideas that teachers can implement right away to overcome obstacles to family-centered care:

◆ Learn every significant family member's name. You can post names in the classroom (bulletin board, class list, or cubbies) so that you can refer to them when you are greeting family members.

◆ Work to greet every family and child when they arrive. Then try to learn one significant thing about every family member (grandpa likes to build model boats, sister plays soccer, dad writes poetry, stepmom makes homemade *lumpia*).

◆ At least once a week, ask each family for information about their child. Ask questions like "What does Lucho like to do when he is home?" "Who does Juli play with when she is at home?" "Are there any things you would like me to know about Sarah so that I can provide better care for her?"

◆ Every day (if possible), give each child's family information about the child's day. Work with your

coworkers to provide classroom coverage that allows each of you time to observe children and to share your observations with family members.

◆ Arrange the classroom so there is room for families to visit. For example, provide a low, small couch or other comfortable seating arrangements for families.

Long-Term Strategies

Many of the changes to support family-centered care need to be made at the programmatic level. Teachers and families can plan, advise, and advocate for these changes, but vision, investment, and support on the part of the program administration and board are essential to the successful implementation of these strategies. Here is a list of ideas for supporting partnerships at the programmatic level:

◆ Provide adequate staffing so that teachers can have daily two-way sharing and communication with families at both drop-off and pick-up times.

◆ Provide time for staff to keep written documentation on the children in their care to be regularly shared with families.

◆ Provide staff with time to plan, carry out, and document regular home visits, parent conferences, and parent meetings.

- Create and support parent advisory committees.
- Invite parents to participate in program planning and evaluation.
- Create written materials (handbooks, questionnaires, newsletters, letters to families) in families' home languages that include and promote two-way communication and partnerships.
- Work to develop a staff that is culturally and linguistically representative of the families in the program and the community.
- Provide training and written materials for staff on community resources for families.
- Provide staff training on family-centered care, including the importance of culture in parenting and caregiving practices.
- Provide staff with training and practice in using two-way communication and problem-solving strategies.
- Provide regular time in staff meetings to discuss specific family partnerships, as well as general strategies for building partnerships with families.

REFERENCES

Iowa's Early ACCESS and Iowa SCRIPT. 2004. Guiding principles and practices for delivery of family centered services. http://www.state.ia.us/earlyaccess/doc/fcs04.pdf.

Galinsky, Ellen, and Bernice Weissbourd. 1992. Family-centered child care. In *Yearbook in early childhood education*. Vol. 3: *Issues in child care*, edited by B. Spodek and O. N. Saracho. New York: Teachers College Press.

González, Norma, Luis C. Moll, Martha Floyd-Tenery, Anna Rivera, Patricia Rendón Raquel Gonzales, and Cathy Amanti. 1995. Funds of knowledge for teaching in Latino households. *Urban Education* 29 (4): 443–70.

Moll, Luis C., Cathy Amanti, Deborah Neff, and Norma González. 1992. Funds of knowledge for teaching: Using a qualitative approach to developing strategic connections between homes and classrooms. *Theory into Practice* 31 (2): 132–41.

Gandhi, Lakshmi, Christine McCluskey, and Rekha Matchanickal. 2000. The past, the future, the present. *Bi-College News Online* 33 (2). www.biconews.com.

DEVELOPING STRATEGIES TO BUILD FAMILY-CENTERED CARE

After reading these lists, do you have more ideas for supports, actions, or solutions for building partnerships that you could implement, collaborate on, or advocate for? Think again in terms of short-, medium-, and long-term goals.

- What could happen tomorrow or this week? in the next six months? in a year or two?
- What changes would you be able to implement yourself? working with coworkers?
- What changes could you work for with administrative staff?
- What changes could you make working with community resources?

Remember that even changes you can make by yourself should be communicated to other staff so that you can maintain and support effective teamwork.

Effective Communication with Families: An Overview

Effective communication between families and the program is central to the success of building family-centered care; it is the cornerstone of the partnership. Communication is a dance involving two or more people in which ideas are conveyed, shared, listened to, and built upon. Effective communication involves articulate expression of ideas and receptive listening. Clear communication necessitates that the speaker understands who the listener is and articulates clearly in a way the listener can understand. In successful communication, ideas often go back and forth until partners are clear that each of them is heard and understood. Discovering the other person's meaning and knowing that someone cares about and will listen to your ideas creates the sense of trust necessary for true partnership. This kind of partnership empowers both parents and teachers through providing expanded resources and a strong base from which to solve problems together.

Effective communication involves using a variety of communication tools: listening well, speaking well, writing well, being aware of nonverbal communication, and using language that is accessible to both families and teachers. Successful communication requires these communication skills and also accessible communication systems: for example, time in a teacher's schedule and the physical space and equipment necessary for the variety of communication involved in the partnership. A teacher may have wonderful speaking and listening skills, but if he doesn't have enough classroom coverage during pick-up time or access to a phone or e-mail, he won't be able to use those skills.

This chapter offers an introduction to communication in family-centered programs and identifies the relationship between communication and each of the family-centered care principles. The four chapters that follow this one cover different aspects of communication in the child development program. Chapter 4, "Daily Communication," focuses on daily communication between teachers and families, including check-ins, telephone calls, notes, and interactive journals. Chapter 5, "Challenges to Communication: Problems Affecting the Child at Home or at School," covers when communication with families involves challenges, including helping families with problems and sharing difficult information with families about their children. Chapter 6, "Challenges to Communication: Conflict between Family and Program," offers strategies for using communication to resolve conflicts between families and teachers, and Chapter 7,

"Formal Communications: Documentation and Conferences," discusses family conferences, handbooks, newsletters, letters, and child and family information forms.

WHAT MESSAGE ARE YOU SENDING?

Communication is one of the simplest and yet most complex things we do with each other every day. People are often surprised to discover that someone misunderstood messages they thought they had communicated clearly. Communicating in ways that both respect and support parents requires awareness of several different aspects of communication including word choice, quantity of communication, tone, language, different communication styles, and nonverbal communication. In family-centered care it is important to be aware of the messages that are conveyed through all communications with families. Here are some examples of messages that support family-centered care:

- Families are welcome in the program.
- The program is inclusive of all families.
- All the people in families are respected by the teachers and staff of the program.
- Families can be proud of who they are in this program.
- The staff knows families are intelligent and knowledgeable about their children.
- Parents are assumed to be competent both as people and as parents.
- The staff is looking forward to learning from families and is open to input.
- Families are invited into a mutual partnership.

Here are some messages that don't support family-centered care:

- Some kinds of families just don't fit in our program.

- We don't have time to listen to parents because we are too busy taking care of children.
- The program has lots of rules that parents have to learn.
- Parents have to learn to do it our way, or they won't fit in our program.
- Teachers know more about children than parents do.

EXAMINING THE MESSAGES IN YOUR COMMUNICATION

Referring to the list of messages above, review some of the written communication in your program. What messages are parents being given through your communication? Are there ways you could more clearly communicate family-centered principles in your communication with families? Discuss with coworkers or fellow students.

RECOGNIZING AND RESPECTING ONE ANOTHER'S KNOWLEDGE AND EXPERTISE

Communication is the main vehicle through which teachers and families can learn about, acknowledge, and show respect for each other's knowledge and expertise. However, families may not automatically share information with teachers because they don't know it would be useful to teachers, they don't know teachers are interested, or they haven't acknowledged to themselves how much they know about their children and family. Because teachers are already seen as the experts by some families, it can be challenging to figure out how to communicate with families that you want to share expertise.

How do teachers convey to families that they are interested in learning about family knowledge? Teachers can convey to families the importance of family knowledge and expertise through statements and questions. A statement in the family handbook or orientation meeting can demonstrate the program's interest in family knowledge. Here's an example:

As your child's first teacher, you have provided love, nurturance, and education for your child during her/his life. We look forward to getting to know you and your child and hope that you will share the knowledge and understanding that you have about your child and family with us so that we can build our partnership with you in caring for and educating your child.

A parent handbook statement like this one can be followed up by questions on the child and family information forms, in the intake interview, and during home visits or daily check-ins that ask families for specific information about their children. Listening carefully to families (another aspect of communication) also counterbalances the notion that program staff are the only experts on children. Listening helps to empower parents as experts on their children. Asking questions, truly listening, and demonstrating an understanding of information from families are crucial to respecting family knowledge and expertise.

Every Family Has Strengths

Most teachers have known families who on the surface appeared to have no knowledge, expertise, or skills at all. It can be challenging to find the strengths in some families. These families may demonstrate little or no care for their children, actively harm their children, or have a style that "pushes our buttons." These families are often facing multiple stressors and challenges with little resource, support, and information. Teachers are often critical or judgmental of these families and find it hard to respect them.

Interestingly, these families probably feel the same way about themselves as you do, at least initially. For that reason above all, as difficult as it

may be, it is still important to use a "strengths-based" philosophy in working with these families. Learning and growth, as well as partnership, need strength to build from. For example, consider this teacher's story about the father of a child in her class:

This dad was unbelievable. George was usually homeless, sometimes high. He might as well have had a big "L" tattooed on his forehead for "Loser." His child lived with her grandmother (George's mother, Martine) most of the time. Martine chain-smoked and literally sat in front of the TV every minute, day and night. The amazing thing was that George managed to get his daughter to our program every day. He would bum rides with friends, take the bus, sometimes drive his car when it was working, but whatever it took, he would get her here. I had all kinds of issues with George, including deciding when to report him to social services, but I had to give it to him for getting it together to get his daughter to our program every day. One day, when he arrived with her, I looked at him and said, "Thank you for bringing your daughter every day. I know it isn't easy and that you do it because she is so important to you." His face lit up, and he made eye contact with me. I don't think he was used to being complimented on his parenting.

This is an example of finding a strength in a challenging family. Finding the strength in a family doesn't mean that you ignore the problems, but it is the first building block in creating the partnership in which the problems can be addressed.

Teacher Expertise

Teachers bring knowledge and expertise to the partnership as well. How can teachers share their knowledge with families in ways that are helpful and understandable to families, yet not intimidating? As families feel increasingly comfortable with their own knowledge and expertise, they will be more interested in seeking information from teachers. Different families will want information in different ways. Some avid readers will benefit from books, articles, and handouts. Many appreciate child development and parenting information when they have an immediate issue with their child. Listening carefully to a family's questions will help teachers find the right resource to share. When teachers offer their expertise and knowledge in ways that meet a family's need, both feel acknowledged and respected.

SHARING INFORMATION THROUGH TWO-WAY COMMUNICATION

Clearly, this second principle is what this chapter is all about! Two-way communication ensures that the family has a voice in the care and education of their child and that needed information is available to both the teacher and the family. Being respectfully listened to and communicated with builds everyone's feelings of confidence and effectiveness.

As important as two-way communication is in family-centered care, it doesn't always happen naturally. Many communications with families have been structured to be one-way. Parent meetings and conferences, parent handbooks, and bulletin boards are all traditional methods of one-way communication. Even daily check-ins can be dominated by teachers' reporting on a child's day in the program. There are visible and invisible barriers to two-way communication. Some of the obvious and visible barriers include parent meetings in which a speaker or an "expert" gives a presentation or parent conferences in which the teacher has prepared a developmental report to share with the parent. Bulletin boards and parent handbooks are also structured as vehicles for the program to give information to parents.

Invisible barriers may be less obvious and include contexts and relationships in which people don't feel they have equal permission to participate, the way language is used, choice of words, and quantity and tone of communication. One might assume that when people are having a conversation with each other, it constitutes two-way communication. However, for some people, conversations with a teacher they believe has more knowledge or more power will be mostly one-way. Thus, even if a teacher is inviting, warm, and open, some parents still might not be able to communicate their ideas. And in situations in which a teacher doesn't have the time, knowledge, or support to open communication with parents, two-way communication is unlikely to happen.

Here are some basic ways teachers can overcome the barriers and support genuine two-way communication in their programs:

◆ Use accessible layperson's language in documents and in conversations.

◆ Choose words that reflect your values and expectations.

◆ Be mindful of the tone of your communication.

◆ Pay attention to the quantity of communication desired by individual families.

Teachers can support two-way communication with families by using accessible layperson's language. Child development professionals are often accustomed to speaking a special language that includes terminology such as "continuity of care," "zones of proximal development," and "psychosocial development." Theoretical jargon may make perfect sense to some teachers, but most parents will feel left out of the conversation if the language used is too technical. Parents are often familiar with the concepts teachers are referring to when they use technical jargon, though they may not have heard the terms before. In writing (for example, in a parent handbook), if it seems that a term is particularly meaningful, it can be used and immediately defined, so that parents can learn it as they read.

We believe that children learn best through play and that their learning happens in an integrated way. For instance, when a child is sliding down a slide, she is developing both her physical skills like balance, coordination, and strength, as well as her cognitive skills, like her understanding of how gravity pulls her down the slide and how the friction of her jeans slows her down.

Word choice is another aspect of accessible communication. The words you use contribute to the tone of the message and communicate your values and expectations. For instance, choosing to use the word "parent" instead of "mother" communicates an appreciation that men are also significant parents. Choosing to use the word "family" rather than "parent" gives a welcome message to the larger family of the child and not just the parent. It also implies that there might be other caring adults in the child's family who are not technically the child's parents. In another example, using the words "challenging behavior" rather than "bad behavior" helps convey that children's behavior is not being judged but instead is seen as a challenge to be solved.

Obviously, word choice influences the effectiveness of our communication. Some people feel offended if they are not addressed as "Ms.," "Mr.," or "Miss." Others feel that they aren't being treated in a friendly way by someone if they aren't addressed by their first name. One parent might be delighted to hear that his daughter was assertive at school today, and another might be dismayed by the same report.

Word choice is complicated by the fact that people have different definitions for and associations with words. Discussing the vocabulary you use and especially some of the word choices in written communications will help you gain a broader perspective on how words are most commonly understood. Considering these issues will help you to choose the words that relay the meanings you intend.

Tone is another way that messages are knowingly or unknowingly sent. Tone is used for emphasis and to communicate feelings. Some-

times tone is used to communicate things that are too hard to say. You can probably remember the way a parent or teacher said *just* your name but implied that you were in big trouble. The meaning of a message can be turned completely around depending on the tone. Even the simple phrase, "How are you?" can mean "This is just a polite, short greeting" or "I'd like to hear all about how you are really doing," depending on tone and body language. One phrase we often say to children, "What was your idea?" can mean "I'm interested in your thinking," unless you put a loud emphasis on the word "what," as in "WHAT was your idea?" With such an emphasis, the phrase becomes a statement that you aren't interested in the child's idea and that the child has made a huge mistake.

You can often be unaware of the messages you are sending with your tone. This can feel disempowering to both you and the parent. Sometimes a frustrated parent or teacher will say through his teeth, "I'm not mad." This can be confusing to both the speaker, who might not have identified her feelings yet, and also for the listener, who is getting a mixed message. The tone says "mad," but the words say "not mad." Similarly, we might say in an unanimated voice to a parent at the end of the day, "Your child's day was o-o-o-o-kaaay." The teacher may not know how to talk to the parent about the difficult thing that happened, yet the parent can hear that there was something that didn't go well. It is uncomfortable for the listener to address the issue that is brought up just with tone, and often she will leave with an uneasy feeling. It would be more helpful to be direct with the parent even if it seems uncomfortable. You might say something like, "We are observing some new behaviors with Charlie. Do you have a few minutes to check in so we can compare notes?"

In addition, your tone may be understood differently from how you intended because of the listener's different associations with tone. You may say, "Oh, I'm so-o-o-o sorry" to someone who has been hurt. One person may interpret it as nurturing, and another may think of it as pity. You can't always predict how people will respond to your tone, but you can be conscious of how and when you use it, your intent, and the reactions of others. This awareness of the significance of tone in all your communications will help empower you to support parent competence and empowerment.

REFLECTING ON YOUR TONE OF COMMUNICATION

Think of some phrases you commonly use with parents. (See the examples below if you need them.) Practice saying the phrases in a scolding, frustrated tone. Then practice saying them in a respectful, supportive tone.

"Remember, five o'clock is pick-up time."

"Could you please bring an extra set of clothes for Ashley?"

"I'd like to talk to you about your son."

Do this exercise with coworkers or fellow students. As you practice different tones, check with your coworkers or fellow students to see what they are hearing in your tone. Are they hearing what you intended? Now, notice the tone you use in all your communications this week. What do you notice? Share your observations with your coworkers or fellow students.

Finally, when planning how to create genuine, two-way communication, it's important to be aware that families may have differing expectations about the quantity of communication they should have. One seventeen-year-old in-home caregiver was eager to share with a mother many details about her child's day, including eating, sleeping, playing, and diapering. However, after several days in which Mom busied herself around the house when she arrived, the caregiver sensed that the parent felt this was too much information to be communicated. On the other hand, a parent may show up looking forward to an extensive report and be disappointed by a simple greeting from the teacher.

Building effective two-way communication happens over time, as teachers and families build trust and as families are given consistent messages in many venues that their voices are essential.

Communication Tips

Here are some ideas to keep in mind in any setting in which you are trying to build two-way communication:

◆ Be curious.

Most of us are naturally curious and interested in parents' ideas, beliefs, experiences, and feelings. Act on that curiosity by showing interest when they talk to you and asking questions to keep them talking.

◆ Start conversations with a question.

Questions communicate that you are interested in the parent's ideas. They set the stage for a dialogue and give you information about the parent's perspective.

◆ Use open-ended questions.

An open-ended question is one that can't be answered with yes or no. These questions draw parents out and give them a chance to talk about what is important to them. Here are some open-ended questions: "What do you think about that?" "What have you observed?" "What have you tried?"

◆ Consider answering questions with questions.

Some questions that parents ask have a clear, short answer that you know and they don't. These need to be answered directly. But often people ask many questions because they already have an idea or they have some information about the topic that they would like to share with you. For example, when a parent asks, "When is the best time to have a second child?" or "When do you think I should start toilet training my child?" you can respond with something like "That's an interesting question. What are your thoughts about it?" or "Hmmm. What are you noticing?"

◆ Share information about yourself.

Part of two-way communication is letting families get to know you. Sharing information about who you are as a person can help families feel more comfortable sharing information about themselves and can contribute to a mutual partnership.

◆ Observe families' preferred styles and modes of communication.

Where and how are families most comfortable talking? Some families prefer to have private conversations, while others are more comfortable talking in the middle of the bustle of the program. If you observe carefully, you can learn how to best communicate with each family. For example, one director spends time in the yard during pick-up time because she has noticed that families who never come to her office will check in with her when she is outside.

◆ Let parents know you appreciate their input, personally and publicly.

Remember to thank parents, individually and in the group, when they offer their input and ideas. This reinforces your message that you want to hear from them. It encourages them to keep engaging in two-way communication.

Addressing both the visible and the invisible barriers to two-way communication is essential to building family-centered care. Dedicating yourself to making every communication avenue two-way will take creativity, understanding, and a willingness to try new things.

SHARING POWER AND DECISION MAKING

Communication is the tool that teachers and families use to share power and decision making. When families and teachers share their unique sets of knowledge with each other, they develop a common body of information both can access to make decisions and provide care and education for children. Some mutual decisions are made easily, with both partners communicating smoothly and agreeing on a course of action. Other decisions involve conflicts between very different perspectives, values, and practices. Sometimes these conflicts are between families and the program, and sometimes different families have different views that must be reconciled. Using effective communication strategies, you can often resolve these conflicts through negotiation and consensus, finding a solution that everyone can wholeheartedly support.

For example, Meena tells this story about a difference of opinion with a family.

We always use disposable plates and cups for mealtime in our program. This year Blue's mom, Sunny, told me that she didn't like her son using disposable plates and cups, because she thought it was teaching him to be wasteful, and she was also concerned that our program was not being environmentally friendly. I told her that we didn't have either plates and cups or a dishwasher, or funds to buy them, so we couldn't really change. She asked if we would be open to using real plates and cups if we had a dishwasher and dishes. I took it to the staff, and their only concern was about who would load the dishwasher. When I talked to Sunny, she said she would work on it. Sunny sent out letters to all the parents to ask for support for a fundraiser. She ended up working with a group of parents who raised the funds to buy dishes and a dishwasher. This group also volunteered to take turns loading the dishwasher at the end of the day. I discovered that there were a number of people on our staff who felt the same way Sunny did and were happy to unload the dishwasher in the morning.

In this story, the families and teachers were

able to come up with a consensus, a decision that everyone was happy with. Another outcome for conflicts is compromise, a solution that isn't necessarily everyone's first choice, but one they can live with. See Chapter 6, "Challenges to Communication: Conflict between Family and Program," for a continuation of the discussion on using communication to solve conflicts in shared decision making.

ACKNOWLEDGING AND RESPECTING DIVERSITY

The interplay between communication and diversity is complex. Communication is critical to respecting diversity, and understanding diversity is essential to effective communication. Because "diversity" refers to cultural, family, and other differences, as well as to language, respecting diversity through communication is a complex undertaking. In addition to language, varying communication styles and nonverbal communication are important to consider.

Communicating across Languages

Programs that include several languages offer a unique curriculum to the children, families, and teachers in those programs. This curriculum can provide immediate, hands-on learning about language and culture different from one's own. In addition to these benefits, there are major challenges in working with children and families who speak a language that is different from the staff. The more languages in a program, the greater the potential benefits and challenges. While the best solution for this challenge is hiring bilingual staff who speak the languages of the children and families in your program, this is often not feasible.

While programs work to find qualified bilingual staff, here are several creative solutions they can use in the meantime.

◆ Contact community groups and cultural or ethnic group organizations for interpreters.

◆ Check with other bilingual families in your program to see if they would be willing to help.

◆ Ask families if they have friends or family members who could help provide interpreting services.

◆ Use interpreters to teach staff key words and phrases as well as to provide interpreting services.

◆ Use interpreters to teach simple words and phrases to other children in the class (for instance, at circle time).

◆ Invite community and family members who speak the languages of the children in your class to volunteer in the classroom as a way to share language and culture.

◆ Translate written materials. You can use them even when an interpreter is not on site.

◆ Be aware of culture as well as language when selecting an interpreter or translator. When an interpreter understands or shares the culture of the family, she can also act as a cultural ambassador.

Building partnerships with families who speak different languages can pose challenges to a child development staff, and monolingual English-speaking teachers sometimes feel inadequate and ineffective in the process. It is important to note that English-speaking teachers (or other teachers who don't speak the language of a child or family in the program) play a significant role in supporting children and families who speak languages different from the teachers'. The gifts these teachers can bring include respect, honor, and admiration for different languages and cultures. The mechanics of learning language are fairly simple compared to building an environment of respect for a variety of languages and cultures. Children and their families are keenly aware of whether they are seen as a burden or an asset to the child development program, and the staff's attitudes are the key factors in this message.

If the staff understands the richness of learning about different languages, cultures, and perspectives, that attitude of inclusion will be communicated to all families.

Communication Styles

We know that even if people are speaking the same language, differing communication styles make it possible to miscommunicate. Styles of communication are influenced by individual personality and temperament as well as the rules of talking that people learn in family and culture. These rules include how much people talk, who talks and when, who initiates conversation, what is appropriate to talk about in different settings, and how to indicate that a conversation is over. Often people are unaware of the rules of conversation they have learned until they meet someone with different rules.

For example, Rita remembers visiting a friend's house as a child: "I thought my friend Leti's family was so strange. When the family would talk at dinnertime, there would be these weird pauses after one person spoke before another person would respond. It wasn't until a few years ago that I realized in my family people always jumped in on the end of one another's sentences. You never waited for an opening because there wasn't one."

Another teacher, Daniella, realized that she had learned rules about gender roles in communication that affected her teaching. "For years, I greeted both men and women family members when they came to drop off their children with me. One day, all of a sudden, I noticed that, unconsciously, I initiated conversation with the women, but I waited for men to start the conversation with me. I thought I was a fairly aware person. This really surprised me. I'm sure I learned it when I was a little girl."

Most of us have noticed that our own communication style changes from one setting to another, and many of us have had experiences with people we thought talked too much, talked too little, interrupted, or were very friendly in one setting and very cool in another. Becoming aware of the communication style rules you have learned and being sensitive to styles that are different from yours can help improve comfortable communication with families.

In addition to culture, personal temperament affects your communication style. Whether you are an introvert or an extrovert, slow-to-warm or quick-to-warm, flexible or structured will affect your communication strategies and the communication style you develop with different family members in your program. Roberto reflects on his personality: "I've always been an introvert at heart. I have to work so hard to approach parents and to be friendly, but I do it. I was so happy when e-mail and text messaging came along. I love to send messages to parents. Sometimes I send them two or three messages a day." While teachers and family members can't change their basic temperaments, they can develop communication strategies that are a good match for each relationship.

A person's style of communication also includes what modes of communication a person is comfortable with, such as letters, notes, e-mail, text messages, in-person conversations, phone conversations, spontaneous conversations, and planned conversations. For example, Tess, a young in-home provider, uses her phone to send several photos and text messages every day to Benji's parents at work.

Recognizing your own style of communication, learning about the communication styles of those around you, and discovering the most effective modes and venues for communication with each family are essential to respecting diversity in your partnerships with families.

Nonverbal Communication

People also communicate through nonverbal means, including eye contact, touch, physical distance, and hand motion, most of which have been learned through family and culture. Nonverbal communication is learned through demonstration, modeling, and practice. It is almost never taught directly. This is why many people are not fully conscious of how they and others use body language. For example, in some cultures, making eye contact is a sign of respect. In other cultures, averting eye contact demonstrates respect.

Most cultures have elaborate rules about who touches whom, when, and how. In certain families hugging, cuddling, holding hands, and sitting close are all expected in every relationship. In other families physical touch is used to acknowledge a greeting or a good-bye, or for comfort. In still other families physical touch rarely occurs. All of these are on a continuum of normal relating, but differences in nonverbal communication can still cause misunderstandings between teachers and families.

For example, Malia tells the story of Ben, who had been in her care for two weeks. Ben's mother went to the director because she was concerned that Malia wasn't greeting Ben. When asked about it, Malia reported that she squatted down, made eye contact, and said, "Good morning, Ben," every day when he arrived. Ben's mother said, "But you didn't touch my child." In this situation Malia was offering her best, most attentive greeting, but it didn't match the expectations of the family for a warm greeting.

REFLECTING ON YOUR OWN NONVERBAL COMMUNICATION

Think about the kinds of nonverbal communication you use and are comfortable with. Have you ever had a conversation with someone that felt uncomfortable because they were standing too close or too far away, because they looked you in the eye too long or not long enough, because they touched you or neglected to touch you, because their facial expression was distracting? Are there people you work with or families in your program who have different styles from yours? Discuss with your coworkers or fellow students.

The better you know your own comfort zone with nonverbal communication, the more you can let people know how best to communicate with you and the more sensitive you will be in reading other's nonverbal communication style. Terri, a teacher-trainer, begins most of her workshops this way:

I want to let you know something about my communication style. I like to touch people on the shoulder, on the hand, on the arm. It is part of the way I communicate. If you don't like to be touched, I will try to read your body language, but feel free to tell me. Also, you are welcome to touch me in the same way. I feel like it is a sign that we are on the same team. Let's take a few minutes in small groups to share what we know about our verbal and nonverbal communication styles with each other. You can let your group know what kinds of communication you are comfortable with and those you are uncomfortable with.

Terri models a way that you can reflect on your own nonverbal communication style, articulate it to others, and give others permission to tell you what works and doesn't work for them in nonverbal communication.

Nonverbal communication also includes how close you stand to someone when talking to them, the use of hands to communicate, and facial expressions. Through observing people in families communicating among themselves, you may learn their style and comfortable ways of communicating nonverbally.

CREATING EXTENDED NETWORKS OF SUPPORT

Expanding communication channels makes it possible to build networks. Exploring ways to enable families to communicate with other families and the larger community opens up opportunities for sharing resources. When teachers create accessible, visible communication avenues for families to use, networks of support begin to develop on their own. Many programs create phone lists for families who wish to share their contact information with others in the program. Other programs make bulletin board space available for family-to-family communication or set aside time during family meetings for networking. There are many ways to identify or implement communication systems that families can use on their own to develop extended networks of support. These systems can be as elementary as a sign-up sheet on a clipboard or as complex as a chat group on the Internet. Using the concept of partnership, teachers and families can collaborate on identifying the support needs of the parent group and brainstorming ideas for communication.

Effective communication is not only the cornerstone of relationships with children but also the foundation of successful family-centered care. Whether communication happens in a simple greeting with a parent or in a parent conference or handbook, it determines the quality of the relationship. Working to learn the communication styles of the families in your program as well as striving to improve the quality of your communication skills will serve to nurture your partnership with families and children.

REFLECTING ON YOUR STRENGTHS AND AREAS NEEDING IMPROVEMENT

What do you consider to be your own personal strengths in the area of communication with families? What do you consider to be your program's strengths? How would you like to improve your own communication skills? your program's? Discuss with coworkers or fellow students.

4

Daily Communication

aily communication can happen orally and in writing between families and teachers. Many teachers and families talk daily in person or on the phone to check in on the day-to-day life of the child at home and in the program. Face-to-face communication gives partners an opportunity to read nonverbal cues, and it also offers children a chance to observe or be included in family-teacher communication. Phone and in-person communication provide immediate feedback and an opportunity to clarify information as it is shared. However, some people are much more comfortable writing notes, journal entries, e-mail, instant messages, or text messages than they are talking in person or on the phone. Written communication also allows families and teachers who don't see each other or have enough time to talk (for example, because of transportation arrangements), another way to share information. Family-teacher partnerships are nurtured and maintained through all these kinds of daily communication.

Many programs see families face-to-face twice a day. This makes communication easier. For teachers who don't see families daily, regular communication takes more effort and planning.

DAILY CHECK-INS

Talking with families daily offers teachers a chance to stay apprised of children's moods, health, family experiences, and out-of-school connections to friends and community. It gives teachers a link to the child's experiences at home so that they can refer to them, acknowledge them, and respond to the child's conversation about them. For families, talking with teachers helps them stay abreast of their children's experiences, discoveries, development, challenges, health, moods, and friendships in school. For teachers and families, daily sharing helps build trust, relationship, teamwork, and support. Daily communication also helps children to integrate their experiences at home and at school. Rather than having two distinct "lives," children can feel that the two parts of their day are connected and whole.

Finding the Time

Seeing families every day begins to set the stage for good communication. It also helps when both families and teachers have time and availability to talk. Check-ins can last between a minute and several minutes. This can be challenging for teachers who have several families and children to greet at the same time and also have responsibility for supervising all the children who are present. Many teachers become skilled at talking to a parent while keeping an eye on the children. Nevertheless, it is important that programs support teachers in these check-ins by ensuring there are enough staff during greeting and pick-up times so that teachers can be free from supervising while they are greeting. Another idea is to close the outdoor space if necessary to minimize the area that teachers are responsible for supervising. A few programs have asked parents to take turns supervising children to free teachers up for greeting. Many programs welcome families to hang out and visit with each other while the teacher greets each family and child personally.

Most parents have time limitations during drop-off and pick-up times. They may be in a rush to get to work or school or to drop off another child. It is useful to talk to parents individually and as a group about the importance of daily check-ins and ways to make them work for busy families as well as for teachers. Individually, you can find out about each family's schedule and their other responsibilities at the beginning and end of the day. You can let all families know that they are welcome to arrive earlier than they intend to say good-bye to help their child transition, to observe, and to talk with their child's teacher. Equally important, you can let families know how much time to allot for drop-off and pick-up. Many parents arrive exactly at the designated drop-off or pick-up time, not anticipating that the transition into and out of care will take some time. Staff can either designate a pick-up time that allows for twenty minutes of transition for children and families or let families know that they need to arrive ten to twenty minutes before closing time.

What about the Children?

Another significant part of the daily check-in between teachers and families is the child's role. At the same time the adults are trying to share

information, the child is making her transition between home and school. It is important for teachers to be aware of greeting both child and adult individually. Also, if the child is present while the adults are talking about her, it is crucial to think about what she is hearing. If the conversation is about her, it is important to include her. For example, you might say something like, "I'm telling your grandmother about how we changed your clothes after you were done playing with the water," or "Your brother is telling me about how you went sledding together." Some programs have a wonderful practice at pick-up time: the teacher and child together tell the parent about the day. Much of the time children are very interested in participating in the conversation; sometimes they just want to quietly watch or play.

When children are involved or are playing within earshot, it's important to be aware of whether the conversation is appropriate for the child to hear. Communications dealing with confidential adult issues from home or school can be scary or confusing for children to overhear. In addition, extensive conversations about a child's challenging behavior can be hard for a child to listen to. If necessary, the teacher can set up a separate time to talk to the parent, saying something like "This is important information. Let's set up a time when you and I can talk alone about this."

Daily Notes and Announcements

Daily written communication can be done individually or with the group or both. Notes also offer parents and teachers a chance to communicate with each other even if the teacher is working later in the day or is gone by pick-up time. Notes between individual teachers and families might include anecdotal observations of the child made by teachers or families, acknowledgements or appreciations, requests or questions. Here are some examples:

"Lori washed babies for most of the morning,

wetting, soaping, rinsing, and drying them, and then starting all over again. What are you observing at home?"

"Davin's grandparents have been visiting all week—late nights and lots of cookies. Are you noticing any change of behavior at school?"

"The kids have been trying to take apart everything. Do you have any broken radios or clocks in your shop you could bring for them to explore?"

"Thank you for bringing your puppy the other morning. The kids have been playing puppy games all week."

Notes to the whole family group might also include appreciations, reminders, information, or requests from either teachers or parents as well as reminders about upcoming events, such as family meetings, home visits, special curriculum activities, class photos, vision screening, etc. These notes to the parent group can be posted on a bulletin board or on a big piece of paper on the door. Here are some examples:

"Remember the potluck on Friday at 5:30."

"Thanks from the Alexanders to all the families who brought us dinners last week."

"Check out the new tree house in the yard."

"Thanks to all the families who participated in the all-center clean up last Saturday."

"Remember to bring swimsuits for water play tomorrow."

"On Wednesday a child safety specialist will be here during pick-up and drop-off to help with any questions you have about car seats."

Some programs have a daily announcement board. If you provide extra pens and paper by the board, families can add their own announcements—for example, "Jani's new baby brother, Sterling, was born last night!" Making it easy for parents to communicate with teachers and with other parents is an important part of supporting two-way communication and building networks. Dry-erase boards can provide another way for families, as well as teachers, to post upcoming events. They can be divided into sections that allow communication from all directions: from teachers to parents, from parents to teachers, and from parents to parents. E-mail offers a new dimension to written communication; it can be sent to one or many families and can be read from many locations.

In one classroom the teacher posts written communication for all families every day. She puts two sheets of paper on the door. The top of one sheet says, "This is what we planned for today," and the top of the other one says, "This is what happened today." In the morning the first one is filled out, and the second one is filled out in the afternoon. She usually writes four to eight lines about the day's activities, experiences, and interests. This is a wonderful way to give all the families information about the day and helps families in talking to children about their experiences in the program. Rather than the typical parent-child interaction ("What did you do at school today?" "Nothing"), the discussion might go like this: "I heard that Josie's dog visited today." "Yeah! He licked me, and it was wet!"

When You Don't See the Family Daily

Sharing information with families who don't come to school every day with their child or who have limited time requires creativity and flexibility. Phone calls, e-mails, written notes, and interactive journals are all ways to communicate when face-to-face time is limited. You can let these families know the importance of regular communication and ask them about what system would work best for them.

Interactive Family Journals

Interactive journals, written daily by both teachers and families, provide a venue for information sharing, as well as for sharing power and decision making. Many programs use interactive journals to record observations, discuss development, and make daily notes and reminders to each other. In these programs, each child has his own journal. Journals usually stay at school, but they can also go home with the family and come back in the morning. Teachers typically write in them at least once a day. Families use them in a variety of ways. Some write copiously, and others never write. Some read daily; others read weekly or not at all. Some families keep them when they leave the program as a precious history of their child's young years. These interactive journals can be an important tool in two-way communication.

Zane, a toddler teacher, describes a decision he made with a family through their daily journal:

Yesenia's mom, Dora, wrote excitedly in the journal one day that she had gotten some number blocks for Yesenia to use at home. The next day she suggested that we should get some at the school, so that we could work with Yesenia on her numbers here also. I thanked her for her suggestion and wrote back describing a few of the number activities we already do with children in our program. Then, *on the weekend, I saw some nice wooden number blocks at a garage sale and brought them in on Monday morning. Dora was so excited. When I showed them to other families that morning, I told them that Dora, Yesenia's mom, had suggested I get them. Dora is pretty quiet sometimes during our daily check-ins. I'm not sure she would have mentioned the blocks to me if we didn't have our written journal.*

Journals don't have to be fancy; a simple set of binders with loose-leaf paper and children's names on the spines works just fine.

MORNING DROP-OFF

During the drop-off conversation parents can share information about their child's health, eating, sleeping, clothes, significant events that happen at home, and family changes. Parents can give any special care or pick-up instructions and ask questions about things their child has said about school. Teachers can share anything about the child's day at school that didn't get shared the day before. They can ask parents for observation of the child at home and give parents updates about upcoming activities, curriculum, and school events. Teachers can offer child development information if parents have questions about certain behaviors.

One family home child care provider establishes trust with families by sharing a little about herself during these check-ins. She says, "I often give a little information about something my kids and I did or a short trip I took with my family. Sometimes I give an example of my child's behavior. I make it very short, like fifteen to twenty seconds, because I don't want to take up our time talking about my family, but I think it helps them get to know me and gives them an idea of the kinds of information we can share about our families." Check-ins during drop-off are important because they can affect everyone's day. If the parent leaves after a sincere and friendly interaction with the teacher, the child starts his day seeing his important adults in good communication, and the teacher has had a chance to share information with the family as well as receive information from them, everyone has a better day.

Getting Ready to Go Home

Even before you consider what information to share with families at the end of every day, it's important to think about the atmosphere you create in the classroom that helps children and families slow down and reconnect when family members arrive. Helping families make a successful transition home with their children is an important part of this end-of-the-day routine. Parents and children generally have differing paces and rhythms during their days. Adults often operate on an accomplishment-oriented, fast pace. Children tend to have a slower, more process-oriented pace. In many instances the child development program can help children and their parents get back into sync with each other and move smoothly into their evening. This approach will pay dividends not only in better evenings for families and children but in easier transitions out of the program for children and thus a much easier end to the day for staff.

Teachers can do a number of things to help children prepare to go home: having good-bye circles; collecting belongings; giving reminders that parents will be here soon; leading songs about pick-up time; making sure the children are dressed and ready to go. For many parents, spending a few minutes observing their child, sharing a book together, talking with other parents, or checking in with the teacher will help them get back on "kid time." It is important to remember that this is one of the times of the day when most parents are juggling many things. Sometimes they just need to have you listen to how tired or overwhelmed they feel. They are the ones who need a personal check-in. Ironically, we spend our days listening to children, and often no one is listening to their parents.

Here's an example of a teacher skillfully helping a parent get in sync with his son. Brett was sharing custody with Damian's mother. He hadn't seen his son for a few days when he came to pick him up. Brett came into the classroom loud, excited, and fast: "Come on, Damian. Time to split." Teacher Tatiana came over to Brett and started talking about Damian's day. Brett repeated, "Come on, buddy." Tatiana came closer to Brett and sat down, giving him nonverbal clues that she was available to talk. Brett still kept his attention on moving Damian, who remained engrossed in the sandbox. At this point Tatiana asked Brett, "How was your weekend?" Brett turned to her and talked for several minutes about his weekend, his body noticeably relaxing. When he came to a natural stopping place, Tatiana said to him, "I bet you are looking forward to spending some time with your son." Brett nodded, and Tatiana began to tell him about how Damian's last few days had gone. Brett then went over to Damian, crouched down low, and said, "Hey, buddy, I see you are digging in the sand." They talked a little bit and left together, hand in hand. Reflecting on her interaction with Brett, Tatiana said that sometimes parents need a little care when they come to pick up their children, before they can turn their attention to the child. Tatiana sees her role as helping both the child and the parent get ready to be together again. She believes that if they can get in sync before they leave the program together, they will have a much better evening together. Sometimes she leaves Damian's shoes off after the last diaper change of the day, so that Brett can have the chance to slow down and help his son get his shoes on before they leave together. It's clear to Tatiana how much Brett loves his son—he has told her how he wants to be a good dad.

Teachers can also structure activities that help parents and children reconnect at the end of the day. Years ago, when I was an afternoon child care teacher, the children and I almost always cooked a late snack together, and parents often joined us at the snack table for food and talk about the day. For many parents who are on a hurried schedule all day long, pick-up at the children's center can be a little oasis of relief in their day.

Sharing Information about the Day

Many families who haven't seen their child all day will be eager for news. Some parents will be wondering if their child missed them. Some will want to know about naps, eating, and diapering/toileting. For the teacher, this is a good opportunity to partner with families by giving them information that helps them feel connected to their child, offering child development information so they can better understand their child, acknowledging parenting skills already in place, and listening to any stories or concerns they want to share. The information you give parents will be determined by your program's policy and practices, what the parent is interested in knowing, and the time you and the parent have available. Many programs use a combination of verbal and written communication. Some programs plan for staggered pick-up times so that all parents don't arrive at the same time. This can help give teachers time to talk with each family.

It is important that you share with families at least one observation of each child from the day. Many families have an underlying worry that their children will be ignored once the families leave. Offering an observation of their children not only reassures them that someone was watching but also models the importance of observing. This observation should be something positive. Even if you need to share information about a struggle or difficult behavior a child is having, it is essential to share, in addition, an observation about something that is going well for the child.

Along with information about the child's play and learning, many parents are very interested in their child's routines. Many programs keep written records on children's food intake, napping, and diapering. Generally, the younger the child is, the more interested parents are in this information. Knowing the ins and outs of their child's day can help them anticipate the kinds of care their child will need at home for the rest of the day. Even if all this information is written down, parents enjoy hearing one thing about the routines. For example, a teacher might say, "Benji loved the oranges today," and then turn to Benji to say, "You must have eaten ten orange sections at snack."

Some teachers do a quick check in their mind at the end of the day to make sure they have something about each child to share. Others keep written notes in their pocket or on a clipboard in the classroom to remind them of what they want to say.

Aside from information about their child's activities and routines, parents enjoy hearing that their child remembered them or asked about them during the day. If you can catch or remember one of those moments when the child visited her family pictures on the wall or looked up at you and said, "Dada?" parents usually appreciate your sharing it. This is also a good time for child development information. Parents may feel guilty that their child is asking about them, and you can reassure them that this is the child's way of remembering and keeping track of their important people. Just the way the parent remembers his child several times throughout the day, the child also remembers her family.

The end of the day is a busy time for teachers with cleanup, supporting tired kids, finding everyone's shoes and artwork, managing siblings in the classroom, remembering what to tell parents, preparing for your own transition to go home. Remember that you don't have to tell everyone everything every day. You might want to think about parent communication over a week. Could you manage to really focus with each parent one day a week? On the other days, could you manage a quicker check-in? Once you have a comfortable relationship established and parents are accustomed to the pick-up routine, they may be able to help and support one another. Many times in the late afternoon, when they are comfortable being in the program and used to slowing down when they get there, parents stand around, chatting with each other about their days, while children finish up play and get ready to leave. While parents can't give each other information about their child's day at school, they can provide a listening ear to one another's stories and stresses. Some programs give "parent volunteer hours" to families for coming at the end of the day and helping with cleanup. This offers parents a way to be active contributors and also frees up teachers for check-ins with other parents.

SHARING CHILD DEVELOPMENT INFORMATION

When teachers think of parent education, the first thought is often about articles, books, or parent meetings. While these are all good ways to share information with families, daily communication can provide wonderful opportunities to offer insights into children's behavior and to explore helpful responses. Parents are most interested in child development information when it directly relates to what is happening with their

child. When Vicki showed up in the morning after a sleepless night with newly walking Kellan, it was helpful for her to learn from Kellan's teacher, Joniko, that children's sleep is often disrupted when they pass a developmental milestone. When Luz told Pete about his four-year-old son Leny's new "poop" vocabulary at school and explained that four-year-olds are fascinated with body language and are testing how to impress people with it, Pete could understand his child's behavior. Teachers can also use journals and notes to share developmental information with parents about their children. (For more on talking to parents about difficult behavior, see chapter 5, "Challenges to Communication: Problems Affecting the Child at Home or at School.")

Some teachers invite family members to observe with them in the classroom. A short observation of children building a spaceship out of blocks can offer families a chance to understand children's ability to learn many things simultaneously: teamwork, science, physics, and physical coordination. Short interactions like these can enable parents to learn important child development information.

REFLECTING ON DAILY CHECK-INS

How are daily check-ins done in your program? Think about the environment, the staffing, the communication systems. What is your program doing well, and what needs improvement? What are your personal strengths in doing check-ins? What skills would you like to improve? Find a coworker or a fellow student, and role-play the kind of check-in you would like to have with every family every day. What would be the first step you could take to implement these kinds of check-ins?

Daily communication provides different kinds of opportunities for strengthening the partnership and keeps teachers and families up-to-date with each other. Both oral and written daily communication offer an ongoing way to learn about each other's knowledge and expertise, to engage in two-way communication, to explore ways to include the diversity of the children and families in the program, and to share power and decision making.

5

Challenges to Communication: Problems Affecting the Child at Home or at School

There are two main ways that problems can arise to test the partnership between families and the early childhood program. One is when a parent is facing a problem with his child at home or dealing with other difficult issues in the family. These issues don't directly affect the teacher or the program, although they are likely to have an impact on the child's behavior in the program. Also, parents may ask for support or need a place to talk. A different kind of challenging communication with families is when a teacher needs to share information with a family regarding the child's behavior at school or concerns the teacher has about the child. All of the principles of family-centered care support communication when there are problems. Families and teachers who respect one another's expertise, engage in two-way communication, and share power and decision making develop a base of understanding and trust that supports clear communication and problem solving when difficult communication arises. Respecting diversity allows for different perspectives on the same problem and acknowledges that there may be a variety of solutions. Networks of support broaden the resources available when there are problems and make it possible for families to seek support from other families as well as from the larger community.

PARENT-OWNED PROBLEMS

Often parents will ask teachers for help with questions or problems they are having with children at home. Sometimes they also share information about issues in the family that are stressful for them. Teachers can play an important role in facilitating parents through their problem-solving process, but teachers aren't responsible for solving these problems. Here are some examples of parent-owned problems: the child wakes several times a night, and the parent is not getting enough sleep; the child won't get ready for child care in the morning, and the parent is late for work and feels frustrated; a parent has differences of opinion with his partner about parenting strategies; and a parent is considering separating from her partner. You can probably name fifty other parent-owned problems from your experience working with families.

Using the principles of two-way communication and of recognizing and respecting one another's knowledge and expertise, teachers can use a strengths-based approach to problem solving. Specifically, the teacher's role is to listen to the parent; to acknowledge the parent's experience, frustrations, and attempts at solutions; to offer child development information as appropriate;

to encourage the parent to access resource networks; and to support the parent in developing a plan of action, if appropriate.

Parents who are feeling overwhelmed, confused, and frustrated are often forgetting they have any skills as parents. One of your roles as a teacher in facilitating parents' problem solving is to remind them of their resourcefulness and acknowledge their strengths. This can be done by directly naming the skills you have observed or by asking questions and making comments that allow them to rediscover their expertise.

For example, an attentive teacher might say something like "I heard you say that you have thought of and tried four different approaches to this problem," or "You've listened to your child, you've offered alternatives, and he is still trying to climb on the table. Even though his behavior hasn't changed yet, he is still learning important things from the way you are talking to him."

Teachers can provide child development naturally throughout the conversation. Child development information often gives parents an understanding of their child's behavior that allows them to feel less worried and more resourceful in responding to it. For instance, a teacher might say, "Some two-year-olds go through periods where they just have to climb on everything. It becomes their main priority. You can't really stop them; they just need plenty of alternative places to climb and test their newfound skills."

The other aspect of strengths-based problem solving is understanding and communicating to the parents that you believe they can resolve this challenge. Often in the midst of struggle parents lose hope that they will ever be able to get through. Your confidence and reassurance can provide the encouragement a family needs: "You've done some really good observation of your child and some creative thinking about ways to respond. I'm confident you will figure this out. Often with behavior that is developmental or typ-ical of the age, it just takes a little more time."

It is also important for teachers to know what to do when these problems are beyond their capabilities to help. Sometimes you will know right away that the issue is outside of your expertise, and other times you will discover this while talking to the parent. Problems such as marital issues, addiction, and domestic violence are clearly beyond a teacher's training to help resolve. There are other, more ambiguous issues such as challenging family and parenting relationships that a teacher may start out supporting a family through. Only after some unsuccessful attempts at resolution does it become clear to the teacher that the family needs outside support. Consulting coworkers, administrators, or community resource people can help a teacher clarify if a family should be referred. In either situation, where a teacher feels unable to assist a family, she can ask other professionals for help.

These situations can be challenging for teachers to handle if they don't feel prepared with information or the listening skills to support the parent. Reviewing child development information and learning and practicing communication strategies will help prepare you for these conversations. It is also helpful for you to be familiar with resources in the community and to have referrals easily available.

Steps for Supporting Families with Problems

Here are some steps to consider when supporting a parent with a problem. These steps focus on listening to encourage a parent to share her thoughts, observations, expertise, and frustrations. They also include the two-way sharing of information and encouragement for the parent to find his own solution and make his own decision. These are suggested steps, starting with listening and moving to facilitating a solution. They don't all need to be used in every dialogue, and they can be used in a different order from the one listed here.

◆ Listen, listen, listen. Ask open-ended questions, and reflect back to the parent.

◆ Restate and reframe the parent's ideas.

◆ Acknowledge the parent's efforts and strengths.

◆ Ask the parent what he or she would like to have happen.

◆ Give child development information as appropriate.

◆ Refer the parent to resources.

◆ Make a plan to check back with the parent, and thank the parent for sharing with you.

LISTEN, LISTEN, LISTEN

Give the parent an opportunity to tell his story. Being really listened to is an empowering experience. In many conversations people are more focused on convincing one another, telling their own story, giving advice, reassuring each other, and agreeing or disagreeing than they are on truly listening to the other person. In authentic listening the listener suspends her own feelings to work to see the perspective of the speaker. Many people don't have experience doing this kind of listening. It can be challenging and may take practice. Authentic listening provides several benefits. It offers you a chance to empathize and more deeply understand the ideas and experiences of the parent, and it gives the parent the chance to voice and reflect on his own ideas. When a parent feels truly listened to, he feels respect for you, gains confidence in his ideas, experiences deeper trust in the relationship, and develops an increased willingness to listen to your perspective. Listening is especially critical when you sense that the parent is getting defensive or tense.

Ask open-ended questions and questions that give you more information about what really matters to the parent. Avoid questions that distract the parent from what she really wants to express. For instance, when a parent says, "Gino got real-ly scared at swimming lessons yesterday," you could respond, "Oh, where is Gino taking swimming lessons?" Or you could say, "Hmmm, what happened at swimming lessons?" The first question conveys more about what you are interested in than responding to the parent's concern. The second question allows the parent to continue with her story. Open-ended questions communicate to the parent that you are really interested and have time to listen. Open-ended questions can also help parents discover things they haven't yet understood or articulated.

You can also use an eliciting statement to help the parent tell his story. For example, you might say something like "Tell me more about that." Even a response as simple as "Hmmm" tells a parent that you are listening and invites him to say more.

Reflecting back what the parent is saying, perhaps in different words or more precisely, helps people name their feelings. It is natural for families to have strong feelings about their children. Sometimes parents can name these feelings; other times they communicate them without naming them. Because feelings can be hard to talk about but are an important part of the partnership, it is useful for you to acknowledge, ask about, or help parents name their feelings. Here are some examples of reflecting back that names feelings parents may not have named for themselves yet:

"That sounds challenging."

"So many nights without sleep sounds exhausting."

"It can be really frustrating when what has been working all of a sudden doesn't work anymore."

"It sounds like you are feeling worried about Gino's experience at swimming."

In acknowledging or naming parents' feelings, it is important to remember that they are the expert on their own feelings and as such it is important not to tell them what they are feeling. Here are some examples of phrases *not* to use:

"That must have made you so scared."

"You're really feeling sad right now."

Instead, use phrases like "It looks like . . ."; "It sounds like . . ."; "I wonder if . . ."; or "Were you feeling . . . ?" in order to engage the parent and allow him to correct you if you have guessed wrong.

Restate and Reframe the Parent's Ideas

When you restate a parent's ideas back to her, it informs her that she is being heard, recognizes her knowledge, and gives you an opportunity to check to see if you have heard her accurately. Hearing her own idea spoken may also give her a different perspective on it. Here's an example: "So, it sounds like you are concerned about how late Genevieve is getting to sleep in the evenings, and you would like us to adjust her nap schedule."

Occasionally, a parent will say something in a way that isn't helpful to the problem-solving process. When this happens, it can be useful to put his idea into slightly different words to offer a new perspective. For instance, when a parent says, "William is just a trouble maker. He always has been," you can say, "It sounds like things have been really challenging with William." Reframing can help a parent reevaluate the problem and see it in a new light. Often it is useful to ask open-ended questions before reframing, so you have more information about what the real concern is.

Acknowledge the Parent's Efforts and Strengths

Often a parent who is struggling unsuccessfully with an issue feels powerless and incompetent. Using the strengths-based approach, you can acknowledge her efforts and expertise and remind her that she has the creativity to resolve her challenge. "It sounds like you have really been working with this." "You have come up with so many ideas for solutions."

Sometimes *facilitative* questions can help the parent discover his own best thinking and communicate your confidence in his ability to solve problems. "What have you tried that works?" "Do you have other resources you could use?" "Is this like anything you have dealt with before?" "What have you figured out about this?"

Ask the Parent What She Would Like to Have Happen

Sometimes parents are clear about what isn't working, but they haven't yet conceptualized their goal for a better outcome. Asking them to think about their goal can help them move toward a solution and also informs them that they have the power to implement change. "How would you like to see this resolved?" "What would you like to have happen?"

This is the point in the conversation at which teachers often want to give advice. Asking parents first what they would like to try gives them the opportunity to experience their own power and do their own creative thinking based on the new information and insight they have gained from the conversation so far.

Sometimes concrete suggestions can be very useful to a parent in a quandary. Before offering suggestions, though, ask the parent if he wants a suggestion. This communicates to him that he is still in charge of the problem-solving process. When offering advice or suggestions, remember to offer rather than direct. For example, you might say something like "Some parents have found it useful to wean their child from the bottle by gradually introducing the cup" instead of "You should wean your child from the bottle by gradually introducing the cup."

Give Child Development Information as Appropriate

Helping parents understand their child's behavior in the context of healthy development can offer parents new insight. In offering parents information about child development, it can be useful to give them an array of possible reasons, rather than just giving them the reason you may believe is the cause of the behavior. "A two-year-old might bite to show affection or frustration, to test for a response, or because she is teething. Do any of these reasons seem to fit for your child?" This empowers parents to actively participate in thinking about their child, teaches them about child development theory, and allows them to share their own observations of and ideas about their child. Letting them know the continuum of normal behavior can also reassure them that they are not alone. Information can be offered orally or through written resources.

Refer the Parent to Resources

Often parents will bring up topics that you don't have the information to help with. You can help parents find resources in other parents, books, or articles. If you are referring parents to another parent, be aware of confidentiality. Both parents have to agree before you can connect them. "Would you be interested in talking to another parent about this? I know a couple of parents who have had similar experiences. I could ask one of them if they would be able to give you a call." When you refer the parent to a professional, it is important that she understand that her concern is important to you and that you are not disregarding it. For example: "This is a really important issue, and I don't feel that I have the experience or training to offer the support you need. Would you like to set up an appointment with the director, or can I refer you to another person who might be able to help?"

Make a Plan to Check Back with the Parent, and Thank the Parent

Telling the parent that you would like to check back to see how things are going lets her know that you care about her family. Additionally, it provides some structure for the parent to follow through on the plan. Even if you aren't the only resource the family is using, you may have a role

in helping them navigate the system. Letting the parent know you appreciate her sharing her concern with you supports ongoing two-way communication. Sharing information, struggles, experiences, and successes with each other is part of nurturing the partnership.

Listening Practice

Find a partner, and take turns talking for five minutes each. When it is your turn to speak, talk about something in your teaching that is important to you. When it is your turn to listen, focus on really listening. Make good eye contact, but don't speak. If you feel like speaking, take note of what you would like to say, but remain quiet. After each of you has had a chance to speak and to listen, compare notes on what it felt like to be listened to. Also, if either of you felt tempted to talk, discuss the kinds of things you wanted to say while you were listening. Did you feel tempted to tell your own story, give advice, reassure the speaker, or something else? Being aware of what makes it hard to just listen can help you improve your attention when listening.

Here are a couple of sample dialogues to help you see how these techniques look in practice. You will probably find that you are already using some of the suggestions!

Sample Dialogue: Thinking through a Problem

Parent: *[Arriving with child, looking hurried and flustered] I can't believe my morning. I thought we would never get out of the house.*

Teacher: *Sounds like a frustrating morning. [Actively listening]*

Parent: *Yeah, we couldn't find the other rain boot, and I couldn't get Mira away from the TV.*

Teacher: *Tell me more. [Eliciting response]*

Parent: *Oh, there's more all right. I overslept*

because I was studying late last night, and her dad is out of town.

Teacher: *You sound like you are juggling a lot: single parenting, schoolwork, dealing with a child who has her own ideas. [Acknowledging parent's strength, restating parent's ideas]*

Parent: *Whew! I've been doing pretty well with it, actually, but this morning I just lost it.*

Teacher: *That happens to all of us sometimes. Congratulations on managing it for so long. [Giving information, acknowledging parent's strength]*

Parent: *Thank you.*

Teacher: *How would you like the morning to be different? [Asking parent what she would like to have happen]*

Parent: *Well, I would really like to have a little time with Mira, rather than just me rushing around and her watching TV.*

Teacher: *I know the morning story you usually read with her helps her feel connected to you for the rest of the day. How do you manage to do that some mornings? [Giving child development information, asking a facilitative question]*

Parent: *Those are the mornings I am able to get up before she does, have a cup of tea, and get everything laid out and ready to go. Then she doesn't even get a chance to turn on the TV.*

Teacher: *Do you have any creative ideas for how to deal with those mornings when you need to sleep in a little? [Asking a facilitative question]*

Parent: *Well, you know, as tired as I am after I finish studying, if I took the time to lay our things out the evening before, I would feel much more on top of it in the morning.*

Teacher: *Sounds like you have a plan. I'd like to check back in with you in a few days to see how things are going. Thanks for sharing your challenge with me this morning. [Make a plan to check back in, and thank parent]*

This next sample shows what a dialogue between a parent and a teacher might look like when the teacher decides to make a referral.

SAMPLE DIALOGUE: MAKING A REFERRAL

Parent: *My mother-in-law is coming to visit this week.*

Teacher: *Hmm-mm. [Listening and making eye contact, eliciting response]*

Parent: *Yeah, she always has lots to say about our parenting.*

Teacher: *What kinds of things does she say? [Asking open-ended questions]*

Parent: *Well, she thinks I'm babying Lee because he isn't weaned and he's already a year old.*

Teacher: *It sounds like you are feeling criticized for your decisions. [Reflecting, restating]*

Parent: *[Sighs] Yes, I've read a lot and thought a lot about when is the right time to wean him, and she just bulldozes in and says that it's time to stop.*

Teacher: *So you have really researched and thought about how and when you want to wean Lee, and she doesn't seem to notice. [Acknowledging the parent's efforts]*

Parent: *Yeah, I know it is hard for her because she didn't get any support for breast feeding.*

Teacher: *Do you have any ideas for ways to handle this? [Asking facilitative question]*

Parent: *No, right now I feel really stuck.*

Teacher: *Would you like some suggestions? [Offering suggestion]*

Parent: *Please.*

Teacher: *This is not my area of expertise. I know we have some books and resources here that refer to relationships with extended family, and I could refer you to other families in our program who have dealt with similar issues. But also, this is a very personal and important issue, and I wonder if you have thought about talking to someone like a therapist about it. [Referring parent to resources, as appropriate]*

Parent: *Well, I've never gone to a therapist before, but I could really use help with this one. Do you know of any you could refer me to?*

Teacher: *I'll do a little research and get back to you this evening. Does that work?*

Parent: *Yes, thank you.*

Teacher: *Thank you for sharing this with me.*

Supporting families with their problems and struggles is an important aspect of the partnership. Understanding your role and having the skills to facilitate, offer resources, and identify when the issue is beyond your scope are essential to the success of the process.

SUPPORTING FAMILIES WITH PROBLEMS

Make a list of the steps for supporting families with problems. Role-play a teacher talking to a parent who has brought up a problem. Remember that these problems need to be "family-owned," for example: child won't take a bath or brush her teeth at home, child runs away from parent at the store, child is fighting with his sibling at home. Have a third person observe the role play to give feedback on the teacher's use of the steps. Discuss how the role play felt for the teacher and the parent.

TEACHER-OWNED PROBLEMS

The second kind of problem that requires communication with families is sharing difficult news with them about their child at school. It can be confusing as well as challenging for teachers to talk to families about some things that happen at school with their children. It is important that teachers understand that the problems you are sharing with parents are ones that you have most of the responsibility for finding solutions to. In these conversations, you don't need the parent to tell you how to solve this problem, and you don't need the parent to follow through at home with the child. You can use the parent as an informational resource, but it is ultimately your responsibility to solve the problem. Here are some examples of teacher-owned problems: a child is excluding other children from play; a child resists diaper changes with the teacher; a child is using hurtful language; a child won't come to group time; a child is hitting, biting, kicking, or shoving other children; a child cries whenever he is not being held while in child care.

Even though these are problems the teacher is responsible for, the relationship with the parent regarding these issues is very important. For the teacher, talking to the parent may help you gain insight into the behaviors in question, give you information about all the different ways this behavior is showing up, and understand what the family thinks about the behavior and how they are responding to it. Talking with the family can also bring you up-to-date on any experiences or changes that are happening with the child or family at home.

For the parents, hearing about their child's challenging behavior at school can be uncomfortable or worrisome. Parents may be concerned that there is something wrong with their child or that their parenting skills are in question. They often feel helpless because they weren't there when it happened. As you talk with them, it is important to keep these things in mind and to be as supportive and informative as possible.

The main purposes of sharing this information with parents is to keep them informed about their child's day, to offer child development information about the child's behavior, and to let them know what strategies and responses you are using. Ultimately, families want to be reassured that their children are "normal" and that you are able to handle whatever comes up or to find help if necessary.

When talking to a parent about his child's challenging behavior, teachers need to keep in mind three guidelines: it's important not to use the conversation with the child's parent as an opportunity to vent your own feelings about the child's behavior; it's crucial that the parent understand that it's not his job to do something at home to change the child's behavior at school; and it's important to be conscious of the cumulative effect on the parent of the information you give him about his child over time. Let's take these one at a time.

Teachers who have been dealing with conflict, testing, and other difficult behavior all day sometimes just need to vent their own feelings of frustration. While teachers deserve the opportunity to let off steam after a hard day, the parent is not an appropriate person to do it with. Using the parent in this way will detract from the partnership and can make the parent feel defensive about her child, critical of the teacher, and worried about the teacher's abilities.

Many times parents feel responsible for their children's behavior whether the children are with them or not. Because of this sense of responsibility, when you share information with a parent about a child's difficult day, the parent might feel that you are asking her to do something at home to follow up on the behavior from school. This is not the parent's job and will probably confuse the child.

When talking with parents about a problem at school, be sure to think about the cumulative effect of all the information you share about a child with her parents over time. Here's an example that will help to explain why: Lyssa's mother, Kate, talks about her experience when Lyssa was going through a challenging period at school. "Every day I would come, and the first thing the teacher said to me was 'Lyssa grabbed toys from so and so. Lyssa pushed so and so down.' Sometimes they would just flash a number of fingers at me to represent the number of times she had hurt someone. It got to the point that I would avoid the teachers when I came to pick up Lyssa. I'd try

to sneak in and get her stuff out of the cubby while the teachers were busy outside."

While it is important to give parents accurate information about their child's day, it is also crucial to remember how a parent feels when bombarded by difficult news. Further, there are always positive things that happen in any child's day. It is especially important to share these things with families when you also have unsuccessful behavior to share. In the end-of-day check-ins it can be helpful to start with something successful about the child's day, then share the challenge, and lastly, end with a sweet anecdote about the child. For example, you might say something like this: "Trevor spent much of the morning having a wonderful time climbing all different ways on the obstacle course. He had a rough time coming to circle, because he still wanted to climb. We told him he could climb again after snack and gave him a choice of being in the reading area or coming to circle. After he made a few attempts at jumping around circle, Nancy took him to stay in the reading area, and he cried for a while. It seems like he is so into physical activity right now that it is hard for him to have to sit still. Later, he helped Nancy pass out snack to the kids at his table." This example talks about Trevor's strengths as well as his challenges and also puts his behavior into a developmental context.

Discussing School Problems with Families

Here are some steps to consider when talking to families. As with the previous set of steps for communication, these are suggestions. You might not use all of them, and you might find yourself using them in a slightly different order.

- Greet the parent, make sure she has time to talk, and share your observation.
- Listen to the parent's feelings, and ask for his observations and ideas.
- Offer child development information, and give possible reasons for the behavior.

◆ Explain to the parent how you are handling the behavior.

◆ Clarify with the parent why you are sharing this information with him.

◆ Ask the parent if she has any questions, thank the parent, and arrange to check in later.

GREET THE PARENT, MAKE SURE SHE HAS TIME TO TALK, AND SHARE YOUR OBSERVATION

A simple greeting can help a parent feel comfortable and welcome. Even though you may be ready to give the parent a full report on his child's day, the parent may have other plans. On days when you want to do more than the normal check-in, it is important to ask the parent if she has time. You can ask for a few minutes or a specific amount of time. You might say something like "Do you have five or ten minutes to talk today? I'd like to share some observations with you and hear how things are going for Carmelita at home," or "Do you have ten minutes anytime in the next few days to talk? I'd like to share some observations."

If the parent doesn't have time to talk at that moment, you might be able to set up an evening phone call or arrange to talk the next day. In most cases, this should be fine. If the parent does have time to talk, then tell the parent descriptively and as objectively as possible what you have observed and experienced in the program.

The words we choose to tell parents about their child's behavior affect the parents' response to what is happening. Using descriptive and non-judgmental language about children educates, informs, and supports parents as well as nurtures the partnership. For instance, use phrases that show the developmental link to children's behavior, such as "Your child is experimenting with swear words" instead of "Your child is insulting everyone with rude language."

It is critical that you also tell the parent about the child's strengths and successes. This can give the parent a clearer picture of the whole child,

not just the challenging behavior. For example, you might say something like "Lulu has been spending a lot of time working on puzzles. She has mastered most of our harder puzzles. She also seems concerned when other children come into the area and will sometimes scream at them to 'go away!'" This gives the parent a clearer context for the behavior and shows the parent that you see the whole child and not just the problems.

LISTEN TO THE PARENT'S FEELINGS, AND ASK FOR HIS OBSERVATIONS AND IDEAS

Often a parent's first response to hearing about his child's difficult behavior at school is shock, anger, or upset. Taking a minute to acknowledge a parent's feelings can help him continue more fully in the discussion. Then reflect back the feelings you hear. Say something like "It can be worrisome to hear that your child is using language that you don't want him to use at school," or "It seems like you are feeling sad and concerned about Riva's hitting." Ask families in a neutral and supportive way about what they have observed at home. This encourages them to share information. You might say something like "I'm interested in your observations of Ari," or "I'm wondering what you are seeing at home." If you ask accusative or yes-or-no questions like "Have you seen this behavior at home too?" or "Is he doing this all the time?" families might feel defensive and be less able to share their observations. Partnering with families to share information about the child's experience at home and at school will give both teachers and parents a deeper understanding of the child. It also reminds families of the teacher's interest in their ideas and experience and reiterates the parents' essential role in the care and education of their children.

Next, ask the parent for her ideas about the child's behavior. In many cases, parents will tell you without being asked, but asking emphasizes that you consider the parent to be the expert on her child individually. Most parents spend considerable time reflecting on their children's growth and development. They often have several ideas about what causes a particular behavior. Even if you think a parent's ideas may be off-target, asking her what she thinks will help you learn more about how she sees her child.

OFFER CHILD DEVELOPMENT INFORMATION, AND GIVE POSSIBLE REASONS FOR THE BEHAVIOR

Explain to parents how their child's behavior fits into child development theory. This helps parents understand what their child is trying to learn, and helps them view difficult behavior as a normal part of development. It offers parents the tools to think about all of their child's behavior in a different way and helps empower parents to be active partners with you. Here is an example of a teacher sharing possible reasons with a parent when his child is biting:

Ari is experimenting with using his teeth on his friends. From my experience children bite for a lot of different reasons, most of them developmental and very normal. They might bite because they are teething, showing affection, showing frustration, or experimenting with cause and effect. Often they bite because they are trying to communicate something, and they don't have words yet. Biting is normal behavior for many two- to three-year-old children. Let's share what we have both observed and see if we can figure out what Ari is working on.

When you offer parents several possible explanations for behavior, it invites them to help you decide what the reason might be for their child.

Here's another example of talking to parents; this one is addressing the parents of a child who is excluding others from play:

I've observed that Raul is exploring some ideas about friendship. Today, he tried to exclude some of his friends from playing when he was in the playhouse area. This is a very common behavior for four-year-olds. They are trying to define friendship. They wonder if they can be friends with more than

one person at a time. They can get confused or over-whelmed playing with several friends, because there are so many different ideas of what to do. They sometimes get excited about a new friend and don't know how to include their old friends in the new play. I can share with you some more of what I observed and listen to what you have seen, and maybe together we can think about what he is trying to figure out through this play.

The right amount of information to offer a parent will depend on the available time, your relationship with the parent, and the parent's interest and existing knowledge about child development.

EXPLAIN TO THE PARENT HOW YOU ARE HANDLING THE BEHAVIOR

Letting the parent know that you have the tools, knowledge, expertise, and resources to help her child through this challenging behavior is one of the most important parts of this dialogue. It not only reassures the parent that her child will be respected and well cared for, but it also clarifies that the parent doesn't have to intercede. You might say something like "We have a lot of experience helping children get through biting. We try to observe when it happens, so we can anticipate it; we give children other things to bite or chew; we let them see that the other person is hurt; and we offer alternative ways for them to express their idea or feeling." It can also be helpful to the parent to know that you have a plan if the behavior continues. "Sometimes the biting stops after a few incidents, and other times, it persists for a while. If that happens, we will make sure there is a teacher close to Ari most of the time to help keep him and his friends safe."

Clarify with the Parent Why You Are Sharing This Information with Him

It is important for teachers to clarify to parents that what happens at school is the teacher's responsibility and what happens at home is the family's responsibility. Sometimes, in frustration, teachers imply that they would like the parents to do something at home, and occasionally, parents feel so bad about the behavior that they take it upon themselves to follow through at home. In either case, it might be useful to tell the parent explicitly, "It is important to me that you know about what happens in your child's day, and that I get a chance to see if you have any information or insight about your child and this behavior. That is why I'm sharing this information. I also want you to know that we followed through with your child here at school, and I'm not asking you to do anything else about it right now."

If you would like the parent to talk to the child or to provide some experiences to help the child with his learning, you can brainstorm ideas or offer suggestions. If a child is having a hard time making friends at school, you might ask if the family would be interested in inviting a child over for a play date. If a child is biting other children because she is teething, you might discuss with the family teethers they could use at home.

If appropriate, you may also need to let parents know if there are any policies in your program that relate to their child's behavior. For example, most programs have a confidentiality policy that prohibits telling families the name of the child who bit or hit their child.

Ask the Parent If She Has Any Questions, Thank the Parent, and Arrange to Check In Later

Don't forget to ask the parents if they have any questions. Sometimes parents have questions that they don't feel comfortable asking. Inviting their questions reminds them that you are interested in a dialogue with them and that you are glad to give them more information.

In closing the conversation, thank the parent for taking the time to talk with you and for her input. This helps to remind them that you value their knowledge and expertise. Then tell them you will check in with them again about this issue later, and be sure to follow up. Knowing that you will maintain regular communication with them about their child's behavior and about their concerns is reassuring to parents.

Reflecting on the Impact of Our Language

Compare these statements: "Riva was making all the other children cry today." "Riva was misbehaving today." "Riva was hitting other children today." "Riva hit two children when they wouldn't let her play in the block area with them." "Riva was experimenting with ways to express her feelings when she got excluded from the block area today, and she hit two of the children who were telling her she couldn't play." Imagine yourself as a parent, and respond to each of these statements. Which one gives you the most information? Which one helps you understand your child's point of view? Which one tells you that the teacher is on your child's side? Discuss with coworkers or fellow students.

Here's a sample dialogue to help you see how the steps above might play out in a real conversation with parents.

Sample Dialogue: Telling a Family about a Child's Challenging Behavior

Teacher: *Hi, Boris. How was your day?*

Parent: *Too long, too much traffic.*

Teacher: *Sounds stressful. Do you have a few minutes to check in about Alvin's day? [Active listening, ensuring that parent has time to talk]*

Parent: *Sure. Is there a problem?*

Teacher: *I just like to regularly check in with families so we can keep up-to-date about what's happening here and at home. Alvin had a busy morning. He spent a lot of time mastering the obstacle course. He tried it over and over again, especially the balance beam. He seemed really intent on doing it perfectly. [Describing child's behavior]*

Parent: *Yeah, he loves that stuff, and he can be such a perfectionist.*

Teacher: *Oh, what have you observed at home? [Asking parent what he has observed]*

Parent: *Well, he gets really engrossed in things and then just screams when he can't figure something out immediately.*

Teacher: *Yes, I've noticed that. He can get pretty frustrated when things don't go the way he wants. Today, he got mad several times and yelled. A few times when yelling didn't work, he pushed some of the kids who were in his way. It seems like he has almost learned to use his words, but when they don't work the first time, he reverts to pushing. This is so typical for four-year-olds. [Describing child's behavior, giving the parent ideas about it, and providing child development information]*

Parent: *Oh, no! He is such a bully. I'm going to have to talk to that boy.*

Teacher: *It can be worrisome to hear that your child has been pushing [Reflecting back the parent's feelings], but you know, Alvin is really not a bully. He is always concerned when a child is crying. He is the first one to jump up to pass out snack. I think he is just struggling to learn what to do when he gets frustrated. [Describing behavior and giving reasons] It would be great if you wanted to talk to him about other ways to express his frustration. [Telling the parent what he can do at home to help] We did several things with him today when it happened. We had him listen to his friend's feelings about being*

pushed. We asked him to put his frustration into words, instead of pushing. After a couple of pushes, we had him take a break from the obstacle course for a while. All of these seemed to help, but it takes some repetition before kids can really change their behavior. [Explaining to parent how you are responding to the behavior, giving child development information]

Parent: *I hope you are right. I'm just so worried about him because his cousin is such a bully and they play together all the time.*

Teacher: *I'd be glad to set up a time to talk to you more. I'd like to hear more about your observations and concerns, and there may be ways you can help him play more successfully with his cousin. [Asking parent for input and planning for a follow-up]*

Parent: *Thanks for the check-in. Maybe we'll set up an obstacle course in the backyard when we get home.*

Teacher: *Thank you for your time. I appreciated hearing your ideas, and I'm really happy to be working with your son. [Thanking the parent]*

DEVELOPING WAYS TO TALK TO FAMILIES ABOUT CHALLENGING BEHAVIORS

Name three challenging behaviors that you have dealt with in the past week. Think about the possible reasons for each of those behaviors, and practice telling the child's parent about the behavior using developmental information.

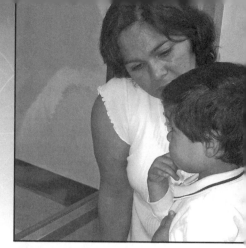

6

Challenges to Communication: Conflict between Family and Program

Even in the most successful partnerships between families and teachers, there are sometimes differences of opinion. While having the potential for conflict, these differences can also offer new perspectives and foster creative thinking. They provide opportunities to use two-way communication and for both families and teachers to learn more about themselves as well as about one another. Listening deeply in the conflict resolution process helps everyone more fully understand the belief system, knowledge, and expertise of the other people involved. The willingness to stay in dialogue even through significant disagreements also deepens the trust in the relationship. Negotiating diverse perspectives is at the core of sharing power and decision making. When people in a partnership have the experience of working together to resolve a conflict in a mutually satisfying way, they both have more confidence in their ability to work together. Learning the steps to resolve conflicts will keep support networks free from the alienation that occurs when there are unresolved problems in any relationship in the network.

For children, seeing their families and teachers work through differences and conflicts can inspire and inform them about their own ability to navigate conflicts. Watching the significant adults in their lives model respect for others and listening, brainstorming, and negotiating skills can give children concrete tools to use in their own relationships. Further, children's sense of security deepens when they see that the partnership between their important people can weather inevitable differences of opinion.

CONFLICT WITHOUT BLAME

Thinking about conflict without blaming each other is the first step toward positive resolution. However, conflict resolution without blame requires a new, different way of thinking for most people. It requires teachers to incorporate the strengths-based focus we've talked about in previous chapters and to respect the knowledge and expertise families bring. This approach asks teachers to reconsider some of the terms they previously used to refer to parents. In order to do this, teachers need to apply what they have learned about children's behavior to parent behavior.

Behind children's challenging behavior lies a healthy impulse. For instance, a child who pushes another child may be feeling crowded or scared and not have the words to express these important feelings. The behavior is not okay, but the child's impulse to protect herself from hurt or from being overwhelmed is healthy, and a teacher's job is to help her learn how to keep herself safe without hurting other children. Similarly, even when they seem most unreasonable, parents are also showing healthy impulses. For example, the complaining, accusing, overprotective, or critical parent might not have the words to express feeling left out, concerned, worried, or guilty. The continually late, absent, or uninvolved parent may be feeling overwhelmed or uncomfortable at the school. The talkative, questioning, or lingering parent may want to learn from you about how to be a better parent. Through a process of listening supportively, asking questions, and observing, teachers can discover a parent's healthy impulse and even the wisdom that drives his behavior. This information enables teachers to work together with parents to share information, discover their common goals for the child, and develop mutual solutions.

This chapter will explore the definition of mutual conflicts between teachers and families, the reasons for conflict, possible resolutions to conflict, challenges for teachers in mutual conflicts, strategies for problem solving, limit setting with families, making referrals, and steps for reporting families to child protective services.

MUTUAL CONFLICTS

Conflicts between teachers and families are called mutual conflicts. Mutual conflicts are those that take full participation, communication, and negotiation on the part of both parents and teachers. Each person has a contribution and a stake in the problem and its outcome. Mutual conflicts are different from family problems (such as a child who is waking several times a night) or teacher problems (such as a child who won't stay on her cot during naptime). (See chapter 5 for more information about solving parent and teacher problems.)

Here are some examples of mutual conflicts teachers and families need to solve together: the parent wants the child to stay inside all day, and the program is an indoor/outdoor program for much of the day; the teacher wants all families to bring extra clothes to keep in the children's cubbies, and one family doesn't do it; the parent is continually late picking the child up from school; the parent doesn't like the way the teacher disciplines the child; the teacher doesn't like the way the parent disciplines the child. Think back over the last week or month of your work with children. You can probably think of a dozen other examples of mutual conflicts between teachers and families.

In a family-centered early childhood program, the first step toward resolving a mutual conflict is dialogue. The purpose of the dialogue is for both people to share knowledge, viewpoints, beliefs, expectations, and concerns and to listen to each other. This dialogue is the basis for shared decision making, which should lead to a mutually satisfying solution or the determination that a mutual solution isn't possible at this time.

Causes of Family-Teacher Conflicts

Most conflicts between families and teachers fit into one or more of these categories:

- Conflicting family and program needs
- Different views of teaching and child development
- Inadequate communication
- Cultural differences

CONFLICTING FAMILY AND PROGRAM NEEDS

Conflicts can happen because there is a program need and a family need that don't fit well together. For instance, a family needs to have child care for their sick child. The program needs to have healthy children in attendance. Late pick-ups are another example. The program needs the child to be picked up on time, and the family needs more child care time. Clothing is often an area in which program needs and family needs are in conflict. Most programs want families to bring extra clothes for children, and some families don't have clothes to leave or don't want to leave clothes at school. Neither is wrong for their need, but there is a conflict.

DIFFERENT VIEWS OF TEACHING AND CHILD DEVELOPMENT

Another source of conflict may be different beliefs about how children grow and learn and different practices in caring for and educating them. Many of these differences are cultural, and all of them deserve acknowledgment and respect. Remember that there are two sides to every conflict: the right side and . . . the right side! This attitude will help you navigate the many different perspectives you encounter. For instance, Miya's family wants three-year-old Miya to learn how to write her name, and they expect her teachers to help her practice at school. The teachers at Miya's school make sure there are plenty of pens, pencils, paper, books to read, and models of writing throughout the classroom, but they are uncomfortable "teaching" Miya to write her name. There is a conflict between the family and the program about child development, about how and when children should learn, and what the adults' role in the learning should be. What's important here is that neither the family nor the teachers are wrong; both approaches are reasonable in the context of their different beliefs about children and learning. Different views on discipline between families and teachers may also fit in this category.

INADEQUATE COMMUNICATION

Poor communication is another reason for conflict in relationships between families and teachers. It can be caused by lack of communication skills or inadequate systems for communication. For example, Brittany's family has been weaning her from her pacifier for two days, but there have been no teachers available for check-in during drop-off or pick-up time, so the family hasn't been able to let the teachers know about the change. The teachers wonder where her pacifier is and why she is so cranky. Another example involves lack of communication skills and different ideas about how children develop. Matt is pulling hair at school when he gets frustrated. When the teacher, Sal, tries to talk to Matt's father, Dave, about it, he gets defensive or blames the other child. Sal would like to have a discussion with Dave about it but feels she doesn't have the skills.

CULTURAL DIFFERENCES

While cultural differences themselves aren't a reason for conflict, there are times when people don't understand each other because they have different perspectives and beliefs. These differences can contribute to miscommunication or misunderstandings between families and teachers. Cultural differences might have to do with food, sleep, discipline, health practices, clothing, and cleanliness, among others. For example, Lee John's parents want him to learn to use the toilet by spending time naked, so he can see when the pee and poop come out. They would like him to be naked at school for at least an hour each day, and school regulations require that children wear clothes. Here is another example of a conflict that is partly caused by cultural differences: Joella's family believes that keeping children healthy means

REFLECTING ON REASONS FOR CONFLICTS

Think about three conflicts you have had with parents in the past. Can you identify the reason or reasons for the conflict using the examples above (conflicting family and program needs, different views of teaching and child development, inadequate communication, or cultural differences)? Does knowing the reasons for the conflict help you think about it differently? Would you work to solve it in a new way based on understanding the reason better? Discuss these questions with coworkers or fellow students.

keeping their shoes on. Often when the family picks her up from preschool, Joella is bounding around the yard barefoot. The family is uncomfortable bringing it up with the staff because they don't want to make the teachers mad. This problem is a combination of differing beliefs about caring for children, a cultural belief in the teacher as an authority figure, and a lack of open communication.

One of the most familiar conflicts between families and teachers is about children getting messy. Most child development programs have lots of paint, ooblick, and other messy activities as part of their sensory curriculum. Some families feel concerned about their children getting messy and clothes getting stained.

Resolutions to Conflicts

Janet Gonzalez-Mena has defined possible resolutions to mutual conflicts between families and teachers (Gonzalez-Mena 2005). Here are four of those resolutions:

- ◆ teacher education
- ◆ parent education
- ◆ mutual education
- ◆ agreeing to disagree

In teacher education the family informs the teacher of their beliefs and practices, and the teacher or program changes practice to meet the family's needs. For example: The Lee family highly values privacy and feels uncomfortable with their child using the open bathroom at school. The teachers talk to the family and carefully listen to their concerns. They come up with a solution of a teacher taking the child to the adult bathroom, which has a latched door, whenever he needs to go. The family feels comfortable with this solution, and in this program there are enough teachers for this to work.

In parent education the teacher informs the parent about the school's practice and beliefs about child development. The parent understands and is able to accept the school's procedures. For instance, Giselle asks that her three-month-old daughter, Maya, be put to sleep on her tummy at school because that is the way she always sleeps at home. The teacher listens to Giselle's ideas, gets more information about how Maya sleeps at home, and then talks with Giselle about the current research that recommends children sleeping on their backs. Giselle thanks the teacher, and together they figure out a way to transition Maya to sleep on her back both at home and at school.

In mutual education the family and teacher share their beliefs and are able to negotiate a solution that might be different from both of their original ideas but is acceptable to them both. For instance, Juanita, Gregorio's grandmother, requests that three-year-old Grego be fed his meals at school the way she feeds him at home. The teacher asks Juanita for more information about her beliefs and the way the feedings go at home. The teacher shares her perspective on the importance of children learning self-feeding skills and her concern about not having enough teacher time to feed Grego his entire meal. After a respectful exchange in which both the teacher and Juanita listen to each other, they decide that the teacher will help feed Grego part of his meal at first and then gradually transition him into feeding himself at school, while Juanita continues to spoon-feed him at home and also begins to encourage him to eat finger foods on his own.

The last possible outcome for mutual problems is called "agreeing to disagree." In this situation, after talking and listening together, neither the family nor the teacher feels able to change, and they agree to disagree about the problem. In this last instance the family and program might decide to terminate the relationship (the family finds other child care), or they might decide to continue the relationship knowing that they have an unresolved disagreement. For example, Caroline, Becca's mom, wants four-year-old Becca to be able to bring her own toys to school on a regular basis. School policy excludes children from bringing their toys, except for sharing circle, once a week. The teachers feel strongly about children keeping their toys at home and using school toys at school. Caroline feels that Becca would be much happier if she could bring her own toys but decides to keep her in the program because she likes the teachers and Becca has so many friends at school. Since an unresolved conflict could result in ongoing resentment and criticism, it may be useful for the family and teacher to continue to check in with each other about how things are going. In the above example, the teachers regularly report to Caroline about what toys Becca is using at school and ask about what her current favorites are at home.

Here's another example. Calvin is continually dropped off late. Calvin's father, Milton, works the swing shift and likes to have a leisurely breakfast with Calvin in the morning. The teachers feel it is disruptive to Calvin and the program to have

him arrive after greeting time and when all of the other children have gotten involved in play, but they do their best to help him adjust once he does arrive. Keeping two-way communication going even when there are ongoing differences helps to maintain the partnership.

REFLECTING ON RESOLUTIONS TO CONFLICTS

How would you describe the resolutions of conflicts you have had with families? Have you resolved conflicts through teacher education, parent education, or mutual education? Can you think of a conflict that was resolved through parent education that could have been resolved through mutual education? Are there ongoing conflicts with families in your program? Are these conflicts in which you are agreeing to disagree, or is there ongoing resentment? Think about ways you could manage or resolve these conflicts. Discuss your ideas with coworkers or fellow students.

Challenges for Teachers

Almost no other work requires the same amount of emotional literacy as working with children and families. Teachers are asked daily to predict, identify, reflect, manage, model, and express feelings—their own and those of others. They are asked to help children discover the boundaries between their own feelings and the feelings of their peers. This experience can be helpful to teachers in their work with families, when they sometimes need to distinguish between their own feelings and those of a family member. When a parent is angry and frustrated, it is important that teachers remember their boundaries; teachers can be supportive and empathetic, but they are not in charge of or responsible for the parent's feelings.

In conflict situations with families, teachers may be challenged by a lack of experience or training in doing problem solving with adults, by difficulty managing their own feelings, and by uncertainty about what to do when criticized or ignored by a parent. These challenges are in addition to the normal challenges teachers may experience in building partnerships with families, as covered in chapter 2, such as lack of time or space, feelings of competitiveness, communication barriers, and cultural differences.

The good news is that conflicts usually arise after there has been some time to build the partnership, so there is a basis of trust from which to solve problems. In addition, teachers get to practice problem solving and managing feelings daily in their work with children.

REFLECTING ON YOUR FEELINGS IN WORKING WITH FAMILIES

Talk about the questions below with coworkers or fellow students. Then make a plan to gather the information and develop the skills you need to manage your own feelings around conflicts with families.

What feelings come up for you in your work with families?

What strategies do you use to manage those feelings?

Do you have safe and appropriate places to explore and express your frustrations, sadness, and anger?

If not, can you find a friend, coworker, or counselor to listen and help you clarify what your feelings are?

Would it be helpful to you and your coworkers to have an in-service with a therapist to learn about some of the feelings that typically arise when working with children and families and learn some healthy strategies for managing them? Perhaps you could suggest this to your director or site supervisor. It can be useful to discuss your feelings with coworkers or fellow students to feel less alone.

If teachers can remember that the underlying causes of conflicts are complex, it can be easier not to take them personally. A parent who is critical is often feeling powerless himself, because of lack of time, worry about his child, or feelings of inadequacy. A parent who always hurries in and out and basically ignores you may feel awkward in a school setting based on her own experience as a child. She may be shy or feel that her input isn't important. She may be juggling work, multiple family responsibilities, and transportation challenges and feeling overwhelmed. She may imagine that you don't like her or are critical of her. Once teachers understand the deeper causes of a parent's behavior, they are in a better position to address these causes directly through the problem-solving process.

CONFLICT RESOLUTION STRATEGIES WITH FAMILIES

Here is a list of suggested strategies for resolving conflicts with families. These strategies demonstrate family-centered principles in action, giving teachers step-by-step ideas for promoting information sharing, respecting different viewpoints, sharing decision making, and using outside resources as necessary. These are suggested steps. They don't all need to be used in every dialogue with families, and they can be used in a different order from the one listed here.

◆ Listen and ask open-ended questions.
◆ Restate and reframe the parent's ideas.
◆ Find common ground.
◆ State your position, idea, and feelings.
◆ Give information as appropriate.
◆ Give the parent the opportunity to respond.
◆ Outline the conflict as differing viewpoints.
◆ Invite, discuss, and choose possible solutions.
◆ Thank the parent, and set up a time to check back in.

Listen and Ask Open-Ended Questions

Listening supports two-way communication by

giving you a chance to learn more about the parent's perspective and helping the parent develop a willingness to listen to your perspective. Listening is a tangible way to acknowledge family knowledge and expertise. A parent's experience of confidence and empowerment is supported through having someone care enough to listen carefully to him. In addition, careful listening models for parents important communication tools. If you listen carefully and patiently to them, without blame or judgment, you may find that they are able to listen more fully to you as well. Listening is a useful strategy when you begin to feel defensive or you find yourself disagreeing. You will probably use it several times during the discussion. You can simply say, "Tell me more," and listen to see if you can better understand the person's viewpoint. Listening is crucial to finding the common ground that you can build your resolution on.

Listen specifically for feelings the parents may be having. Acknowledging their feelings and showing caring and empathy can help the parents feel safe and think more clearly about what is happening. Often people have feelings they haven't even noticed they are having, until someone names them. You can acknowledge their feelings with statements like "I wonder if it was discouraging for you not to be allowed to play with bugs" or "It can be so frustrating to be up with a sleepless baby all night." It is important when reflecting someone's feelings that you only share your observation and don't try to tell the person what they are feeling. For instance, "You must have felt . . ." or "You are feeling . . ." are statements you can't make, because you don't know for sure what a person is feeling. But you can say, "It looks like you might be feeling . . . ," "It sounds like you are feeling . . . ," or "I wonder if you were feeling. . . ." You can also always ask, "How are you feeling about this?"

Open-ended questions help the parent share more of her experience and let her know you are interested. Here are some examples of open-ended questions: Can you tell me more about that? What else did you do? How did your child respond? Then what happened? What did you observe about your child? How did you feel about that? Open-ended questions can also help parents discover things about themselves that they haven't acknowledged before. For instance, Carlito's mother, Esperanza, was talking to Luz, a teacher, about wanting Carlito to stay clean at school. As Luz gently asked Esperanza questions and encouraged her to talk, Esperanza remembered that as a child she had been fascinated playing with bugs but she had gotten in trouble numerous times when she slipped outside to dig for them. Once she made this connection between how she was treated as a child and her current expectations for her son, Esperanza was able to reevaluate her request for Carlito to stay clean at school. She decided to bring play clothes for Carlito to wear at school to get dirty in and nice clothes for him to change into to wear home.

Restate and Reframe the Parent's Ideas

Restating the parent's ideas confirms that you are listening and checks to see if you heard what he was really saying. You might find yourself saying something like "So this is the third jacket Wyoming has lost at school?" or "You are really hoping your child does well in kindergarten?" or "So your priority is that she has time to play outside every day?" If your replay of the parent's idea doesn't match what she thought she said, she can clarify her message. As obvious as this step seems, it is absolutely helpful in effective two-way communication.

Reframing a parent's idea in a new way can help her understand the problem from a different perspective. Sometimes a parent will state an idea in a way that makes it hard to solve the problem. "None of the teachers listen to what I say!" can be reframed as "Sounds like you have some ideas you would like to be heard." Similarly, if a parent says, "All kids do at this school is just play," it can be reframed as "When kids are running around having so much fun, it can be hard to see that they are learning anything." You can even reframe statements that you know fall outside licensing regulations or other program parameters, without contradicting parents. For example, if a parent says, "If Dashani doesn't do exactly what you tell her, you can just give her a swat," and you know that licensing regulations and program policy absolutely forbid staff members from ever hitting children, you can still reframe the parent's statement as "It sounds like respecting authority is very important to you."

Find Common Ground

In conflict it is very important to identify common goals. These common goals are the basis for shared decision making and are a way to acknowledge the mutual expertise and knowledge of the family and the teacher. Often, when people are in conflict, they are not aware that there are any areas of common ground between them, when in fact in almost every conflict there are many areas of agreement. This is a key concept in negotiating diverse perspectives and opinions. As in the last example above, people who believe in spanking and people who don't believe in corporal punishment usually agree that they both want the child to learn right from wrong. People who believe in using flash cards with two-year-olds and people who believe in using blocks both want children to learn math and be successful in school. Naming the shared belief helps people align themselves on a shared starting point from which to resolve the conflict more constructively. To help find common ground, you can say something like "It seems like we both want children to learn right from wrong," or "I think we are both in agreement about how important it is for children to learn math concepts."

State Your Position, Idea, and Feelings

Once the parent knows that you have heard his perspective, it is time to share yours. When you share your position as your own, rather than as the truth, it shows respect for the family knowledge and expertise, and you are strengthening the partnership with the family. For example, rather than saying, "It is better for children to use blocks instead of flash cards to learn math," you can say something like, "From my experience, children learn math concepts through touching, moving, lining up, and stacking blocks." Rather than saying, "Spanking just teaches children violence," you can say, "What I've noticed is that it can give children a mixed message when we tell them to be gentle with their friends and we also spank them."

As professionals, we need to be thoughtful about when we share our feelings at work. In order to decide whether or not to share your feelings with a family in the process of conflict resolution, ask yourself questions like these:

> "Will it be helpful to this parent to know my feelings about this, or do I just need a place to vent?"

> "Am I already communicating feelings nonverbally?"

It can be useful to share feelings with parents when your feelings are about something they did that affects you directly. Sharing frustration about a parent's late arrival can be helpful in problem solving. However, sharing your frustration after a hard day at work is not helpful in resolving conflicts, and it should be saved for coworkers or friends outside work.

The other thing to consider is the importance of naming feelings that are already being communicated nonverbally. If a teacher says through clenched teeth, "Just get your child's things and leave," to a late parent, it leaves the parent no constructive way to respond. If the teacher says, "I know there were a lot of good reasons for your lateness, but I still feel frustrated when you are late because I need to get home to my family," the parent can better hear and respond to her honest expression of feeling.

This promotes two-way communication.

When sharing feelings with adults, it's important to use I-messages. When you use an I-message, you take responsibility for your own feelings. This eliminates blame and makes it much easier to resolve conflicts. For example, rather than saying, "*You make me* so frustrated because you don't pick your child up on time," consider using an I-message, saying something like, "When you don't come on time to pick up your child, *I feel* frustrated." The structure involves "When this happens, I feel . . ." Parents can usually respond less defensively when you share your feelings in this way. When you use I-messages, you are also modeling for parents a tool they can use to express their own feelings.

Give Information as Appropriate

Often, teachers have a different view of children from that of families because of their training in child development. This information can be useful to parents in understanding their child's behavior and growth. It can also be useful in understanding program practices. Giving parents a number of possible reasons helps them think more deeply about their child. For instance, Vince was concerned because his four-year-old daughter, Demetra, was using swear words at home that she had learned at school. Teacher Linda shared with Vince that children might swear at age four because they are exploring the power of language, imitating language they have heard, trying to discover different people's reaction to this new language, experiencing stress at home or school, and/or trying to impress their friends. Linda also shared that she thought that Demetra was trying to get the attention of a particular group of friends, and she talked to Vince about other ways she was helping Demetra make friends. Sharing child development information in this way gives the teacher and the family more tools to understand the child's behavior, promotes dialogue, respects the family's expertise, and simultaneously nurtures their partnership.

Give the Parent the Opportunity to Respond

Regularly during the discussion, it is important to make space for the parent to respond. Occasionally, a teacher might get so involved providing information to the parent that he fails to notice if the parent understands him or has an idea or question. This space can become an invitation to the parent to engage in two-way communication. It demonstrates the belief that the parents have expertise to share, and it reminds parents that they are an essential part of the discussion and decision making.

Outline the Conflict as Differing Viewpoints

Often when people are in conflict, each feels like the other person is the problem. Defining the problem as two relevant but differing beliefs honors diversity, sets the stage for shared decision making, and helps people take the next step in solving the problem. Here are some examples of defining the problem this way:

> "So it is really important to you that someone takes Allen to the bathroom every half hour, and in our program we don't have the staff time to do that."

> "So you don't want your child coming home loaded with sand, and sand play is an important part of our outdoor curriculum."

Outlining the problem like this gives parents another chance to hear your viewpoint and to be reminded that you have heard their idea as well. It is another way to reiterate that there are two valid viewpoints in the discussion.

Invite, Discuss, and Choose Possible Solutions

This is an important step. At this point you may have at least one great idea for a solution. However, if you jump in with your idea, it doesn't offer a chance for the parent to share her expertise and contribute to the solution. Working together on the solution keeps the partnership mutual, invites shared decision making, and offers a broader and more creative base from which to brainstorm solutions. It is much more inclusive to say, "Let's think together about possible solutions to this problem," or "Do you have any ideas how we might solve this problem?"

Once there are some ideas for solutions on the table, you and the parent can both offer more information to help determine which solution might work best. For example, you might offer a compromise solution, such as "We do have enough staff time to take Allen to the bathroom hourly. Would that work for you?"

Thank the Parent, and Set Up a Time to Check Back In

Thank the parent for bringing the issue up and making time to talk with you. Engaging in conflict resolution can be unfamiliar and scary for people. Sharing differing ideas and feelings is not something that most people do regularly. It takes courage and time for parents to participate with you in these dialogues. Thanking the parents acknowledges the effort and expertise they demonstrated, supports two-way communication, and invites their future input and sharing of knowledge.

When teachers and families decide on a solution, they don't know for sure how it will work. Letting the parent know that you are interested in evaluating how things are going communicates that you really want this conflict to be resolved, even if it takes time and multiple efforts. It also conveys that part of shared decision making is experimenting and evaluating things together. Further, it communicates your understanding that working out the partnership is an ongoing, two-way process, rather than an isolated event.

This list of strategies relates to situations in

which the parent raises the issue. If you, the teacher, are raising the conflict, start with stating your position, your concern, or what you have noticed. Then use the other steps as appropriate. Make sure, as always, to listen to the parent.

Here are some sample dialogues to show how this conflict resolution practice might play out in your everyday life in early childhood programs. In the first situation, the parent brings a concern to the teacher. In the second, the teacher is the one who raises the conflict. There are also exercises to help you practice conflict resolution with your coworkers or fellow students. This is a complex process, and it takes lots of practice to feel comfortable!

SAMPLE DIALOGUE: WHEN THE PARENT RAISES A CONFLICT

Parent: *I don't want Nico to play with water. It's a big mess, and his clothes get soaking wet.*

Teacher: *Sounds like you are concerned about Nico getting wet. Can you tell me more? [Listening and asking open-ended question]*

Parent: *Well, he has been getting ear infections every other month, and I hate for him to get cold and wet, because I think it is too much for his little body.*

Teacher: *Seems like you feel really concerned about his health, and you feel like getting cold and wet makes him sick. [Actively listening and restating parent's ideas to confirm that you have heard the concern]*

Parent: *Yes, I know the doctor says that getting cold and wet can't make you sick, but it seems like every time he plays with water, he gets sick again.*

Teacher: *So your observation is that getting ear infections is related to his water play. [Reframing parent's idea]*

Parent: *Yes.*

Teacher: *This is kind of a challenge for us because sensory activities like water play are an important part of*

our curriculum. In my experience children learn physical skills, science, math, and measuring skills as well
as social skills when they are playing in the water.
Water play is one of our standard activities, and Nico
is one of the kids who really loves it. [Stating your
position or ideas and giving child development infor-
mation] At the same time I'm also concerned that
Nico stays well. [Finding common ground]

Parent: Yes, I just wish his ears weren't so sensitive.

Teacher: I wonder if we could think together about
some solutions to keep Nico healthy and also provide these important play experiences for him.
[Defining problem and inviting solutions]

Parent: Yes, I don't really want him to stop his wonderful play. Do you have anything that could keep
him dry while he is playing?

Teacher: We do have plastic aprons. We could make
sure he has one on every time he plays in the water.
We also have other dry pouring activities that we
could put out more often, which would give him
many of the same experiences but would allow him
to stay dry.

Parent: I could also send two sets of extra clothes.
Would you be willing to change him quickly if he
does end up getting wet?

Teacher: Sure. I'll let the other teachers know that
he needs to wear an apron and be changed as soon
as he gets wet. We will also talk about our sensory
curriculum to make sure we have a balance of dry
as well as wet pouring activities available. [Choos-
ing solutions]

Parent: Thank you. I feel much better now that I feel
we are working together to keep him healthy.

Teacher: I also want to thank you for bringing this
issue to me. It is so important that I know when you
are concerned about something, and I appreciate
the opportunity to work together with you on solutions. [Thanking the parent] Let's check back with
each other next week to see how things are going.
[Setting up a time to check back to see how things
are working out]

PRACTICE RESOLVING A CONFLICT RAISED BY A PARENT

In a group of coworkers or fellow students, divide
into groups of two or three. Role-play or discuss
how you would use these steps to work through a
mutual conflict brought up by a parent. Use the
example below or one from your own experience
when an angry parent brought an issue to you. If
there are three people in the group, the third person can observe (especially body language and
tone, as well as choice of words) and give feedback and support to the "teacher" in coming up
with effective responses. Here's a possible parent-
raised conflict to start with: "My daughter came
home yesterday with two scratches on her face,
and nobody said a word to me about it. What kind
of a place are you running here?"

SAMPLE DIALOGUE: WHEN THE TEACHER RAISES A CONFLICT

Teacher: Hi, Skip. Do you have a few minutes to
talk?

Parent: Sure. What's up?

Teacher: I notice that you have been bringing Eli to
school around ten o'clock for the last couple of
weeks. [Stating your concern or what you have
noticed]

Parent: *Yeah, I've been working graveyard, and I've been trying to catch a little sleep before I bring him in.*

Teacher: *Sounds like you have been short on sleep. Has your shift changed? [Listening and asking questions]*

Parent: *Yeah, I got switched, and I'm having the hardest time getting everything done, showing up to my class, and getting enough sleep.*

Teacher: *That sounds hard, trying to fit in sleep with your new shift and everything else. Your sleep is so important. Especially as a parent, you need to get enough sleep. [Actively listening, restating parent's ideas, and finding common ground] Skip, I've noticed when you bring Eli in at ten o'clock, you and I don't get a chance to check in with each other. I really miss checking in with you. I like to let you know what is going on with Eli at school, and I miss hearing about the two of you at home. [Stating your position, idea, and feeling]*

Parent: *Yeah, I started wondering if you didn't work here anymore.*

Teacher: *It sounds like you need time to sleep, and we would both like to have our morning check-in with each other. I wonder if we could think of solutions. [Defining problem and inviting solutions]*

Parent: *Well, on Wednesdays and Fridays I don't have class and could sleep later in the morning after I drop him off at nine o'clock.*

Teacher: *Great—we could check in on those mornings. I could also ask Mayo if he could switch breaks with me on Mondays so we could check in that morning at ten o'clock. That just leaves Tuesday and Thursday. Would you be willing to write me a little note on those mornings, and I'll leave you a note in your cubby? [Choosing solutions]*

Parent: *Sure, if you don't mind my horrible spelling.*

Teacher: *Skip, if you take the time to write me a note, I'll be so glad to read it. Thank you for making the time to figure this out with me. Let's check back in next week to see how our plan is working*

out. [Thanking the parent and making a plan to check in]

PRACTICE RESOLVING A TEACHER-RAISED CONFLICT

In a group of coworkers or fellow students, divide into groups of two or three. Choose an example of a mutual conflict that the teacher brings up, or use the example below. Role-play or discuss how you would use problem-solving strategies to work through this issue with a parent. If there are three people in the group, the third person can observe (especially body language and tone, as well as choice of words) and give feedback and support to the "teacher" in coming up with effective responses. Here's an example: Three-year-old Dora comes to school each day with her lunch box full of cookies and sugar drinks. You would like to talk to her family about a sending a more nutritious lunch.

SETTING LIMITS WITH A PARENT

Some conflicts that happen between teachers and parents aren't fully open to a negotiated solution. For example, a teacher may need to set a clear limit with a parent when a parent drives a child to school without a car seat; a parent is continually late picking his child up; a parent hits her child in the classroom; a parent comes to pick up a child and is drunk or high; and any other situation in which a school policy is repeatedly ignored or a child is endangered. Even though teachers need to set clear, firm limits in these situations, they can still be respectful, compassionate, and supportive toward parents. In addition to the strategies suggested above for resolving conflicts with families, here are some specific steps for communication with families in limit-setting situations:

◆ Share your observation with the parent.

◆ Ask for information.

◆ Give information.

◆ Set a limit with the parent, if needed.

◆ Follow through.

Share Your Observation with the Parent

It is important to begin by letting the parent know what you have seen. If you can describe or state what you have seen without blame, often the parent will recognize and name the problem. If the parent acknowledges the problem, instead of your doing it, she will probably feel less defensive and more in control. This allows you to support her in setting her own limit, rather than being the enforcer. For example, here's how a brief conversation like this might go:

Teacher: *I noticed that Sean was standing up in the front seat of the car when you drove into the parking lot this morning.*

Parent: *Oh, I know it's illegal and so unsafe, but he keeps wriggling out of his car seat.*

Teacher: *Since it is so unsafe and illegal, it is important to solve this problem with Sean. Shall we talk about ways to help him stay in his seat?*

Ask for Information

Asking the parent what she knows or has tried in this situation can help to remind her that she has knowledge and experience with this situation and can support her confidence and encourage her to be her best self. For example, in the above example, you might ask one of these questions:

"Can you tell me what you have tried with him before to keep him in his seat?"

"Do you have other ways you use to set limits?"

"How are you planning to solve this?"

Give Information

Often parents feel isolated in their struggles. You can reassure them by letting them know that most of the issues they face are typical parenting struggles and by giving them child development information so they can understand what is going on with their child. They may also appreciate some specific strategies. You might say something like "A lot of parents have struggled with this issue," "It is normal for a child to resist sitting in his car seat. He doesn't have a clue about the danger he could be in outside of his seat," or "There are several strategies parents can use to help their children stay in their car seats. Have you tried a basket of special toys, just for the car?"

You may also need to give information about why the limit is so important, by saying something like "We both know that it is extremely dangerous for a child to be in a car without his car seat," or "It is hard for your child to see other kids getting picked up when you don't arrive on time."

Set a Limit with the Parent, If Needed

There are times when a parent doesn't recognize the limit and the teacher needs to state it. In order to show respect to the parent, it is important, if at all possible, to speak to the parent privately, out of earshot of children and other families. If there is immediate danger, the teacher might need to set the limit before any of the other problem-solving steps. If that is the case, the limit can still be offered empathetically. For example, you might say something like "I know kids can be so frustrating at times, but because of the no-spanking policy in our program, I can't let you hit your child here," or "Children need to be picked up on time. It is school policy, and it is necessary for me so that I can meet my own family's needs."

Often the limit can be followed by an invitation to resolve the conflict together. For example, you might say something like "Children have to ride in car seats. I can't let you go until I'm sure your son will be safe in his car seat. We absolutely need to figure this out for both safety and legal reasons." Even in very difficult limit-setting situations, you can still be respectful with the parent, by saying something like "I can't legally let you drive with your child when you've been drinking. I know how important your child is to you. I know that you wouldn't want to do anything to put your child in harm's way."

When you need to set a limit with a parent, it can feel as if you are opposing her. Reminding her that you have the same basic goal is a way of acknowledging her expertise and staying on her team. You can do this by saying something like "I know that we both care deeply about Sean's safety."

As well as setting a limit with a parent, it can be useful to help her figure out what else she can do. Inviting the parent to think about other ideas reminds her that there are alternatives. Here are some ways to do that:

"Can we think together about other ways of setting limits with your child?"

"Do you have some ideas to solve this late arrival issue?"

"Would you like to think together about other things you can do when you feel really frustrated with your child?"

"Do you have any other ideas about how your child could get home?"

It can be helpful to offer your expertise at this point. Parents might be looking for some specific information and help. It is still useful to offer rather than to direct, by using questions like these:

"Would you like some suggestions about other ways to discipline?"

"I might know of some other families who could help with picking up your child on time. Are you interested?"

"I have some literature on child car seats. Would that be helpful to you?"

Even when you need to set a limit with a parent, you can still acknowledge the various feelings the parent might be having. This is part of respect and maintaining the partnership. You can do this by saying something like "It can be really frustrating when you are trying to drive and your son keeps crawling out of his car seat."

Follow Through

Following through is particularly important in limit-setting situations, because there is often no flexibility in the limit. Following through may involve checking back with the parent the next day, informing the parent of the consequences of her action, making a referral, or calling child protective services or the police. If the parent is in agreement with the limit, checking in by phone or in person the next day is probably adequate follow-through. You could say something like "Why don't you call me in the morning if you still can't get him in his car seat," or "Let's check in Friday to see how your no-spanking plan is working out for you."

If there is a question about the parent's willingness or ability to adhere to the limit, it may be appropriate to explain the possible consequences if he doesn't adhere. You may need to say something like "There is a late fee charged for every five minutes of a late pick-up," "It is part of my job to call child protective services if I feel that your child is being hurt," or "If we can't figure this out, I will need to call the police, as driving under the influence and endangering a child are illegal." As hard as this is for teachers and family members, it is an important part of the partnership, and often families are ultimately grateful for the fact that someone cares so much about them and their child.

Here are a couple of sample dialogues to show how the limit setting we're talking about might work in a real situation.

Sample Dialogue: Setting a Limit with a Parent

Teacher: *I saw that you spanked Jesse when she ran away from you. [Sharing your observation]*

Parent: *Every day it's the same thing. That girl never learns. She is going to run off someday and get herself good and lost.*

Teacher: *It can be really scary when she runs away. [Actively listening]*

Parent: *Sometimes I get so scared I don't know what to do.*

Teacher: *It is such an incredible responsibility to be a parent. [Reframing parent's idea]*

Parent: *Yes, and she acts so fearless. I'm just trying to keep her safe.*

Teacher: *I agree with you that it is important for her to learn to be safe in the world. [Finding common ground]*

Parent: *Yeah, but how is she ever going to learn?*

Teacher: *That is what I'd like to talk with you about, both because we have a policy that prohibits spanking at school and because we might be able to figure out some other ways to help her learn. [Setting limit and asking for ideas]*

Parent: *What's wrong with spanking?*

Teacher: *Well, even though spanking can give a child a clear message about a limit, it also teaches the child that hitting is acceptable and doesn't give her any information about why the limit is there and what else she could do. The other problem is that children get used to it after a while, which can cause the punishment to increase. [Giving information] I'm wondering what else you have tried with her. [Asking for ideas]*

Parent: *Well, I've tried talking and yelling, but neither seems to work.*

Teacher: *It can be frustrating when you tell her something, and her behavior doesn't change right away. [Actively listening] But talking can be an important part of helping her learn. Are you available later today to meet with me so that together we can come up with some positive limit-setting tools? [Following through and asking for ideas]*

Parent: *I have to work late today. Will tomorrow afternoon work?*

Teacher: *Sure. How about four o'clock in the office? I'll get someone to cover the classroom for me.*

SAMPLE DIALOGUE: SETTING A LIMIT WITH A PARENT

Parent: *[Coming into the classroom, obviously agitated] Goddamn little brat, ran that Hot Wheels down the side of my car and keyed my brand new paint job!*

Teacher: *[to both parent and child] Oh, it sounds like you guys are having a really hard morning. You were playing with your car, and your mom's brand new paint job got scratched. [Actively listening and reframing]*

Parent: *Yeah, I wonder where the little asshole is going to come up with six hundred dollars to get it fixed.*

Teacher: *Let's step out of the room so we can finish talking about this. [Setting limit]*

Parent: *I don't have time to be talking to some smart-ass teacher all day. I have to get to work.*

Teacher: *Your son and I don't like to be called names. It is really upsetting to have your new paint job ruined, but I still can't let you swear and call people names in the classroom. You can stay here and talk to me about it without swearing, or we can schedule a time later to talk about it when you've calmed down. [Stating your feeling, giving information, listening to feelings, and setting limit]*

Parent: *I don't want to talk about it. I'm leaving.*

Teacher: *Okay. I'd like you to say good-bye to your son. We'll see you at pick-up time. Thank you for letting me know what happened this morning. [Thanking parent for sharing information]*

Depending on the relationship between this teacher and parent, the teacher might call the parent at home that evening or ask the next morning if they can set up a time to talk. Follow-through is important when the issue doesn't get resolved on the spot. The teacher would need to spend some time listening, asking the parent for information, and sharing information about what the child might be feeling, making it clear that the guidelines in the classroom protect people's emotional safety as well as their physical safety, discussing alternative ways to express anger, and helping to brainstorm with parent solutions to the new paint job problem.

PRACTICING LIMIT SETTING WITH FAMILIES

Choose one or more of the examples below. Role-play or brainstorm with coworkers or fellow students how you would set limits with parents in these situations:

1. Lucille's Aunt Sally often picks her up from child care. You have had cordial conversations with her in the past. Today, when Sally shows up, she smells strongly of alcohol and seems tipsy. She tells you that she has had a horrible day. What do you do? How do you respond?

2. Katarina's father works two jobs and goes to school. He has been coming later and later to pick Katarina up, and today, he is thirty minutes late. You have tried to hint to him about coming on time, but it hasn't seemed to make a difference. What do you do? How do you respond?

3. When John and his mother arrive in the morning, you notice little round red welts on his arms. When you ask his mother about them, she says that she doesn't know anything about them but he has spent the weekend with his dad. When she picked him up from his dad's, his father seemed angry and said he was spoiled and needed more discipline. What do you do? How do you respond?

MAKING REFERRALS

There are several kinds of referrals teachers can make for families. The easier ones are voluntary referrals that help families access community support and resource organizations. The more difficult referrals to make are involuntary referrals to legal agencies, such as child protective services. Even though laws vary somewhat state to state, essentially all people who work in a professional capacity with children are required by law to make a report to child protective services if they have a reasonable suspicion that a child in their care has been or is being neglected or abused. It can be useful for teachers to ask for the support of their director or administration if they feel a need to make a referral to child protective services. However, even if the administration doesn't agree with the teacher about the need for a referral, the teacher is legally bound to make it, if she has a reasonable suspicion of abuse or neglect.

Family-centered principles can be an essential part of making these referrals. Even if the referral is involuntary, you can keep communication open, respect family expertise, share power by offering choices, and work to make the referral agency a part of the network of support. In many instances the teacher can let the family know that she is making a referral. There are several options that teachers can offer parents before the referral is made. Parents can be given the choice to make the call themselves in the company of the teacher or to be with the teacher while she is making the report. This allows the family to know what is being said. Interestingly, many parents who are given these options will choose one of them. Further, a teacher can offer to accompany the family for any visits or interviews they have with the agency. Families are often afraid and uninformed about the role of child protective services. It is important that they receive as much information about the process and the intent of the program as possible.

As difficult as these conversation with families are, maintaining two-way communication through the referral process can be supportive to the partnership and improve the services families receive. Here are some suggestions of things you can say to a family when you make a referral. Depending on your relationship with the family and their responses to you, some or all of these might be appropriate to say.

- *I want to let you know that I need to make a report that I hope will help your family. I've been concerned about the red marks on Jenna's legs and am uncertain about how she got them.*

- *Because I am a teacher, I am required by law to report this to child protective services. This is an agency that provides help and services to children and families who are having trouble. Do you know anything about this agency? I can tell you that their goal is to help families keep their children safe and to keep children together with their families whenever possible.*

- *I need to make sure that the report is made, but either you or I could make the call. If you would prefer to make the call yourself, you could do that from my office with me. Or you could be with me while I'm making the call so you could know exactly what I am reporting.*

- *I want to tell you what will happen after I make the call. They will either call you or come to your house for a visit and an interview. They might interview your child or examine her. Sometimes they come to school to see your child there. After they review your case, they will make recommendations for your family. Sometimes they recommend parenting classes or other interventions.*

- *I want to stay in touch with you and with the agency during this process. I want to support you and to be available if you have questions or if you would like me to be there when you are being interviewed. I know this can be scary, and I also know that it can help us work together to keep your daughter safe.*

Child protective services can provide information about their procedures before you make a referral. If you are uncertain about how they might handle your report, you can call them up before you make the report to ask what their procedure will be after you make the report. In this way, you will have accurate information to give the family about what to expect.

In other cases teachers decide not to tell the family that they are making a call to child protective services. If the teacher fears for her own safety or for the safety of the child, it is best to make the call without the family's knowledge. Likewise, if the teacher believes the family might flee, it is best not to inform them first.

REFERENCES

Gonzalez-Mena, Janet. 2005. *Diversity in early care and education: Honoring differences.* 4th edition. New York: McGraw-Hill.

Formal Communications: Documentation and Conferences

It is especially important that a program's formal communication embodies family-centered principles. Because formal communication is thoughtfully written and/or planned ahead of time, it is the place where a program can communicate its philosophy and make it a reality. This chapter focuses on family conferences (planned, individual meetings between a teacher and family) and on formal written communication, including program brochures, parent handbooks, contracts, family information forms, child information forms, newsletters, bulletin boards, articles, and letters, among others.

Family conferences provide a more formal venue for face-to-face communication than daily check-ins. They offer a chance to build trust and partnership through two-way communication; increasing mutual knowledge and respect; having uninterrupted private time to talk; sharing information about the program, the child, and community resources; and developing mutual goals for the child.

PREPARING FOR THE CONFERENCE

Setting the stage for a family conference involves preparing the schedule, the space, and observations of the child in the program. It also means letting parents know what to expect and how they can participate in the planning. Initially, parents can learn about family conferences through their orientation to the program, the program handbook, a newsletter, and/or a parent meeting. It is useful for families to know that family conferences are a regular part of the program before they are asked to schedule one. Some parents may have negative associations with "being called into the principal's office" because of their experiences as a child. These families might feel like a family conference signifies that they or their child is in trouble.

In preparing for the conference teachers can make observations and fill out any assessment forms used by their program. They can talk to coworkers about any information they would like shared with the family. Teachers can do research, if necessary, so they will be prepared to address questions, topics, or concerns families have shared with them. Teachers can also create or expand children's portfolios to share with families.

Preparing for conferences can be challenging for teachers with limited to no preparation time. Working cooperatively with coworkers and inviting family participation can help. Keeping observation clipboards and cameras (if available) accessible in the classroom makes documenting more convenient. Inviting families to help take, print, and sort pictures supports the partnership and saves time. Some programs have been able to find creative ways of staffing the program to allow release time for preparing for conferences. Advocating with the administration, the board, and/or a funding source for more preparation time is another vital strategy. It is important to remember that the most significant part of the conference is just having some uninterrupted time to talk with families and build the family-teacher partnership through two-way communication, the sharing of knowledge and expertise, and collaboration on goal setting and decision making.

Preparing Families

In notifying families that conferences are going to be scheduled, it is useful to reiterate the purpose of a conference and how they can prepare for it. You can tell parents that you will be sharing information about the program as well as observations and information about their child. In addition, you can ask them some questions to remind them that you are looking forward to hearing from them during the conference as well.

Here are some questions to consider suggesting to parents before the conference. These questions could be included in a letter, handout, or daily check-in or on a bulletin board where parents can sign up for a conference time.

- What things would you like to be addressed in the conference?
- What information can you share with us about your family and child so that we can get to know and provide better care for your child and family?
- What are your goals for your child this year?
- Do you have questions about our program?

Before a conference, families also need to know who should come (are children and other family members invited?), where it will be, how long it will be, and what program staff will be there.

Scheduling the Conference

Finding a time that is mutually convenient for both teachers and families is the first consideration in scheduling conferences. It is helpful when programs can provide release time during the day for teachers to prepare and hold family conferences. However, daytime is not always the most convenient time for families. In some cases, evenings, early mornings, or weekends may be the only time a family has available. It is important that program administrators allow for release time or paid time for teachers for these after-hours conferences. Another scheduling challenge is providing child care. If the program can address this, it will make conferences much more accessible for some families. In addition, for families in which separated parents are not communicating comfortably with each other, there may be a need to schedule two different conferences. You should also consider how long each conference will be; this will be affected not only by the amount of information you want to share but also by the number of conferences you need to plan and the family's availability.

Conference Agenda

What might your time with a family look like? Here is a sample agenda that promotes the idea of two-way communication, acknowledgment of both partners' expertise, and shared decision making:

FAMILY CONFERENCE AGENDA

- *The parents and teacher each talk about what they would like the conference to include.*
- *The parents share information, observations, and updates on the child and the family, and they ask questions.*
- *The teacher and parents discuss the parents' input.*

- *The teacher shares information about the child (development information, anecdotal information, assessment and evaluations, as applicable).*

- *The teacher shares the child's portfolio, if applicable.*

- *The parents have time to comment on the portfolio or ask questions.*

- *The teacher and parents discuss which parent observations and information to add to the child's program records.*

- *The teacher and the parents discuss possible ways for the family to participate in the program and the classroom.*

- *The parents and the teacher discuss goals for the child and make plans for working toward them at home and at school.*

Creating Portfolios

Children's portfolios are dynamic representations of their work, growth, and development. A portfolio is a notebook or file that includes samples of work, photos, quotations from the child, observations, and video or audio recordings. Some portfolios include paintings, drawings, collages, or notes the child has created. Photos can show a child during routines, circle time, or other curriculum activities and might be of children alone or with friends, teachers, or family. Teachers can include captions with the photos that describe what the child is doing and learning. Teacher observations are an important part of the portfolio and are often used to demonstrate a competency or meet a standard. Documentation of children's language through written observations or audio or video recordings can show a progression of language development. Video clips can bring another dimension to the portfolio.

In some programs children help to create their portfolios. Teachers set up a box or folder for each child in the classroom and invite the children to add the work they would like to keep in their portfolios. The family's contribution to the portfolio is equally important. Families can be invited to add observations of children at home or school, photos, work samples, family goals, and letters to their child. In some programs families assemble all of the portfolio materials into a scrapbook, which they design and decorate. Once families are included in making the portfolio, they will bring their own creative ideas to the process. Conferences as well as family meetings can provide space and time to look at and add to a child's portfolio.

Finding Space for the Conference

Setting up the environment for a family conference can be challenging. Many programs have limited choices for a place to meet individually with families. Teachers have creatively held conferences on tiny chairs in children's classrooms, cramped offices, storerooms, or public spaces. Sometimes teachers can find a nice spot outside when children aren't present. Hopefully, a comfortable place can be found.

Things to consider in creating a space for a family conference are:

- Comfort: Use adult-sized chairs or other comfortable seating, when possible.

- Privacy: Meet in a room with a door that closes, where you will be assured of privacy.

- Aesthetics: Use flowers, children's artwork, or other simple things to make the space welcoming.

- Friendliness: Arrange the chairs in a comfortable setup, around a table if possible, where all participants can see each other. If there is a desk, set the chairs in front of the desk, so that the desk is not between the teacher and the family.

- Food: If possible, bring a simple snack and/or water, tea, or coffee.

If there is not an adequate space available in your program, research other community agencies that might have a space you could use.

Conducting the Conference

The most important thing in starting the conference is to establish a sense of trust and comfort for the family. Here are some good ways to set the stage:

◆ Thank the family for sharing their time with you.

◆ Offer a snack.

◆ Ask about how things are going for them.

◆ Ask for their ideas and goals for the conference.

Acknowledging the information and questions families have shared with you about the conference beforehand will remind them that their input is crucial. You might say something like "I remember that you were interested in getting more information about her play with other children," or "You have asked that we talk about ways to encourage him to speak more Spanish. Would you like to do that now or after we have shared our observations of him at home and school?"

Even as you share your ideas for the conference agenda, you can stay open to changing it based on the family's ideas or needs. Depending on the family and what they have told you about their ideas for the conference, you may start by giving them information or by asking them questions.

Asking Families Questions

Many families will eagerly share information about their family and child with you without any probing. With less talkative families, thoughtful questions may encourage them to share their knowledge with you. Questions can also let families know what kind of information is useful to you in your understanding of the child. Some families don't know that changes at home might influence a child's behavior. When you ask for specific information, it informs families about what to look for. You might ask something like, "Are there any changes at home

or special things happening that we should know about?"

In addition to specific questions, it is also important to ask open-ended questions that help to share power with families and communicate to them that you are interested in what they feel is important. Here are some good open-ended questions for parent conferences:

"What else would you like me to know about your child?"

"How could we provide better care for your child?"

"What is the most convenient way for us to share information back and forth?"

"How would your family like to be more involved in the program?"

Giving Families Information

Most families are eager for information about their child. Many are also anxious about what they might hear. If you begin your report with an encouraging statement, most families will relax enough to hear whatever else you have to say. Even if you can't say, "Your child is right on target for a four-year-old," you can probably say, "Your child is making progress," or "Your child has developed some new skills since he has been here."

When you have difficult information to communicate, it is important to share with the family what plans and strategies you have in place to work with the issue and to ask for their input in understanding their child. It's also important to give the family information about development, temperament, or environment that might help them understand the behavior. For example, you could say something like "It is typical for four-year-olds to exclude other children from their play," or "It seems like her hitting happens mostly during transitions. We've observed that she tends to get overstimulated when things are noisy or chaotic. This seems like a part of her temperament." One of the most important things to remember is to keep a strengths-based perspective on the child when sharing information with the family. Include all of the child's strengths, skills, and areas of growth. A child may be a year behind his peers, but if he has made progress, it is cause to celebrate.

Setting Goals Together

Setting goals with families can be an exciting and challenging collaboration. Once information has been shared back and forth, goals may start to emerge naturally. For example, you may find yourself saying something like "You said you were really interested in her learning to play with a variety of children. Should we make that one of our goals?" or "You mentioned that you were interested in kindergarten readiness. Shall we look at the prekindergarten skills list to help us develop our goals?" or "You were concerned about him learning his numbers, and I would like to see him work on large-muscle skills. Shall we make both of these goals?" It can be challenging when families come up with goals that seem unrealistic or inappropriate to teachers. Often, teachers can find a common ground with the family and think about the developmentally appropriate steps to the family goal, thus working together with the family.

Here's a sample dialogue that shows a teacher finding a way to work with a parent's goal:

Parent: *I would like Henry to walk by eight months.*

Teacher: *Wow! It is exciting to think of a child's first steps. Eight months, huh? From my experience, I'm not usually in charge of when a child walks, but I would love to talk with you about steps (ha ha!) we could take so he will be a strong and confident walker when he is ready.*

An important part of goal setting and of sharing power and decision making with families is to talk about how families and teachers can work together toward the goals they have set.

Teachers can share their ideas with families and ask for the family's thinking about curriculum, activities, and interactions to support children. For example, this dialogue shows the family and teacher in the previous example making plans to support a child's walking:

Teacher: *I would like to set up some obstacle courses inside as well as outside to provide a space for him to practice his crawling on different surfaces, including little hills. Do you have ideas of things you want to do at home?*

Parent: *I know he loves the couch cushions. I think I might take them off the couch, so there is a step he can climb from the cushion to the couch, and I could make sure he gets some time in the walker every day.*

Teacher: *That kind of safe climbing is wonderful preparation for the strength, coordination, and balance needed for walking. I wonder about the walker. Ironically, children don't get to practice the skills they need for walking when they are in the walker. However, some children like to use them to pull up on and push around before they can walk on their own.*

REFLECTING ON FAMILY CONFERENCES

With coworkers or fellow students think about ways conferences could become more family centered in your program. Use questions like these to focus your thinking:

What is your program's current practice with parent conferences?

What are the strengths of what you do now?

How could conferences in your program be improved?

What parts of doing parent conferences do you feel most confident about, and what parts are you unsure about?

Use role play and discussion to practice an easy conference and a challenging one.

Family conferences are an important building block of the partnership between teachers and families. They offer the time to discuss issues in more depth, to reflect together on the learning and teaching process, and to deepen relationships. Sometimes hard questions or conflicts arise during conferences because parents feel safe and sense that there is enough time to work through them. Challenging as these are, they present an opportunity to broaden the understanding and the trust between teachers and families.

WRITTEN COMMUNICATION

Written communication transmits as much information about your program as any other form of communication. Written communication is an essential part of the two-way communication that is central in building family-program partnerships. Some people, parents and teachers alike, are more comfortable and articulate with written communication than with talking in person or on the phone. The written word gives people a chance to read over and fully understand information. It allows communication to happen when people are not available at the same time. When you know what kinds of communication families prefer and use them, your interactions with them will become more effective. Using a variety of communication techniques ensures that you are reaching a wider number of families.

In order to be effective, written communication must be two-way; it should provide opportunities for families to communicate with the program as well as giving parents information. It also needs to acknowledge the diversity of language, literacy, and communication styles that exist among families. Communication to families and invitations for communication from families can recognize family knowledge and invite shared decision making. Written communication provides a wonderful framework for networking. The following sections discuss several elements

of effective written communication, including purpose, tone, layout, length, aesthetics, and language.

> ### REFLECTING ON THE MESSAGES YOU WANT TO COMMUNICATE
>
> Think about the underlying messages you would like your written communications to transmit to families. How do you want families to feel about their children, their family, your program, their role in your program, their ideas, and their knowledge? Make a list of messages you hope families will receive through reading your program's written communication. After you have made your list, talk with coworkers or fellow students about their lists and compare them to some of the ideas in the following section.

Building the Partnership with Written Communication

It seems obvious that the purpose of written communication is the transmission of information, but if we look at written communication as a tool for building family-centered care, its purpose grows. The written word can be a two-way vehicle for sharing knowledge and expertise. A parent handbook can inform families about the program's practices and policies, and it can also recognize family knowledge, invite families to share their expertise, and outline ways families can communicate with the program.

The written word provides opportunities for diverse styles of communication. Some families are more comfortable writing a letter to communicate with teachers than they are talking in person. Writing also allows for communicating in a person's home language, even if there is not an interpreter on site at all times. Books and articles from different cultures and languages can also be included in programs, even if the staff are not bilingual. Written materials can be made available in a variety of reading levels to provide access to people with a range of reading skills.

Written resources also contribute to network building by making information about community support groups accessible in one place. Resource notebooks, brochures, and Internet sites can all be used to help families create networks of support in the larger community. Written communication is also an easy way to help families connect and interact with each other. Family-to-family bulletin boards, family mail cubbies, notices, and sign-up sheets on the door about family events all help with building networks of support within the program.

Setting a Respectful Tone

We are often aware of our tone in talking to children or adults. We are less likely to consider the tone of a written document. However, the tone of written communications says as much about the program as the words. On the one hand, program staff want to be clear and thorough in presenting information to parents in order to avoid misunderstandings. On the other hand, if the tone is cold, authoritarian, and condescending, families will feel less empowered and less able to participate in a partnership with the program. Using a tone that conveys warmth, respect, inclusiveness, openness, and clarity will help set the stage for effective partnership building.

Compare the tone in the two statements below about diversity:

"We welcome all families regardless of race, religion, cultural heritage, political beliefs, sexual orientation, marital status, or differing ability."

"We welcome *all* families and know that the inclusion of families from many different ethnicities, religions, cultures, sexual orientations, abilities, political affiliations, and family structures will enrich our program."

The first, more traditional diversity "disclaimer" doesn't exactly extend a feeling of embracing all kinds of families. The word "regardless" is intended to be the inclusive word, but, instead, it conveys a message of reluctant tolerance. The tone in the second statement goes beyond tolerating the differences; it respects and embraces them.

Here's another exercise in understanding the tone of written communication. Read the two examples of lost and found notices below and think about the tone and the language used in each.

"Lost and Found" Note 1:

Families,

Our lost and found box is overflowing with clothing eagerly waiting to being reunited with its children. Please take a careful look through the box this week. At the end of the week, any leftover lonely clothing will be delivered to Goodwill. Another hint: There is a permanent marker at the end of the cubbies. If you don't get a chance to write your children's name on their clothes before you leave home, feel free to use our marker.

Thanks,

Children's Center Staff

"Lost and Found" Note 2

Parents,

Our school has a problem because parents have neglected to check the lost and found box, and it is stuffed with lost clothes. You must look through the lost and found box. Any of your children's clothing that you haven't claimed will be given away to Goodwill at the end of the week. Also, parents have not properly marked children's clothing. Otherwise, it wouldn't be in the lost and found. If you would use the marker we provide at the end of the cubbies, we wouldn't have all this trouble with lost clothes.

This needs your attention IMMEDIATELY!

Children's Center Staff

First, check in with yourself. If you were a parent encountering these notes as you dropped off or picked up your child, how would you feel? Which one makes you feel more or less cooperative, more or less ashamed, more or less inclined to talk to staff members?

Notice the words used in the first note: "eagerly," "reunited," "lonely," "please." What effect do these words have on the tone of the note? Notice the words used in the second note: "problem," "trouble," "neglected," "must," "not properly." How do these create the tone of blame, punishment, and chastising? Also notice the use of humor and the encouragement to parents in the first note.

Now look at one of your program's written communications to parents. Discuss with your coworkers the tone in your program's writing. Are there ways the tone could be improved with a different choice of words or phrases?

PRACTICE WRITING NOTES TO FAMILIES

Practice writing a letter to parents about bringing extra clothes for their children (or about any other issue that is current in your program). Write one letter that is demanding and condescending. Write another one that is respectful. Compare the letters. Look at the different word choices you used. How would you feel, as a parent, to receive each of these notes?

Considering the Appearance of Written Communication

Often there is so much focus on getting information to families that there is no time for thinking about the appearance of written communications. When people first look at a document, they begin to make some assumptions about it. On first glance, readers want to know if a document is interesting, relevant, understandable, and manageable. If a document looks overwhelming, many people won't even try to read it. What can you do to help parents feel comfortable with the documents your program uses?

An important start is to begin the document in a friendly way. If it is a handbook, starting with a welcome and philosophy statement invites parents to read. Some programs use a table of contents or tabs to let parents know right away what content is going to be covered. Short paragraphs and headings are another way to make a document understandable and manageable. Use enough white space around text so that text doesn't look crowded on the page; this helps the page look accessible.

If parents feel like you are handing them an encyclopedia, they may be too intimidated to even open it. Programs always need to strike a balance in providing families all the information they need without overwhelming them. If a handbook is becoming too long, consider eliminating some text or creating another document to cover some of the supplementary topics.

Aside from the layout and the length, it's important to consider the colors, fonts, illustrations, paper, and binding used in your documents. Even though bright colors are often used in child-related communications, colored paper or type can be tiring for a reader in a long document. Similarly, using many different fonts can create a too busy or unprofessional look.

Illustrations are a very important aspect of written communications. Often programs want to use child representative photos or drawings. Ironically, even though child development programs have access to lots of great kid art, many use pictures drawn by adults to look like children's work. Some of the most wonderful handbooks and brochures feature children's line drawings as illustrations. This not only creates a soft and friendly look but also demonstrates a respect of children's creativity and artwork. Including children's names and ages on the drawing further adds to the authenticity.

Photos are also a wonderful enhancement to written communications. Photos of children and families used in program documents demonstrate concretely that children and families are central to the program. With digital photography more widely accessible, it is becoming easier to include photos in many different forms of written communication. Remember to get parental permission for the use of children's photos or artwork. Some programs ask parents to sign a release at enrollment giving permission for the program to use photos of children and their artwork in educational displays or for program publicity purposes. There should be a separate release if photos are going to be used on the Internet. When using children's photos and artwork in written communication, it is important to make sure that each of the children in the program is represented somewhere (the newsletter, the bulletin board, classroom displays).

Some programs use commercial illustrations in their written communications. These pictures can convey an idea or feeling that simple written text doesn't. It is important, however, to be sure that these illustrations portray the message you want them to. Many commercial illustrations neglect to include ethnic and cultural diversity or do so in a stereotypical way. Illustrations can also portray stereotypical images of male and female children as well as adults. For example, often the only teachers shown are women, and only boys ride bikes, while girls are identified by having long hair and wearing dresses. Further, look carefully at illustrations of families to verify they represent the diversity of family structure, physical ability, and gender roles you want to invite into your program. It is also important to look at the whole collection of illustrations you use. One picture alone cannot represent the full diversity you want

to include. Some programs choose to use a few different pictures in a collage to communicate an inclusive message.

Taking Care with Language in Written Communication

There are two major considerations regarding the language used in written communication. First is the availability of materials in the languages spoken by the families in the program. Second is the way language is used and choice of words. Complete multilingual communication can be a challenging goal, depending on how many languages are represented in your program and what resources you have available in those languages. Obviously, it is most desirable for all the written communications from the program to be readable by every family. If this is not possible, consider whether you have the resources to translate some of the most important materials or whether you have someone who could act as a translator for the family in reading and filling out written materials. Note that when you are arranging for either written or spoken translation, the closer the translator's culture is to that of the family needing translation, the more accurate communication you are likely to have.

Classroom signs and labels in different languages can help teachers learn words and phrases. Even when a family is bilingual, they usually appreciate it when staff make an effort to learn some phrases from the family's language to use with the family and child. Family members can often be a resource in translating or creating written materials. Bilingual families are sometimes willing to help make written labels in the classroom so that all the languages of the classroom are represented through the written word. In one classroom there are welcome signs in five different languages on the door to the classroom, including a photo of a parent signing "Welcome" in American Sign Language.

The way language is used and word choice are

also important considerations in written communication. Formal documents like parent handbooks can sometimes use theoretical language in describing philosophy or child development. Keeping language friendly and defining theoretical terms help to honor the expertise of both the family and the program. Equally important are other word choices that convey subtle or complex meanings, as well. While everyone has his or her own associations with particular words, some words are more inclusive, respectful of diversity, and less authoritarian than others. Here are some examples:

"Teachers will provide education for children in the areas of physical, social, emotional, and cognitive development." (less inclusive)

"We look forward to working together with your family as partners in providing for your child's physical, social, emotional, and cognitive development." (more inclusive)

"We invite you to a Mother's Day party!" (less respectful of diversity)

"We would like to invite you to a celebration of the important women in your family and community!" (more respectful of diversity)

"Families are required to volunteer at least two hours a month." (more authoritarian)

"We ask families to share in supporting our program through volunteering two hours a month." (less authoritarian)

THE BEGINNING OF THE PARTNERSHIP

Families and programs need written communication from each other starting at the beginning of their partnership. This communication can make program expectations, philosophy, and policies clear to families, and it can offer a way for the program staff to get to know a new child and family. Comprehensive information for families

about the program usually comes through family handbooks, brochures, information sheets, or Web sites. Written information from families comes through questionnaires, notes, or letters.

Family Handbooks

Handbooks are probably the most common form of written orientation for families. Families need to know the program's philosophy of teaching and learning, including its thinking about child care and child development, before they decide to enroll their children. They need to understand program goals in relationship to families and community building in your program. Families benefit from knowing your philosophy about children's curriculum and environment and your beliefs about diversity. In addition, they need information about

◆ the structure of your program

◆ ages of children

◆ hours of operation

◆ fees and payment schedules

◆ group sizes

◆ ratios of teachers to children

◆ schedule of the day and schedule of the school year

◆ your policies about attendance, clothes, health and safety, nutrition, discipline

◆ permissions and forms required.

Families are also interested in how long your program has been in operation, the education levels of your teachers, and the roles of all the staff in your program (whom to go to for what). Equally important, families need to know what you expect of them in the program, about family participation in the program and classroom, about field trips and special events. In many programs this information is included in a parent or family handbook.

Philosophy Statements

A philosophy statement articulates the underlying beliefs and the overarching vision of a program. It communicates to parents what a program is trying to achieve. It frames goals that are intended to inform program practices. When families read a philosophy statement, it gives them an opportunity to compare their own goals to those of the program. A philosophy statement establishes expectations about how a program will function and creates a starting place for discussions about nurturing and teaching children. It can also provide a reference point for dialogue when there are differences of opinion about program practices. It is useful for both families and program staff to regularly review the program's philosophy state-

ment to see if it accurately reflects the program's current goals and to verify that present practices are truly representing the stated philosophy. A philosophy statement can be a part of a family handbook or brochure, or it can be a stand-alone document.

Here are a couple of sample sections from philosophy statements. They are just parts of a program's entire philosophy, which would be included in a handbook or other written communication. Use them to inspire your own ideas. It is important that the statement for your program reflects the uniqueness of you as a teacher, your program, and the community of families you serve.

WRITING A PHILOSOPHY STATEMENT

Write a philosophy statement for a family handbook that communicates to families your belief in family-centered principles (see list below). This is a good exercise to do with coworkers. You can work on the statements together, or each of you can write your own and then discuss them. After discussing them, compare them to the examples below.

Family-Centered Care Principles

Teachers and families

- recognize and respect one another's knowledge and expertise
- share information through two-way communication
- share power and decision making
- acknowledge and respect diversity
- create networks of support.

After you have written a draft of your philosophy statement, make a list of all the ways your program actually implements that philosophy. Compare your philosophy with your program practices. How could your program more closely demonstrate your philosophy, or does your philosophy statement need revision?

RESPECTING KNOWLEDGE AND EXPERTISE

We are honored that you have chosen our program for your child. While our staff has considerable training and education about children in general, we are eager to learn from your expertise and knowledge about your particular child, family, and culture. You are your child's first teacher. We look forward to mutual sharing and learning so that together we can provide the best care and education experience for your child. We invite your voice, your perspective, and your participation as an advocate for your child and family as well as for the community of children and families.

ACKNOWLEDGING AND RESPECTING DIVERSITY

Our program is fortunate to include a diverse group of families, children, and staff. We believe that the different perspectives, skills, knowledge, beliefs, and life experience offered in a diverse group of people enriches each person as well as the group. We look forward to having conversations and shared experiences that will allow us to learn from each other about our differences as well as our similarities. Our goal is to be inclusive of all cultures, ethnicities, languages, family structures, genders, and abilities. We continue to grow in our understanding of ways to be inclusive and look for-

ward to discussions with you about ways we can be fully welcoming to all children and families.

BUILDING NETWORKS OF SUPPORT

We know that the job of nurturing and supporting your family is one of the most important and challenging jobs parents can have. Every family deserves support for the significant work they are doing teaching and caring for children. Our program recognizes this need and works to build and encourage networks of support among families and in the larger community.

The Family Questionnaire

Families have essential information to communicate to programs at the beginning of the partnership. One important tool to support this two-way communication between families and the program is a questionnaire. It is customary to have families fill out forms as part of the enrollment process. Some of these forms are legal, official, or part of the contract that the family is making with the program and cannot be altered to be more accessible or less intimidating. However, you can always write a cover note to let parents know why you need this information.

Other less formal questionnaires provide a way for families to share information about themselves and their child. Some programs call these "child information forms" or "family information forms." Including these forms with the enrollment package communicates to families from the start that you are interested in two-way communication. It can help families make the transition to care because they feel that they are being listened to and that their child's teacher will have information about them and their child. This information also helps teachers to provide more consistent and culturally responsive care to the child. While not all families are comfortable with filling out forms and questionnaires, this can be a very effective communication tool, and for some families it can be even more comfortable

than face-to-face communication. If you have a sense that a family is not comfortable or doesn't feel competent writing, a teacher could use the form as a basis for an interview with the family. Remember that any time you are talking to parents and writing down what they say, it is important to let them know what you are going to use the notes for.

Amy, a veteran teacher, talks about how she does the questionnaire with the family.

We always have an hour-long interview with the family before the child begins. We do it during naptime, when the other teachers are with the children. This is after the parent and child have spent three hours visiting our program. My co-teacher, Margarita, and I talk to the parents because we really want to get to know their family before their child starts. We used to have the office assistant do the interview, but we realized that we were missing an opportunity to begin our relationship with the parents during that interview. We do an orientation and let them know a little about us; we touch a little on what we do and our policies and procedures, and then we spend most of the time hearing from them. We want to know who is in their family. We need to know so that we don't speak inappropriately about their family. I don't want to say to a child, "Where is your dad today?" if that child doesn't know. We ask how the child asks for things and if there are special words or phrases the child uses or words the child uses that might be hard for us to understand.

We want to know who has cared for them before and what the child's experiences were in that situation. We ask them all kinds of questions about eating and sleeping, for instance. Does the child nap? How does she nap? Do you help her? Does she nap alone or with someone? Does the child let you know she is tired, or is there a set time? Do you put her down for a nap? What do you do? How does it work? Is there anything special that she sleeps with? Can you bring it to school? Does your child like to be touched?

We are really interested in the child's tempera-ment, so we ask about that. Tell us about your child's temperament, her personality. How does she show she is happy? Is she open? Timid? How does she react to new people? Does she like being hugged? How does she show affection? How does she react when she is angry? Does she show anger the same with you? siblings? friends? What hap-pens after the child is angry?

These are just some of the questions we ask, but you get the idea. We write this all down, and we share our notes with all the other teachers before the child starts in the program, because we want our teachers to be as prepared as they can for this child and family.

Amy concludes, "You know, sometimes parents start the interview, and they are kind of reserved and quiet. At the end of the hour there is a noticeable difference; there is less tension, they are more relaxed, and they usually leave smiling."

WHAT INFORMATION WOULD YOU LIKE?

Imagine a child you have never met before. Make a list of all the things you would like to know about him so that you can understand him and provide the most familiar and best care for him. After you have made your list, talk to coworkers about what they would like to know, and compare your list to the one in the next section.

The Child and Family Information Form

The child and family information form gives families a chance to introduce themselves and their children to you. While the information from families about children is very important, you may find that once you get to know the child, you have a somewhat different set of information about him. This is not because families are wrong about their children, but because the child has a different relationship with each person in his life,

and everyone experiences the child through his or her own unique perspective. Family information and perspectives about a child are always an important part of knowing that child. In design-ing a child and family information form it is important to think both about what information you would like to have and about the best way to ask the questions.

As in Amy's story above, you will probably find that it is useful to ask about a child's tem-perament, communication style, language(s), feel-ings and ways of expressing them, learning style, routines (sleeping, eating, washing, dressing), preferences (likes and dislikes), and favorite activ-ities; a child's past experiences with family, child care and education, traveling, moving, and signif-icant events; the important people (family and friends, adults and children) in the child's life and their relationship to the child; and the child's health and developmental history. There will probably be other topics that you want to ask, depending on your personal and professional experience, your program, and the child.

In addition to information about children, in family-centered care it is important to have infor-mation about families. Some programs have a separate questionnaire, the family information form. Other programs include questions about family on the child information form. You may find it useful to ask about the family's goals for the child and for parents and other members; the family's beliefs about child rearing, teaching, and discipline; other beliefs, customs, and traditions the family holds; favorite activities as a family; the family's skills and interests; the ways the family is interested in contributing to and being involved in the program; and questions the family has for the program.

Janessa, a parent, tells a story about when she was filling out forms for her child to attend preschool, and the program had a form for each parent to fill out. "My husband and I were each busily working on filling out our forms when Maisha's older brother, eight-year-old Leo, asked, 'Where's the form for the older brother?' I asked the program if they would give me another copy of the form, and Leo carefully filled it out, and we turned in all three forms. I really appreciated that they were so interested in our family. They gave me those forms back when Maisha graduated, and I still have them."

WRITING EFFECTIVE QUESTIONS

As we have discussed before, the way questions are phrased communicates as much information as the question itself. Here, again, it's important to use open-ended questions as much as possible. Some questions contain a lot of assumptions. For instance, "Does your child have her or his own room?" is a closed question. It can only be answered with a yes or a no. It also often has an implied "right answer." It would be easy for a family who answered no to feel judged, wrong, or inadequate. A more open-ended question would be "Can you tell us about your child's sleeping arrangements?" This allows families to share information about their children without being compared to some predesignated measure of success. In writing more open-ended questions consider using words like "describe" or "tell us about" that encourage families to tell you about their children in their own words.

It is also helpful to think about different family structures and cultures when you are asking questions. Often simple questions about the parents in the family can be hard for some families to answer. Can any family fill out your family information form without feeling "outside" of your box? The first blanks on many forms are for a mother's name and a father's name. These forms don't fit children who don't live in this kind of family structure. Programs have struggled with finding appropriate and inclusive wording on intake forms. "Guardian" seems formal, yet some programs use it to be the most inclusive. Some forms have up to four lines, each labeled with

"Parent." The form could also include an explanation, such as, "Parent, the adult(s) responsible for child."

Likewise, it is useful to be thoughtful about any questions that ask about culture or religion. Here's a story that helps to explain how these questions can affect families in your program. Lakesha, a teacher of three-year-olds, recalls,

I remember a few years ago we had a child whose religion did not support the celebration of birthdays or other holidays. We had some very interesting conversations with the family, who were, luckily, willing to educate us about their beliefs. We made a lot of changes in our curriculum that year and have thought about holidays and celebrations differently ever since then. But one surprising thing came up for us about our family information form, which we had thought was a very good model. We knew not to ask how people celebrated Christmas, because we were aware that many families didn't celebrate Christmas. However, I guess we thought that every family must celebrate something, so we ask the questions, "What holidays does your family celebrate? What are some of your family's traditions and practices on these holidays?" After our discussions with that family, we understood that our form was making assumptions that made them uncomfortable. Our form now reads, "What beliefs, traditions, or holidays are important to your family? What would you like us to know about them? How might you like to share them with the program?" There is probably some family who will educate us about this one, but so far it has been working better for us.

Another thing to consider in developing questions is how to ask them in a way that is understandable to most families. You might want to know about a child's temperament, but you are not sure if most families understand that word. You could ask a variety of questions to help families tell you about temperament. Here are some examples:

"How would you describe your child's personality?"

"How does your child respond to new situations?"

"Describe your child's energy level."

"What words would you use to describe your child? (for example: active, curious, quiet, talkative, thoughtful)"

Note that when you give parents a choice of words, they will often pick from your list, even though the words on it were just suggestions, rather than come up with their own. In some instances, you might still offer words to give parents an idea of what you are asking about.

PRACTICE WRITING OPEN-ENDED QUESTIONS

1. Rewrite these questions to be more open-ended.

- Does your child have a regular bedtime?
- Does your child put him or herself to sleep?
- Does your child have healthy eating habits?
- Does your child live with his or her mother and father?
- Does your child have a place to play outdoors?

2. Write five questions that you would like to see on a child information form. Then look at any questionnaire your program gives to families (exclude forms that are asking for hard data, like immunizations, permissions, and emergency contact information). Are the questions asking for the information you want to know? Are questions mostly open-ended or closed? Do your questions communicate the messages you want to be shared with families? How would you rewrite or add to this questionnaire?

Cathy teaches in her own family-run preschool and always has parents come in for a conference at the beginning of each year. Parents can also request more conferences with her as needed.

Here is a sample of the questions that she asks parents in the interview:

What sparks your child's interest?

What activities engage your child's focused attention?

What can we build on here that your child is currently exploring?

What is your child's most endearing quality?

Do you have any special concerns about physical, social, cognitive, or language development for your child?

What else in your child's or family's life might affect his adjustment to school?

What behaviors are you finding the most challenging to deal with right now?

What questions do you have about policies, procedures, philosophy, or curriculum?

How could we better meet your child's needs?

What would you like to see your child accomplish this year?

What goals would you like us to work toward together this year?

Cathy's questions reflect not only who she is as a teacher and what her interests are but also something about the families in her program.

Any time you ask a series of questions and you want to communicate your authentic belief in two-way communication, it is important to ask, "Is there anything else you would like us to know about your child?" This reminds families that they are the experts. It covers any area you might have forgotten, lets families know that you value *all* of their input, and invites their initiative in sharing important information with you.

It's also useful to tell families why you are asking so many questions. While some might feel excited to have an opportunity to share their family information with you, others might wonder why you are asking them questions and what you are going to do with the information.

In many programs, families are asked regularly to update their information forms so that teachers have up-to-date information about the child and family. Here is a sample "update information" form used by one toddler classroom.

Winter Update Form

Welcome Back!

Child's name_____

What activities has your child been enjoying over break? _____

What have you been enjoying about being a parent? _____

What has been stressful about parenting? _____

Are there any changes in your child's health? _____

What foods has your child been enjoying eating? _____

What foods (if any) does you child not like? _____

Does your child have any food allergies or sensitivities?
If so, describe. _____

Does your family have food preferences that you would
like us to honor?_____

What time is your child typically going to sleep at night
and waking in the morning? Is he or she waking during the
night or sleeping through? _____

At what time and for how long does your child nap during the day?_____

How does your child transition into sleep? _____

Is there anything else you would like us to know? (examples—child's
fears, changes in your household, important events, future changes
to think about, support you would like, concerns, etc.) _____

_____

WRITTEN COMMUNICATION: CONTINUING THE PARTNERSHIP

Once a family has made the transition into the program and the handbooks and questionnaires have been shared back and forth, the second phase of written communication begins. This ongoing, two-way communication covers program and family news, child observations and updates from teachers and families, developmental reports on the child, information about curriculum and classroom happenings, requests from families or teachers, parenting articles, program and community events and resources, and opportunities for parent involvement and interaction with the program. This time-sensitive information may come through bulletin boards or posters; newsletters to all families; notes or letters to individual families; notes to all families on clipboards, dry-erase boards, or e-mail; family conferences; or parent library or article files.

Newsletters

Newsletters to families offer a venue for many different types of communication. Newsletters can include calendars, information on family events at the program, news of community events, documentation of children's school experiences, program information, child development and parenting information, family-to-family communications, and program policies. Newsletters should be available in the home languages of families. (Biliterate families may be able to help with this.) If it is too difficult to translate the whole newsletter, programs may still be able to translate part of it or to include a bilingual parent education article. Newsletters may be distributed as often as weekly or as infrequently as quarterly.

Newsletters provide a natural medium for two-way communication. Parents can be involved in writing and publishing the letters. Families might contribute recipes, stories, photos, drawings, resources, ads, and so on. Parents can be

interviewed or can conduct interviews. Stories about staff and children's families might be included. Parents teaching parents (language, parenting tips, book reviews, and so forth) can be added. Surveys included in the newsletter are another opportunity for families to share their voices and ideas.

Calendars in newsletters might include information about upcoming children's or family events in the program or in the community. Calendars can also cover classroom information, such as planned curriculum and activities, menus, and field trips. They can also provide due dates for program information (tuition, immunizations, getting forms in, and so on).

Communicating to families about children's experiences at school is another important role of newsletters. A newsletter can give an overview of a curriculum unit or a project. It can cover what the group of children are working on over time as well as what individual children are working on. It can describe both the children's activities as well as the learning that is taking place through the curriculum. Pictures or samples of children's work or quotes from children all add an authentic quality to the communication. Also, newsletters often include anecdotes about children's accomplishments, discoveries, and questions.

Samuel and Jessica were watching a trail of ants near the garden. They were looking for the beginning and the end of the trail. After watching for a long time, Jessica looked at Samuel and said, "These ants have to wait in a really long line to get their strawberries from the garden."

When using children's work or pictures in the newsletter, it is important to make sure that all children in the program are represented at some time. Families could be involved in this documentation as well. Teachers might ask a parent to come in and take pictures of the activities in a particular curriculum and add their comments to the article written about it. Similarly, when a parent comes in to do a special activity with children, it is important to document it with photos, if possible, and a write-up in the newsletter or on the bulletin board.

The newsletter can also be used to share information about the people in the program. Teachers, children, and families can each be featured in a "Family of the Week" or "Teacher of the Week" column. This could be as complex as having a parent or a teacher interview a family and write it up as a featured story or as simple as having a family answer a short list of questions. Here's the list one program uses:

"What does your family like about this city?"

"What is your family's favorite food?"

"What does your family like to do together?"

"What does your family like about Rolling Hills Preschool?"

"Anything else you would like to share about your family?"

How a program includes information about people in the newsletter is not so important. The fact that the newsletter is used for the sharing of information among families and between staff and families will open doors for people to share about themselves in other ways. Helping all the people in the program get to know each other better will support the building of relationships, networks, and the sense of community.

If the newsletter is a vehicle for two-way communication, how do you handle it when a parent wants to put something in the newsletter that you don't feel comfortable with? Charlene, a teacher and director of a bilingual preschool, shares a story about this situation.

We have a wonderful newsletter in our program, and parents periodically make contributions to it. A few months ago, a parent approached me and said that she had gone to a workshop on discipline. She was so excited about what she had learned that she wanted to write it up in the school newsletter. I thanked her for her offer and encouraged her to write the article for the newsletter. A few days later, she came in with an article about a kind of discipline that is very different from what we do in our school. I didn't know what to do. I didn't want all the families to think that we were advocating this kind of discipline, and I also wanted to honor this parent's initiative and voice. I decided to put a few comments before her article in the newsletter. As an introduction I wrote, "This section of the newsletter is from families to families. We invite you to share your stories and articles here. This week, Marylee, a parent in the blue classroom, has written an article about a workshop on discipline she recently attended. Thank you, Marylee. This is a different kind of discipline than we usually use at Rainbow Preschool. Marylee's article might stimulate some interesting discussion. We look forward to your questions and comments." I also decided to make available a small selection of different articles on discipline to parents that week.

This story is an example of not just two-way communication but the multi-way communication that is so important for building networks. It also provides a good example of respecting one another's knowledge and sharing power and decision making. The director wanted Marylee to have the freedom to share her perspective, and the director also had the freedom to express her views.

Short child development or parenting articles are also a wonderful addition to newsletters. Programs can use this vehicle to share articles with families about relevant topics. In the fall, many families will have questions about helping children have a safe and comfortable Halloween. This can also be a good opportunity to let families know about the diversity of beliefs about holidays. Other times in the program there are topics of mutual interest, such as toilet learning, reading with children, and biting. Using quotes or excerpting a paragraph from a book can show parents about books they might be interested in reading. Book reviews by and for parents can be included in newsletters, as well.

Each program will have its own unique needs and resources for a newsletter. If a program doesn't have a newsletter and would like to start one, it could be a discussion item at a parent meeting, teacher meeting, or special committee of parents and teachers who are interested in developing one.

Bulletin Boards

Bulletin boards are another tool for multi-way communication, sharing expertise, and building networks. In many programs bulletin boards hold vibrant, interesting, current displays. In other programs bulletin boards consist of a series of out-of-date papers stapled to an out-of-the-way board. In family-centered programs bulletin boards should be informative, dynamic, aesthetic, and relevant, and they should serve as a communication tool for family-to-family, program-to-family, and family-to-program interaction.

There are yards of bulletin board borders available for sale in teacher supply stores, but actually plentiful bulletin board decorations lie under every teacher's nose right in the classroom. Using chil-

dren's art, collections, and photos for decorating bulletin boards saves money, lets children display their precious things, and communicates to families the value of children's creativity. Bulletin board borders can be made out of paper strips children have decorated, leaves they have collected, or unclaimed paintings cut into border strips. Photos of children and other children's art keep the bulletin board reflective of the children's program.

Bulletin Boards: Communication from Families

As a venue for families to communicate with each other and the program, bulletin boards are an exciting part of expanding multi-way communication. Offering a place where families can dialogue with other families and share resources and ideas is a powerful networking tool.

Consider designating a regular section of the bulletin board for parents to contribute ideas and resources. A parent or a teacher can coordinate this. Parents can contribute ideas weekly or monthly. One month they might share some of their children's favorite recipes; another month they might share favorite places to go with children. It can be as formal as parents bringing in typed recipes to share with everyone or as informal as a blank piece of paper and a felt pen hanging from a string. You might want to post big graffiti paper with questions for discussion or sharing. Here are examples of questions that have provoked interesting discussions:

"Has anyone seen the new kids' movie *Boomba*? What do you think about it?"

"We are looking for an inexpensive vacation spot to take our two kids (two and four years). Any ideas?"

"What do you appreciate about the teachers in this school?"

Equally important is a place for families to share resources or events with each other, a place to post helpful articles, newspaper stories about families or children, flyers for community events, names of family resources, and reviews of favorite children's or parenting books.

Families also need places to post notices. For example, you might see notices like these:

"We are looking for a used crib. Does anyone have one for sale?"

"Betsy's grandma is coming to town for two weeks and needs an inexpensive place to stay. Any ideas?"

"We've finally grown out of our double stroller. It's free to a good home."

"I'm interested in starting a Spanish-speaking play group with children who speak Spanish and children who want to learn it. Anyone interested?"

"We are looking for a family who wants to exchange child care one night a week."

When programs give families one more way and place to communicate with other families and program staff, they increase available resources and strengthen parent competence, the teacher-parent partnership, and the networks of support in the program.

BULLETIN BOARDS: COMMUNICATION FROM TEACHERS AND THE PROGRAM

Teachers are typically most familiar with bulletin board information offered to families from teachers and the program. Here is a review of some of the traditional uses of bulletin boards:

- information about the program: daily schedules; menu and curriculum information; announcements for upcoming program events and meetings; reminders; health, safety, and emergency information; parent hours information
- information about community resources and events

- news, articles, and book reviews related to child development and parenting.

Less traditional ideas include teachers posting information and photos of themselves and their families. Staff might do a "family appreciation board" ("We appreciate families because . . ."). Teachers can use bulletin boards for displays of children's work and documentation of curriculum projects. Bulletin boards can provide information about children's play and learning by using photos of children demonstrating the learning that happens throughout the classroom and curriculum.

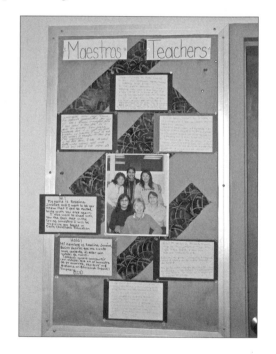

Creating Successful Parent Meetings and Events

When bringing families together, some programs focus on education, some on getting work done, and some on fun and networking. Parent meetings, parent workdays, fund-raisers, parent and family social events, and community advocacy events all provide opportunities to build family-centered care. Each of these activities has the potential to create and sustain support networks, acknowledge family expertise, share power and decision making, strengthen the appreciation of diversity, and provide multi-way information sharing between families and program. This chapter will offer information on planning and structuring parent meetings, including choosing topics, setting goals, and developing activities for meetings. The chapter will also provide information on planning and implementing family social events, fund-raising with families, and family workdays.

PARENT MEETINGS

Parent meetings provide an important forum for family members and program staff to come together. They offer an opportunity for all of the parents in the program to get to know one another. While traditional parent meetings have been used to orient parents to the program and to provide parent education, parent meetings have the potential for much more. Because they allow for focused adult conversation without the distractions of the classroom, parent meetings can provide time and space for both families and teachers to reflect on the important work they are doing in caring for and educating children. They can afford opportunities for families to learn about the program and for the program to learn about families. Parent meetings provide a venue for planning, sharing goals, learning new information, acknowledging the work of teachers and of families, discussing common issues and concerns, sharing news from school and home, and learning about community resources. Usually parent meetings are for adults, with child care provided for younger family members.

Setting Goals for Parent Meetings

Before developing an agenda and deciding on a topic for a meeting, it is important to think of the goals of that meeting. Programs and teachers have broad goals for all parent meetings, as well as specific goals for each meeting. Family-centered care principles would be a good basis for setting goals.

WHAT ARE YOUR GOALS FOR PARENT MEETINGS?

If you were going to name five to ten goals for parents in a successful parent meeting, what would they be? Make a list, and look at your goals. (Don't read further until you have made your list of goals.) Do your goals reflect the principles of family-centered care (two-way communication, respect for family and teacher knowledge, sharing power and decision making, respect for diversity, and building networks)? Are there goals you would add after reviewing these family-centered principles? You can do this exercise by yourself or in a small group. Share your ideas with coworkers or fellow students.

Here's a list of goals for parent meetings based on family-centered principles. How similar or different are they from the goals you listed above? What are the differences? As a result of parent meetings, families will

- feel safe and supported
- experience a sense of community with staff and other families
- identify and work together with other families and teachers for common goals
- participate in collective decision making
- build and nurture networks of support
- share their expertise and stories with other parents
- participate in asking and answering questions
- experience themselves as competent and resourceful
- learn child development and parenting information
- share their own culture and learn about the culture of others
- discover resources in the program and community for their child and family.

Do you see how these goals reflect the five principles of family-centered practice?

Planning for Parent Meetings

Planning for parent meetings can be as important a partnership activity as the meeting itself. Planning parent meetings from a family-centered perspective involves new thinking and procedures. Often program directors and teachers have been the sole planners of parent meetings; however, many families are interested in and able to participate in the planning as well. Families can be involved at essentially every step, sharing dialogue, expertise, resources, and decision making. They can choose topics, develop the agenda, find speakers or panelists, and chair the meeting. Parents enjoy organizing food, welcoming families, and designing notices. Families can also be involved in setting up the meeting space, arranging for child care, and cleaning up afterwards.

Families might participate on a parent meeting planning committee, which would plan meetings and also identify other families who might be interested in contributing ideas, energy, and resources to meetings. Teachers can encourage families with questions about their children to participate in planning a meeting on that topic. Family participation can also happen on a per meeting basis, with a request coming from teachers before each meeting. Here's an example of a notice one program sent out about six weeks before the meeting date:

Our next parent meeting is scheduled for April 14th from 6:00 to 8:00 p.m. The topic parents voted for in the last survey is "nurturing strong sibling relationships." We are looking for parents who would like to help plan this meeting. Are you interested in this topic? Do you have resources to share? Do you have ideas for speakers? Would you like to participate on a panel on this topic?

Choosing Topics for Parent Meetings

Teachers traditionally have lots of ideas for parent meeting topics. In addition to the content that you want to include in parent meetings, however, there needs to be ample space for family-chosen topics. You might get an idea of what parents are interested in or concerned about from looking at family information forms for questions, interests, concerns, or specific topics. You could also survey individual parents or the entire group. Written surveys can be distributed before meetings or a "parent meeting topic" suggestion box can be set up by the door.

Posting a big piece of paper and pens on the classroom door or bulletin board with several topics for parents to vote on supports networking by giving families a chance to work together to choose. A blank piece of paper where parents write down their suggestions for topics provides an open-ended forum for ideas. Teachers can keep an up-to-date list of relevant topics by listening to parents' questions and concerns during daily check-ins and writing them down. Sometimes events in the classroom will bring up a topic parents are all interested in discussing. Timing can be important for topics. Because children are growing and changing so fast, questions parents had a few weeks ago are often replaced with new questions and challenges. Keeping alert to current issues will help staff come up with the most relevant topics.

Structuring Parent Meetings

How can meetings be structured so that they are interesting, engaging, informative, and worthwhile? What would a meeting look like that incorporated the goals discussed earlier? Most people have had the experience of being in a meeting that they couldn't wait to get out of. Knowing what a meeting shouldn't be like is just the first step toward discovering what it should be like. Structuring a parent meeting from a family-centered perspective compels teachers to look at the agenda in a new way.

For example, let's consider ways to create a sense of trust in parent meetings. Because "trust" and "safety" mean different things to different people, this would be a good discussion to have with parents. Building a sense of trust might include making name tags, providing food, outlining the agenda ahead of time, creating ways for parents to meet other parents, greeting parents individually as they arrive, and providing something to do while parents are waiting for the meeting to begin. As well as including as many aspects of trust and safety as you can think of, you can ask parents at the beginning of the meeting to share what helps them feel safe.

Parents have different temperaments as well as different cultural backgrounds and communication styles. Planning an agenda that will meet this diversity of learning and communication styles requires creativity. If you want parents to tell their stories, ask and answer questions, and share about their family and culture, they will need to talk or communicate to the group in some way. Some parents won't feel comfortable talking in the large group. Activities such as talking in pairs or small groups and writing ideas on individual notepads or on shared charts will offer these parents a chance to have their voices heard.

SMALL GROUPS

Many people feel safer talking in small groups. As parents get to know the other people in their group, it becomes a comfortable place for them. Parents might be divided into groups based on the ages of their children. In those groups parents could make a list of things children like to do, challenging behaviors and possible solutions, or their goals for their children in school. Small groups could share experiences and discoveries of being parents. They could share information about their culture or family history. Small groups of parents could develop skits of parent-child interactions, using positive discipline strategies presented in the meeting. These groups might do an art project, like creating a mobile to hang in their children's classroom.

DYADS

Similar to small groups, dyads are sets of two people who talk together. Dyads offer people an intimate setting to begin their sharing with the parent group, and they can be used to introduce people to the group. Some people who may feel shy introducing themselves would be able to introduce their dyad partner and be introduced to the group by them. In dyads parents might share observations of their children, successes or challenges of parenting, or information about their family. After families hear a presentation or read an article, dyads can give parents a place to discuss the new ideas.

Interestingly, many people will become comfortable talking in the large group after they have had a chance to speak to one other person or participate in a small group. Similarly, small group discussions and projects will offer parents a sense of community building, working together, and developing networks.

A VARIETY OF ELEMENTS

A well-balanced parent meeting should include variety. There needs to be useful content, including learning something new and relevant about children, parenting, or teaching. Equally important is time to discuss the content and to reflect

on one's own knowledge and experience. Parents also need time to think about ways to apply the new information to their child and family. Families need opportunities to talk with each other informally. (Some teachers say that the best learning happens during the meeting's break time.) Usually there is also some business that needs to happen: communication of center events, deadlines, and procedures. Always remember to include some fun.

Activity Ideas for Parent Meetings

Many different kinds of activities, projects, and presentations can be included in parent meetings to support family-centered care. This section will cover opening activities that help families be comfortable and that set the tone for networking and multi-way communication. Included also are displays that share information about children and their learning, interactive projects that give families a chance to work together to create materials for teaching and learning, networking opportunities for building support groups, family culture activities that provide a forum for the sharing of family beliefs and expertise, and interactive presentations that offer information and resources in a multi-way communication format.

OPENING ACTIVITIES

One of the most awkward times of a parent meeting is the arrival. Using an icebreaker or opening activity can help people begin to meet each other and feel more comfortable. Here are some activity ideas:

- Person bingo
- *Conocimiento*
- Hands-on activity tables
- Treasure hunt
- Introductory questions

Person Bingo

Person bingo is a bingo grid with squares for people to fill in about the other people at the meeting. Parents might be asked to find the person who lives the closest to them, who has a child the same age as theirs, who speaks two languages, who has the same number of children as they do, who can sing a children's song, who likes the same kind of food they do, who has a similar hobby to theirs, who knows how to make playdough from scratch, who has changed more diapers than they have this week, who has been awake with a child in the night this week. Teachers can make up questions that are appropriate for their families in their program.

Conocimiento

Conocimiento is a Spanish word that means "working knowledge." In this activity people share their working and life knowledge with each other. Families use *conocimiento* to help them name the needs and interests of their children. *Conocimiento* is a channel for families to provide the agenda and define the problems to be solved; it gives the thinking capacity to the families, not just the teachers. It is usually done as a series of interactive posters with a question at the top of each. Parents have felt pens to write their ideas on each chart. Here are some sample questions: What are your child's strengths? What are your family's strengths? What do you hope your child learns in this program? What is the most enjoyable thing about your child? What is the most challenging thing about your child? What are some of your questions about children? What do you like to do for fun? What was a favorite childhood game of yours?

Again, the questions you use will depend on the families in your program and the topic of the parent meeting. This activity gives parents an opportunity to engage in a hands-on activity, to socialize with other parents, and to see some of the ideas of other parents. This can help parents feel that they are a part of a community as they read that some other parents have ideas and experiences similar to theirs.

Hands-on Activity Tables

Activity tables can be set up with a child's activity for parents to explore. Setting up a table of children's books, playdough, ooblick, paint, gluing, blocks, or matching games gives parents a chance to explore some of the materials their children use and to understand some of the learning that takes place in the activity. Along with the activity can be cards describing the kinds of learning children do in that activity as well as questions for parents to answer about their experiences with the material.

Treasure Hunt

One of the ways to help parents explore the children's learning environment is to set up a treasure hunt—a search through the classroom looking for designated objects. Cards can be given to small groups of parents instructing them to look for an activity that promotes children's creativity, an activity that helps children learn to read, an activity that helps children develop hand-eye coordination, and an activity that helps children learn language. Teachers can create many different kinds of treasure hunt cards.

Introductory Questions

Introductory questions allow parents to get to know one another. Beginning a parent meeting by asking people questions can set the stage for partnership for the entire meeting. If the group is small, people may feel comfortable responding to the questions with the whole group; otherwise, parents should be divided into smaller groups. Questions serve to help parents reflect on their children, families, and parenting; remind parents about their expertise; help parents formulate their own questions and concerns; and invite parents to partner and participate in the parent meeting. Teachers often want to ask parents what their questions or challenges are in order to provide relevant information. However, questions that remind parents about their strengths and successes are important companions to the challenge questions.

Here's a list of possible questions:

"What are three words that describe your child?"

"What would you like your child to learn at school this year?"

"What do you hope your children will learn in your family?"

"What are three things you learned as a child? Are any of these things you want to teach your own child?"

"What have you learned since becoming a parent?"

"What are three pieces of advice you would offer to new parents?"

"What are your favorite activities to do outside with your child?"

"What went well for you as a parent this week? What are your current challenges as a parent?" (These two questions go particularly well together.)

In addition, questions can be posed to the whole group throughout the meeting to encourage parents to offer ideas to others. For example, you might use questions like "Has anyone else had the experience of a child waking several times a night?" or "Has anyone discovered strategies for dealing with siblings wanting the same toy?" or "Does anyone have an idea to share about this?"

DEMONSTRATION AND DISCUSSION

Visuals—such as pictures, slide shows, videos, PowerPoint presentations, and displays of children and their work—can provide information about each specific child to the parent group and also teach general concepts. These visuals can demonstrate how children learn physically, socially, emotionally, and cognitively. They might explain curriculum theories, such as how to create curriculum based on children's ideas. Video clips can illustrate things such as circle time, conflict resolution, children's language development, and specific teaching strategies. It is always interesting to show a video of a challenging behavior and then to stop it for discussion of problem-solving ideas. After the discussion, the video can be continued to show what actually happened with the conflict, and there can be more discussion. This is an exciting example of respecting teacher *and* family knowledge and expertise. In some programs, family members share in the taking of the photos and videos and in putting the displays together.

INTERACTIVE PROJECTS

Parent meetings that focus on interactive projects rather than on lecture or discussion can be useful for families in several ways. They are fun, they offer parents an active learning experience, and they let parents see how important hands-on learning is for children. Teachers of young children know a lot about setting up interactive projects. Ideas borrowed from the schools in Reggio Emilia, Italy, include parents working together to make musical instruments or other learning materials and collages and mobiles for classroom decoration. Other ideas include making books or story or song tapes for children, toys for sorting, laminated pictures, collages, "feely" boxes, and lock-and-latch boards.

For example, Ultima set up an interactive project that included children as well as families. Toddlers in her classroom had begun experimenting with painting on objects around the classroom. Protecting her classroom as well as the toddlers' ideas, Ultima brought in eucalyptus bark for children to paint. After these dried, she brought them to the parent meeting so that parents could write on them their goals for their child. She then posted them by the door to the classroom. Lainey has the families in her program make a quilt every year to hang in the classroom. Each family makes a square at a parent meeting, and the squares are put together as a class family quilt. In addition to making things for the classroom, family members can also experience the activities and explorations that children do in the classroom, but in an adult format. Some parent meetings are set up for parents to do more challenging activities than are used with the children, such as adult puzzles and brainteasers, so that they can experience and identify the steps to learning that children and adults need to take.

Networking Opportunities

Networking happens naturally through interactive activities at parent meetings. However, there are some specific experiences that can be set up to help parents network with each other and with community agencies. Parent panels give both the panelists and the parent participants opportunities to share expertise, learn about each other, and develop support relationships. Interest groups can be identified at parent meetings, either verbally or through written sign-up sheets. Teachers can ask questions like these: "Who would be interested in helping to coordinate a dinner calendar for Osha's family?" or "Who would like to be on a committee to organize a community resource referral Web site for the families in our program?" In one

program, a group of parents wanted to create a support group for single mothers. After discussion about other parents feeling excluded, the decision was made to invite any interested parent to attend. One parent who wasn't a single mother became a regular participant in the group.

Parent-generated questions can also be a jumping off place for networking. Instead of trying to answer parents' questions yourself, you can refer them back to the parent group. For example, you might say something like, "That's a good question about the different styles of kindergarten classes available in our community. I wonder if there is a group of parents who would like to do some research to bring back to our parent group," or "I know that there is a La Leche League in town. Does anyone else know of a breast-feeding support group?" In one parent meeting in a college child care center, there was a discussion about family frustration with limited finances and tight budgets. From the discussion, families and the teacher decided to build a barter network, on which people exchange services without using money. They put up a barter bulletin board, and several exchanges happened. One person exchanged evening child care for some computer training; another exchanged gardening for a homemade dinner.

Building Networks of Support

What have you or your program done to nurture support networks for families? Have you observed families initiating these networks themselves? What kinds of support do you think the families in your program need? Can you think of a way to help families create networks around these needs? Share your ideas with coworkers or fellow students.

Family Culture Activities

Parent meetings can be an important forum for

learning about and honoring the diversity of culture among families in the program. Inviting family members to bring cultural stories and artifacts to share can promote wonderful opportunities to strengthen the relationships and networks in the parent group and to help everyone understand families and cultures better. For example, here's an announcement from one program:

> In our next parent meeting we are asking families to bring something that is important in their family or culture. (It could be a photograph, a story or song, a boot, a recipe, a cookie press, a cornhusk, etc.) We are looking forward to learning more about all the cultures and families in our program.

As families get ready to share their things in the meeting, you can ask them to reflect on some questions. Here are some questions that have been used in other programs: "How is your object important in your family? How is it used? Are there values or beliefs associated with it? Is there anything else you would like to tell us about it?" As people start talking about what they brought, other questions will come up. It is important to have a backup plan for busy families who forget to bring something. You can ask them to talk about something that they would have brought or about a special tradition or event in their family. In Vicki's class there is a year-long culture share in parent meetings. Every meeting, two or three families share with the group. After the sharing, Vicki asks the families' permission to display their objects in the classroom.

Families can also be invited to bring food that is special in their family and culture. This can be part of a potluck or as snacks for the meeting. It is important to acknowledge the significance of this food to the person. A family member could describe to the group how this food is important or could write on a card to put on the serving table next to his dish to tell about it. In a potluck the table can be covered with paper and pens to encourage each family to write something about the dish they brought.

INTERACTIVE PRESENTATIONS

Speakers at parent meetings may be parenting experts, medical people or safety consultants, nutritionists, therapists, curriculum specialists, and family support workers. Sometimes in the spring, preschools put together panels of kindergarten teachers to talk to families about the transition to kindergarten. In addition to traditional experts, programs can look to their own staff and families to offer presentations at parent meetings. Teachers can talk about children learning through play, helping children resolve conflicts, and homemade toys, among other topics. Parents can share many kinds of expertise with the parent group as well.

Even though people think of the content of a parent meeting as the time when somebody stands up in front and talks, information sharing and learning also occur throughout the meeting in the kinds of activities discussed previously. In addition, speakers and panels can provide useful information and resources. When there is a speaker or more formal presentation, it is important to check with parents about what they already know on the subject. This accomplishes two things. It gives the speaker an idea of the audience's level of knowledge and what their questions might be. It also provides an opportunity for the parents themselves to reflect on and acknowledge what they do know. It helps them to see themselves as knowledgeable people who are going to learn more rather than ignorant people who are waiting for an expert to enlighten them. This prepares parents to be open, interactive participants in the presentation.

There are a variety of ways for parents to share their expertise. For example, if a presentation was on school readiness, they could be asked at the beginning or during the presentation, "What do you know about school readiness?" and "What would you like to know about school readiness?" These same questions could be asked even before the meeting occurs. Parents could write their responses to questions on a chart on the bulletin board in the center the week before the meeting or as they arrive at the meeting. Here are some more ideas for questions on the topic of school readiness. You can create similar questions for any parent meeting topic:

◆ What have children learned in preschool that will be helpful to them in kindergarten?

◆ What are your child's feelings about going to school?

◆ What are your feelings about your child going to kindergarten?

◆ What are your memories of kindergarten?

◆ What are you doing at home to help your child get ready for kindergarten?

Besides giving parents a chance to share their knowledge with the group, these kinds of questions serve to create a sense of community and let parents know they are not alone in their experiences.

FAMILY SOCIAL EVENTS

Family social events offer opportunities for families to play together with their children and other families, to build new relationships and networks, to get to know teachers in a less formal setting, and to have fun and relax. Some social events are for adults only, and others are for all family members. Adult social events might include fund-raisers such as silent auctions, formal dinners, wine tastings, musical performances, dances, and award dinners. Even with fund-raisers it is important to structure the cost on a sliding scale so all families can be included. Social events for the whole family include play days, picnics, potlucks, puppet shows, sing-a-longs, art-in-the-park events, graduations, and award ceremonies. Most of the events on this second list lend themselves well to

the inclusion of many different family members (siblings, grandparents, and so forth).

Family social events are events that parents often like to help create, coordinate, and organize. Some programs develop a "signature" event that they do every year, like a sing-a-long with local children's musicians or a picnic and bonfire at the beach. Some children's centers in Reggio Emilia, Italy, hold art events in the town plaza, including hands-on art projects for children to do along with displays of children's art and posters explaining the significance of children's art. Many programs in the United States host family play days at the child development center or a local park or community center. The booths at the play day can include many of the normal program curriculum activities, such as clay, wood gluing, water play, and planting seeds. Special activities like face painting, homemade books, or gymnastics demonstration and lessons can also occur.

FUND-RAISING WITH FAMILIES

Many of these social events can double as fund-raisers for the center. Play days, art, drama, and singing events can be opened to all of the families in the community. Fund-raisers provide opportunities for community building, networking, teamwork, and community education, as well as raising money for special projects or program support. When parents are involved from the beginning, they often share power by becoming the primary movers behind fund-raisers. Some programs have fund-raising committees that coordinate all the fund-raising efforts for the year. Others put together special committees for each event. It is important for teachers and program staff to be partners through two-way communication in the planning of the events. Fund-raising events should reflect the program philosophy as well as the interests and resources of the families in the program.

When sharing decision making with a committee to plan a fund-raiser, it is important to identify goals for the fund-raiser. Some fund-raisers are not particularly profitable but are important because they provide education, resources, and outreach to the parent group or community. Other fund-raisers may be less educational but more profitable, and some fund-raisers may turn out to be neither. For example, after an ice cream sale at the country fair one summer, parents of one program looked at each other and figured they had earned about fifty cents an hour. Unless their presence at the country fair promoted their program or educated the community about the needs of children, those parents will probably reevaluate that particular fund-raiser. On the other hand, the spaghetti feed and raffle with entertainment by Jordie's father's band raised about $2,000 for the program and was a wonderful social event for both the program and the community.

In another community the annual tamale sale is something that both the program and the community look forward to. All families sell tamale coupons for a few weeks before the tamale-making event. Then for two days a group of parents and teachers get together and have a huge tamale-making party. People are called to pick up their orders from the school. This is a very effective fund-raiser and also provides a wonderful teamwork experience for the teachers and parents involved. Each year a handful of parents and teachers learn how to make tamales for the first time during the event. In yet another program there is an ongoing flea market table where families donate outgrown children's clothing. When a parent or child finds something she wants on the table, she puts fifty cents in the can and takes her find home. A few parents in the program take responsibility for putting out clothes, making the signs, and keeping the table neat. This provides a steady source of income for the program and low-cost clothes to families.

Providing education, resources, and community building and raising money are all important goals. It is helpful at the beginning of the planning process to be clear about the purposes of each event. It is also important to evaluate whether the event has a possibility of meeting its goals before deciding to embark on it.

Deciding how to use the proceeds from fund-raising is also an important issue. Some programs have a standard procedure for using the money, such as all funds go to scholarships for the program, all funds go toward buying materials and equipment for the program, all funds go for children's books, or all funds go to the benefits fund for teachers. In some programs a deficit caused by a funding source drying up or an increase in expenses may necessitate a fund-raiser. Parents in consultation with program staff sometimes make a decision about how to spend the funds raised. Whatever the procedure is, it is important that both parents and teachers understand how the decision to spend the money will be made.

FAMILY WORKDAYS

On family workdays, teachers and families work together to build, clean, repair, and maintain the child care program's environment and materials. Family workdays provide opportunities for using as well as expanding networks of support. They provide a wonderful forum for families to share their expertise and their knowledge.

The more that families are involved in the design of the day and in decision making about tasks they can do, the better turnout there will be. Families receive a lot of satisfaction when they feel that they are supporting the program with their labor. Attaching some fun and food to the event can encourage families to get involved. There might be a potluck lunch or a lunch with soup children made the day before. There can be a celebration of diversity by inviting families to bring their favorite CDs. For some families, an obstacle to participating is that they don't want to spend time away from their children on the weekend. Some programs arrange for work-with-children tasks and work-without-children tasks. The inside area can be for one group, and the outside area for another. This allows parents who want to bring their children to participate. Despite the challenges in setting up a workday with children, there are also many advantages. Giving children a chance to work alongside their parents and a chance to see their parents investing in their school helps children to feel a part of the larger community and lets them see the partnership between their teachers and families in action. Workdays can also be arranged with some of the parents doing child care for children who need to be on site but cannot be in the work area.

as they arrive. If there are many parents who need directions and only a few teachers, people might end up standing around waiting to start.

Preparation is the other essential element. Making sure the tools, supplies, and materials are there so that the tasks can be done without interruption is key. Again, teachers can be the ones to organize this, or it can also be a parent task in preparation for the day. If teachers have several specific tasks they want done, it can be useful to write up detailed job cards and assemble the materials so that parents can get to work as soon

9

Classroom Environments

The classroom environment conveys messages to families about the program's expectations for them. One environment might say, "Please drop your child off quickly and leave. This is a place for teachers and children, not families." Another environment might say, "Come in, look around, get comfortable, observe children, interact with children. We want to get to know you, and we want you to get to know us." These messages might be conveyed through interactive journals, bulletin boards, family languages and stories on display, daily note boards, family idea boxes, teacher and family mailboxes, and furniture. The environment can communicate respect for diversity through pictures, books, language, and family and cultural artifacts. Evidence of networks of support might include announcements for upcoming single-parent support groups, a clothing exchange table, and a community resource display or notebook. Arranging the environment with families as well as children in mind will help to send a sincere welcome message to families. Helping families feel welcome in the classroom is the first step to inviting them into the teaching partnership.

There are many excellent books and resources on developing children's learning environments, including *Designs for Living and Learning* (Curtis and Carter 2003), *Child Care Design Guide* (Olds 2001), *Infant/Toddler Environment Rating Scale* (Harms, Cryer, and Clifford 2006), and *Early Childhood Environment Rating Scale* (Harms, Clifford, and Cryer 2004). It's not my intention to duplicate the information in these resources, which have many good ideas about developing classroom environments to serve children and families. Instead, this chapter focuses on supporting family-centered practice and developing relationships with families through the classroom environment.

WELCOMING FAMILIES: THE PHYSICAL ENVIRONMENT

The physical environment—the arrangement of furniture and space—can convey to families that your program invites two-way communication, recognizes family knowledge, wants to share decision making, respects diversity, and builds networks of support. Here are some aspects of the environment that can support family-centered care: comfortable, accessible furniture; space for more than one family; an area for parent-child good-byes; a family resource area; teacher and family mailboxes; and accessibility for people with disabilities.

Many child care programs are not in rooms that are specifically designed for children, much less families. Thinking creatively about ways to adapt your space to be welcoming to families as well as children may take time and staff and administrative support. Remember, also, that families may be interested in joining you in helping to redesign space. Tapping family knowledge and expertise, and making decisions together as a community are two key components of family-centered care.

As you think about how to help families feel comfortable and at home in the program, consider these elements and areas of the environment:

◆ furniture that welcomes families

◆ accessibility

◆ parent areas

◆ parent education areas

◆ parent communication, support, and networking areas

◆ parent storage areas

◆ good-bye areas.

WHAT MESSAGES DOES YOUR SPACE GIVE FAMILIES?

Think of all the spaces in your environment where families interact with your program. Are they designed to be welcoming to families? What furniture can families use? Are there spaces for them around the classroom or in just one place? What do you observe at drop-off and pick-up time? What is the traffic flow like when parents and children are there together? Are families staying awhile to observe, chat with each other, check in with the teacher, and listen to their child tell about their day? If you were going to make one change in the environment to improve the environment for families, what would it be? Discuss these questions and ideas for change with coworkers or fellow students.

Furniture that Welcomes Families

Furniture can serve to welcome or to discourage families to stay. Places for adults to sit invite family members to come in and stay awhile. If there is not space for couches or cushions, low benches or risers also provide a space for adults to sit somewhat comfortably. Seating close to the different activity areas invites parents to spend some time watching their child play. Space for teachers and parents to talk while simultaneously observing children invites parents to take some time to check in. Places where parents can visit with other families invite networking.

Do the classroom furnishings feel comfortable to families from a variety of socioeconomic backgrounds? Your program's choice of furnishings can make a difference to the comfort of the families. Classrooms that are totally furnished with new, expensive educational materials can feel uncomfortable to families who don't have the means to buy such toys. They can also communicate that these materials are essential to a child's education. If your environment includes some homemade and recycled educational materials (cardboard boxes, plastic water bottle shakers, coffee can shape sorters, soft sock balls for inside throwing), as well as purchased ones, many families will feel at home. These kinds of materials can also serve to respect the learning environments families provide for their children in their own homes.

Accessibility

Is the classroom set up to be accessible for parents with disabilities or other special needs? Can a parent in a wheelchair get out to the yard to watch her daughter going down the slide? Does an elderly family member have a place to sit? When thinking about the comfort of adults in the classroom, it is still important to think about the safety of children. Finding furniture and equipment that meet both children's and families' needs can be an interesting challenge. When one program was setting up a new infant room, the teachers found foldable couches made entirely out of very firm foam. These couches are used by parents and teachers as well as infants, who can safely pull up on them.

Parent Areas

Some programs have an area of the classroom or building specifically designated as a parent area. In most programs this isn't a special room but just a small area of the classroom or lobby. Depending on its size and location, this kind of an area can offer a parent or family a place to rest, study, read, write, or talk with other parents. Refreshments and a basket of children's toys and books provide a special welcome to families. A parent area offers one more reminder to families that their presence in the program is valued. Some programs are fortunate to have an observation window as part of their parent area. An observation window allows parents to see the program in action and to make observations of their child. As well as providing a restful place to sit and talk, parent areas can provide a place for parents' belongings while they're visiting the program and for parent education and networking.

PARENT STORAGE

Parents have lots of their own belongings as well as their children's belongings that they bring into the classroom. They may have their own backpacks, purses, briefcases, phones, keys, coffee cups, and books. Planning for parents' belongings can offer a clear welcome to families and can ensure safety for children in the classroom. High shelves or cubbies can provide a safe storage for most parent paraphernalia. One classroom has a little basket by the door for keys, which helps prevent the syndrome of lost keys when parents want to leave.

PARENT EDUCATION

A parent area might include a parent library of books and videos to use or to check out, a child development article file, and a computer with family resource Internet sites. Programs can support parents as teachers by providing homework activity boxes and a children's book lending library for families to check out and use at home. Parents also enjoy looking at curriculum documentation scrapbooks and photos of children in the classroom, as well as children's artwork. Some parent areas have workspace for parents to upload and print photos, create displays, laminate pictures, cover books, work on scrapbooks, or make materials for the classroom.

COMMUNICATION, SUPPORT, AND NETWORKING

To encourage two-way communication and support networks, programs can provide family and teacher mailboxes, parent-teacher interactive journals, a file of community resources for families, and a variety of bulletin boards. A children's clothing exchange encourages networking among families.

A few programs have staff available in the parent area who can provide drop-in counseling, parenting support, or technical assistance. A program that does not have this kind of resource might offer "peer support," staffed by volunteer parents for a couple of drop-in hours a week or set aside an hour a week when the director is available to talk. Programs can create the parent areas that work best for them, taking into consideration the needs of both families and teachers, with the resources and space they have available.

Good-Bye Area

It is important that the arrangement of the environment provides a space for parents and children to transition into and out of child care every day. In many programs the sign-in area is set up across the classroom from the door to encourage families to come in. In one program the parent sign-in was on an adult-level table with a vase of fresh flowers every day. This communicates clearly to parents that they are valued and planned for. That same table could also hold some quotes from children, a thought for the day, or several copies of a new parenting article.

Enough space in the greeting area for several parents and their children to arrive at the same time prevents parents from feeling pushed out the door and allows for some informal networking. Well-marked and easily accessible children's cubbies make transitions easier, and family mailboxes supplied with writing implements encourage two-way communication. A conveniently located lost and found box, close to the cubby area, can be easily checked by families on their way in and out.

Space can also be arranged so that children can wave good-bye to their parents and watch them through the window as they leave. Soft pillows and low family pictures can create a cozy family area for children to spend time with their parents and for children to hang out in after they have said good-bye.

THE PHYSICAL ENVIRONMENT AND FAMILY-CENTERED CARE PRINCIPLES

Think of each of the family-centered care principles, one at a time. For each of the principles, think of examples in your program's physical environment (or a child care environment that you are familiar with) that support that principle. If there is a principle that is not evident in your environment, think of a change that would incorporate that principle. Discuss with coworkers or fellow students.

In some programs parents are asked to take off their shoes or put on booties to keep the classroom floor clean for babies. If this shoe area is put together thoughtfully with attractive and neat places to store shoes and benches to sit down while removing or putting on shoes, it gives a message of welcome to families.

WELCOMING FAMILIES: DISPLAYS AND PICTURES

The visual environment—displays, pictures, photos, aesthetics, and bulletin boards—is an essential element of a family-centered care program. Displays can offer examples of and opportunities for the principles of two-way communication and knowledge sharing. For example, one family created a display of homemade musical instruments with a dialogue poster above it for other families and teachers to share what they like about music, thus demonstrating both of these principles. Families can be invited into shared decision making through posted surveys on family meeting topics and brainstorm charts for curriculum ideas. Respect for diversity is demonstrated by including all families, cultures, socioeconomic groups, gender roles, and abilities in the decorations, photos, books, and pictures on display. Additionally, a posted invitation to families to bring things in for display acknowledges diversity and encourages networking. The visual environment gives families some of the clearest and most obvious messages about program values.

Photos, Pictures, and Collages

Pictures can serve to welcome families. Many classrooms display photos of children and families. Photos provide a wonderful grounding for children and families in the program, offer images of diversity, broaden the definition of family, and help families feel welcome. Many programs use general images of families and children as well as specific photos of the families and children in the program. This is useful because teachers can purposefully choose images that portray a diversity of family structure, physical ability, socioeconomic class, gender roles, culture, and ethnicity that extends beyond the immediate families in the program.

Socioeconomic class is particularly important to keep in mind when choosing pictures and books for the classroom. Some picture sets and books available from educational supply stores depict a variety of differences but still feature only middle-class families. Would a homeless family or a family who was living in a trailer or shelter feel represented in your program? It can be challenging to find images that respectfully represent healthy families living in these circumstances, but worth your effort, even if you have to take them yourself. Family structure can also be challenging to portray. Is there an image in your classroom of a child who lives in two different houses or a child with two dads? Families might even be a resource for some of these pictures. Combined with inclusive puzzles, books, and dramatic play props, these images reinforce the program's commitment to inclusion. Further, these messages communicate to prospective families that they will be welcome.

In using family photos there are several things to consider. Some families may not have lots of photos of themselves for economic or cultural reasons or because of migration or moving. Some families may feel very protective of their photos as a part of their family history that they don't want damaged with pin holes and children's fingerprints. Some families may feel self-conscious or be uncomfortable having pictures taken of them, although many will be delighted to bring in pictures to share and/or to have the teacher take pictures of them. As you propose to families that you would like to have pictures of them in the classroom, it is important to be aware of these considerations. The sample note below is one example of a respectful way of asking families for photos.

We like to have pictures of families in the classroom to help build our sense of community and to help children feel comfortable. We can post your pictures, copy them, and give you back the original, or take pictures of your family with our camera. If you are uncomfortable with pictures, there are a number of other ways that your family could be represented in the classroom. What would work best for you?

Simply posting photos in the classroom is a

significant act. There are many ways to create and present photo displays that promote family partnerships. What are all the ways families could be involved in creating a photo display? Some programs hold parent meetings and provide supplies for families to create photo collages or picture frames to prepare the photos for display. It would be important in setting this up that you made sure everyone who came had some pictures to use. For example, the sample announcement below shows one way of handling this:

Announcement! Our family photo collage night is happening next Tuesday at 6:00 p.m. Sign up early if you need child care. Thanks to Leti's mom for offering to provide all the paper, glue, and decorations. We will need pictures of your child and family for you to make collages with. Do you have some to bring, or shall we take some of you with our school camera? If you want us to take some family pictures, let teacher Dena or Larry, AJ's dad, know by this Friday. They are the ones who know how to use our school camera. See you there.

Families can also participate in creating collages from children's photos. This invites the sharing of family expertise and creates an opportunity for shared decision making and informal networking. In one toddler classroom the teacher took pictures of each of the children sleeping. In a subsequent parent meeting she asked each parent to decorate the picture to make a nap collage to post over each child's nap cot. In another classroom the teacher collected photos that had been taken of the children in her class and put them all out on a table at a parent meeting. Also on the table were poster boards on which were written the goals for children that families had shared at the previous meeting. Parents went right to work creatively sorting and gluing the photos onto the appropriate posters that were displayed in the classroom the next day.

Another way to partner with families on displaying their family photos is to ask them to write something about their family to post with the photo. Many programs already post photos and short biographies of staff for families to see. If every family has a similar way to introduce themselves to the group, the program has taken a big step in creating a sense of community. In one classroom teacher Eric set up an adult-level writing table with paper and pencils for parents to write notes to post. This also provided wonderful modeling for children of adults' writing. At different times Eric asked parents to write about different topics. Once he had them write about their favorite childhood game, and he posted those family stories on the bulletin board. This activity offered wonderful opportunities for networking among families as they wrote together and read each other's stories. Time might also be made in a parent meeting for people to write something to post with their pictures. Special paper can be made available for parents who prefer to do their family story as homework. Teachers can be sensitive if there are parents who would rather dictate than write their own story.

Information Cards in the Classroom

Written messages to parents throughout the classroom serve several purposes. Posting information

in the classroom that helps parents navigate on their own contributes to their sense of empowerment. Signs directing parents to the lost and found, the adult bathrooms, their family mailboxes, or their child's artwork collection all communicate that you want them to know their way around. When parents are helping with curriculum or doing activities with children in the classroom, labels on cupboards or in the storeroom help them get their own materials without having to ask a teacher. Instructions on how to use the dishwasher and the laundry help parents take the initiative in doing their parent hours. By thinking creatively about what posted information would be useful for parents, you can make your environment more accessible to families.

Posted notices convey information to families as well as significant messages about where in the classroom they are welcome to be. Notices to parents centrally located on a bulletin board encourage parents to stand at the bulletin board and read. Information cards displayed throughout the classroom invite parents to come in, to look around, and to explore different areas. Notes to parents in many different areas of the classroom send a clear message that parents are wanted here. The written word in the classroom is an important area to be inclusive of the languages spoken in the program. Translating these notes into all the languages spoken in the program shows the program's commitment to including all families. Through these notes teachers can share information about children's learning and play with parents. Here's a sample of an information card that could be posted in a block area and translated into the languages spoken by families and staff in the program.

BLOCK PLAY INFORMATION CARD

Block play offers children a chance to learn math concepts like shape, size, number, sequence, comparison, spatial awareness, and weight. They also learn the physics of balance, gravity, and motion. Physical and social learning is also part of block play. Children develop muscle strength and coordination through building with blocks. They practice social skills such as cooperation, teamwork, and negotiating differing ideas. Children also demonstrate cognitive skills through all of the above and also through using blocks for representation. Listen, and you'll hear children say things like "This is the baby's bed." "This block is my skateboard." Vocabulary that children might learn through building with blocks includes balance, wood, block, shape, square, triangle, rectangle, arch, build, tall, long, wide, big, enclosure, building, heavy, matching.

The language used in this sample is not a match for all families in all programs. Adding drawings or pictures would make the note more interesting for all parents, and simplifying the language would make it more accessible to some parents.

In addition to providing families with information around the room, two-way and multi-way communication can be encouraged. Families can be invited to share information through the posting of notes and comments. A running dialogue sheet in the different learning areas can be a place for observations of children's play and comments about their learning. Clipboards strategically located around the room give families and teachers easy access to note-writing materials. Families can specifically be invited to make observations for their own child's portfolio and assessment.

Displays in the Classroom

Displays in classrooms provide information and add to the aesthetics of the environment. Most classrooms have some displays aimed at children and some aimed at families. Strategically placing displays around the classroom for families as well as children is another way to invite parents in. Teachers, children, and family members can create displays. They can be about the curriculum that is planned, or they can document curriculum that is in process. They can be about children, children's learning, families, events at school or in the community, and events at home. They can be decorative and/or informative. They can represent different aspects of culture. Many times, teachers' use of the classroom display space can invite parents and children to contribute to the space as well. For example, teacher Bonnie hangs her aunt's patchwork quilt in the classroom to give a sense of hominess. Teacher Arlae asks family members to bring in natural things to add to a family mobile project that now hangs in the classroom. Don, a parent who is a beach enthusiast, brings in his collection of shells to display in the classroom. Teacher Luz creates a special table for Día de los Muertos and invites families to bring pictures and objects to display. Roberta takes pictures of another parent making corn muffins with children and displays them in the children's cooking area. Miguelito collects all his drawings and some of his friends' drawings and carefully tapes them up on the wall near the art area. Teacher Eddie posts a note describing Miguelito's project.

Nancy Spangler, a veteran teacher of young children and advocate for families, developed a family shelf in her classroom that holds and displays family artifacts. Each family brings in a small collection of things that represent their family. At different times the shelf has held special cloth, books, pictures, candles, newspaper articles, ceramic cups, twigs, rocks, articles of clothing, poems, letters. Families sign up to bring in things to display for two weeks at a time. Children in Nancy's room see different families helping to decorate their classroom. Families have a chance to share something about themselves and their cultures and to learn about other families. Nancy also invites families to bring in an article of clothing or toy from their child's babyhood to permanently display on the birthday wall. Anyone coming into Nancy's classroom can see that families are welcome and valued there.

Compartiendo Nuestra Cultura Familiar
Family Culture Share

Displays can also promote partnerships by documenting parent activities and participation in the program. After a parent workday, a chart can be posted (parents might even make it during the workday) describing with words and/or pictures the work that was done and thanking the participating families. After Lon comes to circle time to teach the children sign language, teachers can make a photo chart documenting the activity and including American Sign Language that children learned in the activity. After Marcela brings her truck into the center's yard and the children help her wash it, the teacher has children dictate the truck wash story at circle time, and the children's story is posted for all to see.

After parents and children march to the state capitol to protect the child care money in the state budget, a chart documenting the trip and its purpose is posted by the front door. Every time a parent who contributed to the program sees a display honoring his work, the parent reexperiences his connection to the community. Every time a parent sees a display honoring another parent's

contribution to the program, she sees one more opportunity to become involved.

NOTES, PHOTOS, AND DISPLAYS IN YOUR PROGRAM

What are the current messages to families in your program's environment? Are there ways the environment reflects the families in your program? Have families participated in creating displays, notices, or photos in your classroom? Name three new ways that you can partner with families to create a welcoming environment. Discuss your ideas with coworkers, and plan how to work together to make some changes.

REFERENCES

Curtis, Deb, and Margie Carter. 2003. *Designs for living and learning*. St. Paul: Redleaf.

Harms, Thelma, Richard M. Clifford, and Debby Cryer. 2004. *Early childhood environment rating scale*. Revised edition. New York: Teachers College Press.

Harms, Thelma, Debby Cryer, and Richard M. Clifford. 2006. *Infant/toddler environment rating scale*. Revised edition. New York: Teachers College Press.

Olds, Anita Rui. 2001. *Child care design guide*. New York: McGraw-Hill.

10

Curriculum in a Family-Centered Classroom

Developing curriculum can involve many levels of partnership for families and teachers. Parents can participate in the concept and the design, developing educational goals and teaching strategies, coming up with specific curriculum topics, brainstorming activities, creating and acquiring curriculum materials, setting up the environment, documenting curriculum, and, finally, implementing curriculum activities. With the participation of teachers, families, and programs, every partnership will discover its best collaboration.

While planning curriculum in the child development program has traditionally been the sole responsibility of teachers and staff, families can play an important role in the process. Families have information about children's and other family members' knowledge, skills, and interests. They know about the current events in their children's lives and in the community. They can share ideas about the kinds of activities they do at home with children. In addition, many families can offer time, creativity, and energy for the development of curriculum. Children's curriculum in a family-centered program can be supported and influenced by family-centered principles. This chapter will look at ways of including family knowledge and expertise in planning curriculum;

keeping the channels of two-way communication open for sharing family ideas, teacher ideas, and curriculum events; negotiating and sharing power and decision making in the development of curriculum; honoring diversity through the inclusion of family needs, cultures, and ideas; and using networks for bringing together resources and ideas for curriculum planning.

CURRICULUM THAT REFLECTS CHILDREN'S LIVES

It is important for curriculum to address important events and interests in the lives of children and families. These events and interests are part of a family's knowledge and expertise. Curriculum that includes them creates an integrated learning experience for children. When a child's family adopts a new cat, and the school provides kitty ears and tails, kitty dishes, kitty pictures, books and flannelboard stories, as well as kitties in the sand table, a child can continue to expand on her interest from home when she comes to school and to bring the ideas from school back home in learning about her cat. This kind of curriculum also honors the child and the family and offers topics that children are naturally motivated to learn about.

Likewise, curriculum that addresses important

events in a family's or child's life can help children understand, process, and manage challenging life events. When Griselda's dad was injured at his job, teachers developed a network of support for the family and then turned their energies toward helping Griselda work through her feelings and understanding of the event. They put together a "hospital emergency room" outside, where Griselda liked to play, and turned the wagons into ambulances. They put out all kinds of sensory activities, including playdough, sand, and water. In the sand table they included people figures with tractors and other machinery. After talking with Griselda's aunt about how her dad was eating in bed at home, they put trays into the dramatic play center in the house. The teachers continued talking with the family about how things were going during her dad's recovery and were able to offer the family information about how Griselda was doing at school through play observations and through stories she dictated and pictures she was drawing.

In one campus child care program Maggie noticed that every semester, around the time of final exams, families and children started experiencing stress. She now brings out the special book *Tucking Mommy In* (Loh 1988), a story about an exhausted mom who gets nurtured and tucked into bed by her kids. Maggie is sensitive to both curriculum and special interactions that support children and families at that time of the semester.

When teachers develop curriculum they feel will address a family need or situation, it can be important to check with the family during the planning process. In one classroom where there were several families with single moms, children began talking about "daddies." Their alert teachers wanted to help children explore their questions and interests about this aspect of families. One teacher collected a group of books addressing single-parent families and daddies who didn't live with their children. The teachers decided that

they needed to have the families look at the books before they put them out, so that families could offer their input and ideas on the curriculum. A very interesting discussion occurred. Families gave lots of input about the topic, teachers received a great deal of new information about the families and ideas for their curriculum, and families were very grateful that they were consulted.

REFLECTING ON THE EVENTS IN CHILDREN'S LIVES

Think about the children and families you are working with now or have worked with in the past. What are some of the experiences or significant events in their lives that might be included in your curriculum planning? If you don't have this kind of information about families, how could you get it? Discuss with coworkers or fellow students.

Recognizing family knowledge and expertise also includes inviting families to share their resources, skills, and ideas in planning curriculum. Group time or circle time is a wonderful venue for parent-inspired activities. With children gathered and other teachers there to support them, family members can provide all kinds of demonstrations and activities. For example, in one program Janet brought her dance troupe for children and their families to watch. Leo brought his Capoeira group and showed children a few moves they could do. Joe brought his pet snake for children to observe and touch when they grew comfortable. Lisbeth brought all her surfing gear and pictures of her on a big wave. Antoine brought his firefighting gear to demonstrate and for children to touch. Hans played German songs on his guitar and taught children a song.

Families can also set up interest or activity areas for children to explore. Here are some ways parents have contributed in early childhood programs: David made latkes with children. Gisela brought whole corn plants from her garden so children could explore the roots as well as the corn in the husk. May brought her knitting and pieces of extra yarn for children to glue. Patti drove her city bus over for the children to explore.

When family members have an idea for an activity to do with children, it is helpful for a teacher to think through the preparation, setup, and timing with them. (See the next section on sharing power and decision making for more information on negotiating curriculum ideas with families.) Teachers can also plan or help parents plan the follow-up activities to a curriculum theme that a parent has initiated.

Families have traditionally participated in field trips with their child's class. In many programs teachers have been the primary planners of these field trips. Talking with families about their ideas and resources for field trips can broaden your possibilities. Many parents work in settings that might be interesting for children to visit. Family members might have community connections that would provide good field trip sites, and some parents might be interested in taking the lead in planning a class field trip.

Two-way communication with families is essential if teachers are going to learn about the important events and interests in the lives of children and families as well as the skills and resources families have. Teachers can learn about these through communication at the beginning of their relationship, through ongoing communication with families, and through children. Ongoing daily check-ins give teachers a chance to hear about the current events in the lives of children and families that might seed a curriculum project. Other ideas for including family input into curriculum include holding a parent meeting with the focus on teachers' and families' goals for children's learning for the year; establishing a parent-teacher curriculum development committee; creating a suggestion box; and sharing input on e-mail, Internet chat groups, or online bulletin boards. Some programs ask specifically on the family information form if families have interests, skills, traditions, or resources they would like to share with the program. Sadie, a teacher of three- to five-year-old children explains one of her channels of communication with families:

Each family has a binder with different sections: one for teacher comments, observations, and photos; one for parent comments and observations; one for children's work; one for the list of measures that we use for child assessment; and the front section has a curriculum web, which represents their child's interests. We develop the curriculum web based on our observations of children, information we have gotten from families during home visits, and other information that parents tell us on a regular basis, but we include the web in the interactive binder to encourage families to look at and add to it. During Raymond's home visit, I learned that he is very interested in airplanes, and I put that on his web. The other day I noticed that Raymond's mother had added "trains" to his web. I'm excited to see families adding to the webs.

REFLECTING ON FAMILIES' CONTRIBUTIONS TO THE CURRICULUM

Think of the families in your program or families you have known. What skills or interests do you think they might like to share in the classroom? How might you find out if families have skills they would like to share? Discuss with coworkers or fellow students.

SHARING POWER AND DECISION MAKING

One of the most challenging principles of family-centered care to implement in planning curriculum is sharing power and decision making. Teachers may feel concerned that families are going to show up with all kinds of ideas that are inappropriate for children, are disconnected from the ongoing themes of the classroom, contradict the program philosophy, or leave no room for teacher curriculum activities. Any of these might happen in a given situation—although, rest assured, they are not all likely to happen at once! However, if we keep the focus on "sharing" rather than "taking over" power and decision making, collaborative curriculum development can be enriching for both families and teachers.

Here are some things to consider as you begin to include families in curriculum planning:

◆ Start small.
◆ Share information.
◆ Make it clear to families what kind of input you would like.
◆ Remember the family's good idea.
◆ Negotiate with families.
◆ Set limits when necessary.

Start Small

If you are just starting and haven't included families in curriculum planning before, you can begin with simple steps like these: asking families about the interests of their children, telling families about upcoming curriculum you are planning and asking them how they think their child might respond, sharing observations with families about their child's involvement with curriculum at school, asking families if they could bring in specific materials to support your project (for example, natural materials for a collage, fabric for a weaving project), putting poster paper by the door with a question like this one: "It's spring! What interests do your child and family have in spring?"

Share Information

Sharing information is a form of sharing power. Letting families know how you think about children and curriculum empowers them with under-

standing and a sense of connection to the activities of the program. Ultima observed that children in her one-year-olds' classroom had been studying the wheels on the small vehicles. So she decided to buy some new sit-on scooters for her program. Before she introduced them to the children, she explained to the families that she wanted the children to be able to explore them in any way they wanted to. She told them that she wasn't planning to "show" the kids how to use them. She asked the families to observe with her how the children explored them. The families became very involved in observing the many ways children discovered they could play with the scooters before they actually figured out how to sit and ride on them.

Make It Clear to Families What Kind of Input You Would Like

When inviting families to participate, it is important to make it clear what their role is going to be. If you say, "We would like families to plan our next curriculum unit," it indicates that families will do this without any teacher input. If, instead, you say, "We would like to get your input and ideas as we are planning our curriculum for the next few weeks," or "Come talk with us if you have ideas of activities you would like to do in the classroom with children. We would love to discuss your ideas with you and make a plan together to put on our curriculum calendar," you are making it clear that planning happens with input from both of you.

Remember the Family's Good Idea

As with any problem-solving situation with families, it's important to find common ground and recognize the strength and creativity behind families' curriculum ideas, even if the ideas themselves don't seem feasible. When a family proposes that the toddlers could fingerpaint with red frosting, for example, it might be hard to appreciate their idea, as you immediately think of toddlers eating that much sugar and red dye, not to mention the sticky residue on the toddlers and in your classroom for weeks. But when you stand back for a moment, you might be able to appreciate that the parent has identified fingerpainting as an appropriate toddler activity. You could start your response with "Toddlers do love to fingerpaint! Has Ethan been fingerpainting at home?"

Negotiate with Families

The best ideas come when families share their unique expertise, and teachers share their special expertise. Once you have acknowledged a family's good idea, you can offer your own expertise. In the example above, you might say something like "Fingerpainting would be fun. I'm concerned about toddlers eating so much sugar and red dye. I wonder what else they could paint with?"

Set Limits When Necessary

Appreciating the parent's good idea is also an appropriate place to start with setting limits. For example, you might say something like "I love your idea of children working with pumpkins, but I can't let them use sharp knives in the classroom. Let's think about some other things they could do with the pumpkins."

Sharing curriculum with families can take creativity and skill. Here are some examples from

teachers describing how they have planned and negotiated curriculum with families. Teacher Mayo helped David figure out how to move the frying pan out of the reach of children to ensure safety during his latke cooking project. Teacher Luz helped Joe set up an enclosure for his pet snake so that the children who were scared could keep their distance. Teacher Nancy negotiated with Ben, a dad who was a professional skater, to bring in a female skater to join in his skateboard demonstration for the children. Teacher Yosi tells this story:

One of the four-year-old boys in my class was really into superheroes. For his birthday his dad wanted to dress up like Superman and come into the classroom and play with the kids. We've been trying to redirect the kids' superhero play into other powerful outlets, but I also really wanted to support this family's idea. I talked to the dad about how interested in costuming the kids are and also about how they can't always distinguish fantasy from reality. I told him I was concerned that if he was in full Superman costume, that some of the kids might be really scared. He suggested that he wear just a simple cape. I said that sounded fine and asked him what he thought the kids might do. He came up with the idea that he would bring in some plain capes that the kids could decorate themselves with fabric paint.

In another example, teacher Denny was planning on doing a Valentine's Day curriculum, setting up doilies and stickers for children to make valentines to send to each other. She wrote up her plan on the curriculum calendar, and Darla, Connie's mother, came to talk to her about it. Darla was uncomfortable with the activity because her family didn't celebrate Valentine's Day. She and Denny each shared their ideas and goals. They discussed the possibility of Connie staying home that day, but neither of them really wanted that to happen. They settled on a post office curriculum, where children could write letters and notes to put into each other's post office cubbies. Darla offered to bring in some pieces of shiny paper so kids could make fancy cards to send each other.

Sharing power and decision making with families is essential in creating curriculum that is developmentally and culturally appropriate. This process requires a commitment from both teachers and families to engage in ongoing dialogue and negotiation. Sharing power this way is well worth the effort because of the quality of curriculum and the deepening of the partnership that result.

PLANNING CURRICULUM TOGETHER WITH FAMILIES

Have you had any experiences when families had an idea for curriculum that you didn't think was appropriate for the children in your program? Choose (or make up) an example, and role-play a discussion between the family and teacher in which you design an appropriate curriculum activity based on the family's idea.

RESPECTING DIVERSITY

Acknowledging and respecting the diversity of the children and families in your program and community are important in designing effective curriculum. Respecting this diversity includes creating curriculum that is inclusive of the different family structures, abilities, ethnicities, languages, cultures, and beliefs in your group. Using families as curriculum resources is one way to do this. Educating yourself about designing curriculum that is respectful of diversity is another way.

One important aspect of diversity in children's lives has to do with family structure. It is essential to a child's healthy development of identity that her family is valued and respected. How can we redefine "healthy family" to make sure that each child in our program feels accepted? Children learn from our language, songs, books, pictures and stories as well as from our attitudes about

family. Something as simple as saying to a child, "What did your mother put in your lunch box today?" conveys assumptions about both family structure and gender roles in families, and it can confuse or alienate a child whose father, grandmother, or older brother packed her lunch. Knowing the families of the children in your care and using inclusive language allow you to avoid making some of these mistakes.

The language teachers use in songs, stories, and finger plays conveys to children information about families. For example, the "Farmer in the Dell" depicts not only a nuclear family but a patriarchal one, at that. In itself, this isn't a problem, but if all the books and songs and stories depict the same kind of family, over 75 percent of the children in child care are at risk for feeling they don't have a proper family. Furthermore, even if every family in your program lives in a two-parent heterosexual family without important extended family members close by, it's still important that those children learn through the examples in stories and songs and the language teachers use that there are many kinds of families. Teachers can look for literature that is inclusive and shows a diverse representation of families. You can write your own stories and songs, and you can alter the ones you already know. Rheta, a toddler teacher, always sings about Old MacDonald and *her* cows, chickens, and so on. Jake uses the "Thumbkin" song to sing about the different families of the children in his class. Asking children who is in their family or using his knowledge of their families, he puts his hands behind his back and sings, "Where is Grandpa Bill? Here I am, here I am," bringing out one finger at a time to represent the different people and pets in children's families. This is a particularly wonderful example because it creates an open framework that can include and describe any family structure.

Developing curriculum with families is a natural way to acknowledge diversity, as families often contribute ideas that reflect their families and cultures. However, defining and understanding culture is not an easy task. Through questions and discussion, teachers can play a role in helping families articulate the special aspects of their beliefs and traditions. Sharing traditional clothes, food, and holidays has been a way that many people have used to understand culture. These are tangible things that we can somewhat easily include in our curriculum and program. While a piece of clothing might evoke a sense of familiarity for a child, it does not adequately represent "culture." This is where a teacher can help. Imagine asking a family to bring in a piece of clothing that is special in their family or culture and nicely displaying the piece of clothing on a "family wall" or bulletin board. Now imagine asking the family to talk with children and other families about the piece of clothing. Ask them to discuss things like: Who wears it? When do they wear it? Is it for a particular occasion? How is this piece of clothing special in your family? What memories are associated with it? Then you display it on the family wall, with a card written by the family about the piece of clothing and a picture of a family member wearing it.

While these are both good steps toward including family culture in the curriculum, the difference between the two is that in the first one people have the artifact to look at and the family has the experience of bringing something of themselves into the classroom, while in the second example families in the program get to experience the relationship the family has to the artifact. They learn about the family's feelings, stories, way of perceiving things, and beliefs and practices. Neither plan tells us all there is to know about a family's culture, but the second one gives a broader window to the family and their culture.

Because culture influences most of what we do, any family participation in the program shares culture. Inviting families to bring special traditions, food preparation, music, and stories to share with children in the classroom teaches children about family and culture. In a different way, inviting a parent to do an art activity, gardening, obstacle course, or science project will also bring culture into the classroom. A parent who practices organic gardening will teach children her values about plants and insects similarly to how a parent who makes pot stickers with children teaches his values about food traditions and eating.

CREATING INCLUSIVE STORIES

Think of your ten favorite songs, books, and finger plays to use with children. How many different family structures are included in these favorites? Are there children in your program who don't have a representation of their family in your curriculum and language? Can you find or make up a song or story to include these children?

Teachers can support curriculum that families bring into the classroom by preparing children and by providing follow-up activities. In Zoe's class a parent brought in her pasta machine to make pasta with the children. She brought in little chef's hats, made dough with the kids, and taught them how to use the machine. They took pictures and put them together on a big chart, so the kids could tell the story of making pasta. Zoe read *Strega Nona* (de Paola 1975), a book about a pasta pot, with the kids before and after the parent came, so the kids had an idea about pasta. After the cooking activity, Zoe made a sequence card game with pictures of the different steps of making pasta for the kids to use in the classroom. After Kai shared her family's Hapa culture with a hula demonstration, teacher Nancy helped children explore different materials they could make hula skirts with.

Partnering with families in developing children's curriculum provides wonderful opportunities to acknowledge and respect diversity. Inviting families and their ideas into the classroom;

engaging in ongoing dialogue with families about values, beliefs, and culture; and creating inclusive stories, language, displays, and activities all contribute to a program that truly acknowledges and respects diversity.

BUILDING NETWORKS

Creating networks of support for curriculum development can provide teachers with a variety of resources, offer families and teachers a chance to work together collaboratively for the benefit of the children, and link the child development program to the larger community. Families can provide invaluable curriculum resources, including ideas, materials, energy, and community connections. A teacher in Pistoia, Italy, answered my question about the origin of all the natural, fresh plants, flowers, and produce in the classrooms there daily: "The parents take empty bags home in the evening and bring them back to us in the morning, full of things." Another teacher gratefully explains, "Manjula came in every Thursday afternoon and cooked an Indian meal for us. There was always enough for children and parents, both, to have some. It was such a gift to the children, the families, and to me. The food was wonderful, and interesting, but really, her presence in the classroom was what was so special to us." Miche, a long-time preschool teacher, tells of another resource: "We had a child in the program whose family had an apple orchard. Every fall, they would save the short trees with the low branches for our preschoolers to pick. We had a field trip to that farm every year for several years, even after Maya went on to kindergarten."

Developing curriculum for the classroom can provide families a chance to work together for a common purpose and to get to know one another. In one program families worked together during one of their meetings to construct "walking boxes" for their toddlers to push around. In another meeting each family wrote a special letter

to their child to include in the child's portfolio. Workdays also provide opportunities for families to build sandboxes and garden areas, to make puzzles and matching games. These kinds of activities allow families to learn about curriculum and also to talk informally, share stories, and build connections with other families, thus creating networks.

Networking with the larger community can provide resources for programs and can also garner the support of the community for your program and for child care in general. In one city what started as a small community outreach grew into a substantial fund-raiser and public awareness campaign. Freda, the director of a child development program, was approached by a family in her program who owned a local small business. The family admired the children's art that was displayed in the classroom and asked Freda if they could put a small display in their store. Soon, other local businesses were inquiring about displaying children's art. Freda worked with some families in the program to create several art displays containing explanations of the key role played by art in children's development and the importance of child care in support of the local economy. Several businesses participated, and many children agreed to loan their artwork to the project. The families went on to make note cards from children's art that were available for sale at various area businesses. The money raised was used to create a scholarship fund for the program.

Community and family networks can offer support and resources for curriculum development in children's programs. And developing curriculum collaboratively with families can build and expand networks of support.

FAMILIES PARTNERING ON CURRICULUM: GETTING STARTED

Let's look at a particular curriculum and think about all the different levels of participation families might have. A new baby has been born into one of the families in the program. It is a good time to do a curriculum on babies. In a beginning step toward family-centered curriculum planning, teachers could meet, invent a curriculum web, make a plan of activities, inform families that they were planning a baby curriculum, and then ask parents to bring in specific things to support their curriculum, such as baby pictures from their families and baby props like toys, carriers, and clothes. In this situation teachers are including family events as part of their curriculum and creating resource networks by inviting families to contribute materials for the unit. They are also engaging in "one-way" communication by letting families know about their curriculum plans. To bring families further into the program curriculum, teachers could invite them to come and tell stories about babies, to teach the children lullabies, or to demonstrate how to change a baby's diaper or give a baby a bath. Parents could be asked to write stories to go with the baby pictures they bring in to post on the bulletin board. These are all wonderful ideas that recognize family knowledge and expertise, yet there is no formal way for two-way communication in which parents could offer their own ways to support curriculum development, suggest their ideas about appropriate baby curriculum, or bring up their own child's questions and interests in babies.

In order to create a more family-centered program, teachers could invite parents to a special planning meeting about baby curriculum or could create a "dialogue" using a poster by the front door that invites family idea sharing. Teachers and parents alike could share their knowledge of children's interests and their ideas for developing curriculum and setting up the environment. Teachers could structure some questions for everyone to think about, such as "What have we observed children doing on the theme of babies? What are some of our children's questions about babies? What experiences have these children had with

babies? What are some developmentally appropriate activities and experiences we could provide? What resources does each of us have to bring to this curriculum? What roles would each of us like to play in implementing this curriculum unit?" Once the plans are made and posted for everyone to see, ongoing oral and written communication about what is planned and what is happening in the classroom keeps teachers and families informed about the progression of the unit. In this last example, all of the family-centered principles helped inform the curriculum planning, implementation, and documentation process.

REFERENCES

de Paola, Tomie. 1975. *Strega Nona: An old tale.* New York: Aladdin.

Loh, Morag. 1988. *Tucking Mommy in.* Illustrated by Donna Rawlins. New York: Orchard Books.

Families as Teaching Partners at Home and at School

This chapter explores ways for teachers and families to work together as a teaching team and to become part of a learning community. Teaching partnerships embody all of the family-centered principles. Many strategies that are essential to the process of creating teaching partnerships have already been introduced in previous chapters: inviting two-way communication; asking families for information about their culture, goals, expertise, interests, and experiences; making time and opportunity for two-way communication; meeting families at home; acknowledging families as children's first teachers; creating family-centered curriculum; sharing decision making about children's learning and curriculum; creating environments and interactions that help families feel welcome in the classroom; and creating networks of support for families and teachers. This chapter will look at implementing these strategies, incorporating others, and reminding teachers that every interaction you have with families has the potential of inviting them into the teaching partnership.

Teaching partnerships involve spending time together working and teaching, observing, talking, and meeting. These partnerships can take many different forms and might include families with teachers and families with other families. Families might participate in a parent co-op, showing up on a regular basis to work as teachers in the program. Some family members love coming in occasionally and doing a special activity with children, like cooking, creating art, working in the garden, reading, teaching language, taking dictation, going on a field trip, or sharing a cultural practice. Other families informally drop in and participate in the classroom. Families also participate in the teaching partnership by doing educational activities at home with their children. And of course, as discussed in the previous chapter, families can contribute to curriculum planning through sharing curriculum ideas, participating in curriculum planning meetings, donating learning materials, sharing family and cultural information with the program, and other ways.

This chapter looks at the benefits and challenges of having families in the classroom, welcoming families into the classroom, and dealing with children's testing behavior when both teachers and families are present. The chapter deals with setting guidelines for families in the classroom, including using redirection, facilitating interactions between parents and children, and setting limits with parents. The chapter also focuses on parent co-op participation, including orienting co-opers, setting up clear roles, offering time to plan and reflect, providing guidelines, and supporting parents who want to plan activities. Finally, the chapter looks at informal classroom participation, other family contributions to the classroom, and supporting parents as teachers at home.

Families in the Classroom

Once a program is successful in creating a welcoming environment, families might actually show up in the classroom. Now what? There are challenges as well as benefits to having families in the classroom. Benefits include families learning from teachers and teachers learning from families, the inclusion of different cultures and perspectives, the modeling of teamwork for children, children seeing their parents as teachers, and more adults and resources in the classroom. Challenges might include parents having different styles of interacting with children, having a lack of experience with child development protocol, holding adult conversations in the classroom, bringing several other children with them, sitting on children's tables and shelves, putting their belongings where children can find them, wanting the teacher's full attention, favoring their own child, using punitive words or actions with children, playing on the equipment, or taking over children's play.

Welcoming parents into the environment is one thing. Welcoming families takes even more planning. Often families bring siblings or elders into the program. Teachers have made creative adaptations for these family members, including building a temporary sheltered area for a baby to play, keeping a basket of baby toys handy, providing a bench outside so grandpa can talk to the child gardeners, involving the older sibling in delivering the snack trays, and offering an older sibling a basket of bean bags and a box of chalk to create a game for the preschoolers on the playground. Teachers don't have to set up a whole cur-

riculum for each family member. Simple gestures of welcome like these will communicate the program's caring and desire to be inclusive.

Children can also face challenges when their parents and teachers are together in the classroom. Children who have become accustomed to having separate relationships with their teacher and their parent might be confused at first when both are together. Because children see both their parents and their teachers as authority figures, they often wonder, "Who is really in charge here?" To find the answer to that question, children may test limits, cling to their parent, and/or express strong feelings. One of the ways to address some of these challenges is to share information and have discussions with families ahead of time. These discussions can help families understand what is going on for the child and can give the teacher and parent an opportunity to decide on ways they can respond. Even on the spot, a teacher can quickly check in with a parent: "Would you like to respond to that behavior, or shall I?" If the child and parent are already in a struggle, a trusted teacher could ask, "Is there anything I can do to help?" Working through these possible challenges is well worth the effort and can serve to strengthen the partnerships between families and teachers.

What Do We Know about Inviting Families into the Classroom?

Think about and discuss these questions with coworkers or fellow students. What are the ways family members come to understand that their ideas and initiative are welcome in the classroom? How do teacher interactions convey this sense of welcome to families? How does the environment support family involvement? How can we structure opportunities for family members to become partners in teaching?

Setting Guidelines for Families

An important factor in creating successful partnerships with families in the classroom is making program expectations for parents clear. Guidelines for parents in the classroom can be discussed starting with classroom visits and orientation. In the parent handbook and in parent meetings it is important to let parents know what the program expects from them in the classroom. In addition, there can be a notice posted in the classroom reminding families about the classroom guidelines for adults.

DEVELOPING GUIDELINES FOR ADULTS IN THE CLASSROOM

In a small group think about all the issues or challenges you have faced with parents in the classroom. Make a list of these challenges. Now make a list of guidelines for parents that deals with these challenges. Look over your list. How would you feel if you came into a new situation and someone handed you this list? Are your guidelines written in a respectful way? Now write a sentence or two of explanation for every guideline. Compare your lists with other small groups.

Keep in mind that any time the program sets up guidelines and expectations for families, it can be a challenge to keep communication two-way. There are a couple of things to consider in promoting two-way communication in this situation: the style in which the guidelines are presented and the invitation to dialogue about them. The style used in communicating the guideline can either say, "We know best, and you have to do it our way," or it can say, "Here is what we have discovered works; here is an explanation of why we have these guidelines; and we would like to hear your feedback about them." Even using the word "guideline" rather than "rule" communicates that these are suggestions based on your experience, but not the only "right" way to do things.

Parent meetings offer a wonderful opportunity to have two-way discussions (or multi-way discussions between many families and the staff) about guidelines. As well as presenting the guidelines and the rationale for them, teachers can ask parents questions like "What helps you feel comfortable in the classroom?" "What kinds of things do you like to do in the classroom?" "Do you have questions about what happens in the classroom?"

Here is a sample set of guidelines one program came up with. This is only one example of guidelines. This is not a complete list. Every program's staff need to develop a complete list for themselves based on their philosophy and the families who are in the program.

GUIDELINES FOR FAMILY MEMBERS IN THE CLASSROOM

Welcome to our classroom. Teachers, children, and other families appreciate the time you spend with us in the classroom. These are guidelines for parents, family members, and other adults who are visiting or volunteering in the classroom. We appreciate that each family has their own style with children, and we want you to feel comfortable here. Please talk to us if you are unclear or uncomfortable with any of these guidelines.

1. Place your backpacks and purses in the parent cubbies. *If you are going to be in the classroom for a while, please put your backpacks and purses out of the way of children. If your bags are accessible in the classroom, children will naturally want to explore them.*

2. Try to stay low and off children's shelves. *You can sit on the chairs, benches, couches, or floor. If you need to stand, please stand to the edge of an area or near a wall. This keeps children's areas clear for them to play.*

3. When speaking to children, get low and on their level, so that you can make eye contact

with them. *Children get distracted with so much going on in the classroom and may not know you are talking to them if you don't make direct contact.*

4. Use positive language with children. *"Please keep your feet on the floor," instead of "Don't climb on the tables." Children respond better to statements about what you want them to do rather than statements about what you don't want them to do.*

5. Support children in doing their own artwork. *Many adults love to use children's art materials, and children often ask adults to make or draw something for them. However, children often get discouraged from doing their own art if an adult is making things in the art area.*

6. Encourage children to use their own feet. *Many children see parents in the classroom and want to be carried, and in many families and cultures, carrying children is a common practice and a way to demonstrate affection. In this setting we would like to encourage children to walk, when possible. This is one way that they build confidence in their own bodies at school. If you would like to be close with children, you can sit down and read a story with them.*

Giving families information ahead of time helps to prevent having to set a limit with a parent who is already in the classroom. However, there will still be instances when a teacher needs to step in. Deciding when to set a limit or redirect a parent takes some consideration. There may be things that family members do that aren't standard practice in your program but are still things you can allow. Parents might play a safe chase game, make little animals out of playdough or draw pictures for children, put puzzles together for children, and tell children "no" and "don't" rather than use positive direction. Depending on your program's philosophy, your relationship with the family, and the amount of time a family member spends in the classroom, you will make

decisions about which issues you want to address and which you choose to ignore.

Here's a story that shows how teachers can use a family-centered approach involving two-way communication to think differently about "problem" parents in the classroom. Ultima, an experienced toddler teacher, tells the story of the semester she spent together with Paul and his daughter, Chelsea, in the classroom:

Paul had separated from Chelsea's mom. There was so much anger and anxiety between the parents that it was hard on Chelsea to be in the same room with her parents together. Her mom, Cindy, didn't trust Paul, and school seemed like a safe place for Paul and Chelsea to be together where Cindy felt like somebody could be with Paul to support him and keep an eye on him. At the time, Paul was homeless and living in his van. He came in and began to hang out in the classroom for up to two hours a day. Some of the teachers in the classroom were annoyed with the amount of time he was in the classroom and with the fact that they felt he was watching them. Paul would come into the classroom and play with his daughter, picking her up and tossing her in the air. His energy in the room could be overwhelming both for teachers and for other children. He sometimes moved our setup around so he could play with his daughter. He was shy and wouldn't interact much with caregivers.

I started spending time with Paul, sitting on the small couch in our classroom. I wanted to let him know how much I respected and valued his willingness to come into this strange environment and spend time with his daughter. I asked if there was anything I could do to help him be more comfortable. He told me he wasn't really comfortable anywhere, but he was so appreciative to be here with Chelsea. I shared observations of Chelsea with him from that couch. I wanted him to understand that observing her could be as wonderful as playing with her.

After I felt that we had started to develop a relationship, I began to share with him some informa-

tion about the culture of the classroom. I told him how important it was for me to create a place for him to be with his daughter and that I also wanted to safeguard the needs of the other children and families in the program. I explained to him that for a one-year-old child, being in child care can be overwhelming and that part of my job was to safeguard children from too much stimulation. One day we observed a lunch delivery person arrive, and we noticed together how it changed what was happening for children. I told him that children loved watching him play with Chelsea but that they also stopped what they were doing to watch.

I think observing sparked the scientist in him. From those observations on the couch he became more relaxed and calmer and began to spend more floor time with Chelsea. As he changed the quality of his time with her, it took the frenzy out of the classroom. Learning to be with his daughter helped him learn how to be with the other kids. He became a part of the team. He would work with teachers to set up the environment. He didn't do a lot of direct teaching with the other kids, but he was always the one to bring me a chewy toy for a child who was starting to bite. He learned to understand what children were expressing in their behaviors and how to support caregivers. I remember once when two children were pulling on one hoop, he got low and on their level (he was over six feet tall) and brought them another hoop. By the end of the semester, he started talking to me about going to school to become a teacher.

Using Redirection with Parents

When a teacher decides to redirect a parent or inform her about a guideline, it is important to give the parent information and appreciate her effort or interest before making a suggestion to her.

Here are some examples of ways to talk to parents in common limit-setting situations:

◆ A parent leaves a backpack on the floor.
"Looks like the kids are interested in your backpack. We have a special cubby for parent backpacks to keep them safe from children. Can I show you where it is?"

◆ A parent wants to talk to the teacher about the family's upcoming move.
"I would really like to talk to you more about this, but my attention is split because I need to be supervising children. Could we set up a time later, when we can talk without being interrupted? I have time for a fifteen-minute phone call this evening."

◆ A parent is sitting on the puzzle shelf.
"It's hard to find a place to sit around here, I know. Could I get you to move to this bench or the couch over there so children can get to the things on this shelf? Thanks."

◆ A parent has spent all morning playing with just her child.
"It looks like Sal would like to join you and your daughter in this area. He loves to use the matching blocks."

◆ Two parents are discussing their boyfriends' erratic behaviors.
"This seems like an important conversation you two are having. I'd like you to be able to have some privacy, and I'm concerned that children might be overhearing you. My office is free for the next twenty minutes if you would like to use it, or you could get a little more privacy in the lobby."

◆ A parent has called a child "mean" after she takes a toy from another child.
"It can be hard to see children take toys from each other. In my experience children aren't doing it to be mean but to try to play with each other. This would be a good topic for our parent meeting. I think a lot of parents and teachers are concerned about how to respond to this behavior."

◆ A parent has moved among several areas of the classroom, directing children how to play in each.

"Do you have time to do a little observation with me? These kids have been playing in the block area for forty minutes. It's so interesting the way each one is contributing their ideas to the play. Juana started building a cave; Tina helped to find the arch blocks; Angel brought those pieces over to be the dinosaurs. For kids, getting to direct their play with their own ideas is as important as the play itself."

PRACTICE REDIRECTING PARENTS IN THE CLASSROOM

Choose which situations you would intervene in. Role-play empathetic redirection with the parent in those situations:

- A parent is making little valentines for children.
- A parent stops children from making their own paper airplanes so she can make them correctly for the children.
- A parent is pretending to be the patient in children's hospital play.
- A parent is jumping on the children's trampoline.
- A parent is talking on his cell phone for ten minutes in the classroom.
- A parent is mixing all the colors of the paint in the art area to make new colors for the children.
- A parent is telling children at the snack table that they have to eat everything on their plate.

Discuss your ideas with coworkers or fellow students. Explain how you decided when to intervene and when not to. Get feedback from your partners about the effectiveness of your empathy and redirection.

Facilitating Interactions between Parents and Children

An important thing for teachers to remember is to always show respect for parents, especially in front of children. This can be challenging if parents are using language or behavior with children that is hurtful or inappropriate. If the teacher determines that the language or behavior is not directly dangerous to children but would still like to facilitate a more successful interaction, she can do something to help mediate the situation. Using "reframing," stating the parent's idea in a positive way, the teacher can show support for the parent, clarify for the child what the message is, and model for the parent a more positive way to communicate the idea. For example, Linda, a parent, was working with the children at the playdough table when Karen began to throw little bits of playdough up in the air, singing, "It's snowing." Linda spoke sharply to Karen, "Stop it! You're making a huge mess." Teacher Scott heard the interaction and came over. "Karen, it looks like you are making snow, and I hear that Linda is concerned about the playdough getting all over the floor. Can you pick up the snow from the floor and make a pile of snow on the table, or shall I bring the dustpan and brush over so you and Linda can sweep it up?" After this kind of interaction with a parent in the classroom, it is important to check back to see how the parent felt about it and to discuss what might happen in the next limit-setting situation. (It could be helpful to use the steps for mutual problem solving with families in chapter 6.)

Some issues with parents in the classroom cannot be dealt with on the spot because the conversation needs privacy and will take more than a few sentences to resolve. Issues such as discipline philosophy and practice, language to use with children, and facilitating rather than directing children's play all require in-depth discussion. These conversations can happen outside of the classroom individually with parents or can be covered in parent meetings.

Setting Limits with Parents

In rare situations the teacher may need to intervene and set a direct limit with a family member in the classroom. If children are in danger, the teacher will need to step in immediately. There still may be room for active listening as the teacher is setting a limit with the parent. Here are some ways of setting limits and protecting children while still respecting the parent involved:

"You seem really upset. I'm going to ask you to take a break."

"This is a hard situation to deal with. Why don't you step out of the classroom for a few minutes?"

"I know you are feeling angry [or: "wanting to set a limit with this child"], but I can't let you hit kids here."

If possible in these situations, ask the parent to step aside with you so you can set the limit with him in private. Having a relationship with the parent prior to this kind of a situation allows you to build on the trust that is already established and also gives you some information about how to best respond to the parent in this situation.

Trina, a family child care provider with a toddler program, tells her story of setting a limit with a parent:

I remember one time Margie, a parent, saying to her daughter, Brenda, "Do you want me to hit you? You need to cooperate, or I'm going to hit you." I moved in really quick. It was so tense. My instinct was to immediately align with the parent. Right then, I didn't try to help the child make sense of it. I wanted to be sure the parent felt my presence, and I didn't want to raise her stress level any higher. I moved my body really close. . . . I mean, really close. I was definitely in her space, and that way I knew the parent was really alert. I talked to Margie through the child, "Oh, Mommy's getting really frustrated right now . . . and I know Mommy's not going to hit right now, because that won't work for the classroom." I could feel Margie start to relax. That really turned around their morning. Margie and Brenda had been in my program for over six

months at that point. From the beginning I knew that we had really different styles. I watched her style with her daughter, and I had already chalked up a lot of conversation with her. In my talks with her I would point out things about her style that worked well for her daughter. She thought I was kind of a softie, but that was okay. She knew that I respected her even though our styles were different. You know, it wasn't really difficult to go up to her in that tense moment with her child because I wasn't really judging her. I was saying to myself, "I understand how that feels."

PARENT CO-OP PARTICIPATION

Some children's programs are parent co-operatives, which are staffed primarily by parents who work along with head teachers. Many schools incorporate a parent co-op component into their regular program. There may be a special day each week when several parents come in to work in the classroom, or a few parents may come in on a regular schedule each day. Some co-op programs may even be organized by parents who hire a teacher to work with them.

The benefits of parent co-ops are many. Families get a chance to get to know each other well through working together, and, consequently, support networks are built. Child care is affordable because of lower staff costs. Parent education is a regular part of the program. There are increased opportunities for parents and teachers to share their expertise through two-way communication. Parents take leadership in the decision making and operation of the school. Teachers get to know the family group well and families get to learn new ways of helping children learn. Partnerships between teachers and families emerge naturally in most parent co-op schools.

Here are some key elements in structuring and implementing a successful parent co-op:

◆ Providing orientation for family members who are going to participate in the co-op

- Setting up clear roles for parents and for teachers
- Offering time to plan and time to reflect
- Providing guidelines
- Sharing information with parents who want to plan activities

Providing Orientation for Family Members

Before parents show up for their first day in the classroom, it is important for parents and teachers to meet together to discuss the schedule of the day, expectations for parents in the classroom, classroom procedures, parents' questions, parents' goals for working in the classroom, and possible responses from children whose parents are working in the classroom. In addition, taking parents on a tour of the classroom, storeroom, and other parts of the facility will give them an idea of where things are. It can also be helpful to pair a parent who is new to working in the classroom with a parent who is experienced in working in the classroom.

Setting Up Clear Roles for Parents and Teachers

It is important that parents know what is expected of them when working in the classroom, especially at the beginning. Some parent co-op programs write up job descriptions on cards that parents can keep with them or wear around their necks. These cards provide a schedule for the parent about what they should be doing at different times during their shift and describe setup and clean-up duties as well as directions for the activity or area the parent has been assigned. It is also important that parents know what the teacher will be doing, where she will be during their shift, and how they can ask questions.

Offering Time to Plan and Time to Reflect

Making time to talk before starting in the class-

room and time to talk together after working with children allows people to work well as a team and to maintain good communication. Parents generally have many questions after every shift they work with children. They may want answers to questions as varied as "What if Benji won't put on a smock?" "What should I do if Pete takes a toy from Leny?" and "Where do the paint brushes go?" Meeting together and discussing observations and interactions with children is one of the most important learning opportunities for parents and teachers and an essential partnership-building activity. As parents get familiar with the routines, they can use these sessions to deepen their understanding of children and teaching and to plan their own curriculum. However, finding time for parents and teachers to meet is particularly challenging because someone has to supervise the children. Different programs have come up with creative solutions to this dilemma. Some have an A and a B co-op team each day. The A team works the morning shift, and the B team comes in to have lunch with the children while the morning crew meets. Every parent works one A shift and one B shift a week. In other programs a special lunch staff is hired to supervise children during lunch while parents and teachers meet. Some programs use naptime to meet, leaving one teacher with the nappers while the rest of the teachers and parents meet in an adjoining room. Many programs hold regular night meetings, as well. While they take creative planning, these discussion groups are invaluable.

Providing Guidelines

It is important to provide guidelines for parents who work with children in the parent co-op. (See the list, "Guidelines for Family Members in the Classroom," on pages 125–26, could be a starting point.) These guidelines can be developed by teachers or by parents and teachers together. Some programs may have a parent co-op handbook that includes guidelines for working with children.

Supporting Parents Who Want to Plan Activities

Often parents have interesting ideas for activities to do with children but don't have a lot of experience working with groups of children. Helping parents develop the plan for their curriculum can contribute to a more successful experience for the children and the parent. Parents might need help to consider things like necessary supplies, the best area of the classroom for the activity, the time needed for setup and cleanup, the number of children who can participate at once, safety, and the kind of assistance needed.

If you're interested in more information on building a successful parent co-op, see the Web site of Parent Cooperative Preschools International (www.preschools.coop), which publishes useful materials and hosts an annual conference.

INFORMAL CLASSROOM PARTICIPATION

Informal classroom participation often happens on a daily basis at drop-off and pick-up times. For example, Janessa's aunt, Bobbi, almost always finds herself surrounded with children as she sits and reads to Janessa every morning. Joaby, Aidan's dad, allows enough time each morning for all the children to see and touch baby Mason and watch him get his diaper changed before he says good-bye to Aidan. Bill and Ariba chat together while they observe their respective children busy at work building an RV with hollow blocks. At pick-up time Jennie often shows up with her camera to take pictures of all the children; she brings in the prints to share the next morning. Some families are more comfortable contributing their talents through fixing the bookshelf, taking home nap sheets to wash, making puzzles out of children's pictures, and repairing torn books. Both formal and informal family participation in the program serves to enrich

the program and strengthen the partnership.

OTHER FAMILY CONTRIBUTIONS TO THE CLASSROOM

Many programs require that parents do some form of "parent hours" each month for the program. These family hours cover a variety of volunteer tasks. The main purpose of these hours is to provide help and support to the program and teachers; however, another, potentially more important purpose is about investment and partnership. Families can pay for their child's care, but truly partnering with the program calls for another kind of contribution. Traditionally, parent-hour jobs include classroom and equipment maintenance, such as painting, cleaning, repairing, building, and washing; volunteering for classroom activities like parties or field trips; shopping for supplies; helping in the classroom; sitting on advisory committees; organizing phone trees; and putting on fund-raisers. Some of these activities encourage the initiative and creativity of family members, and yet program directors often report that they have a hard time persuading parents to do their hours.

Using a more family-centered approach, programs can find ways to invite the knowledge and expertise of families and to share decision making. Providing a wider range of opportunities for families to communicate their skills and talents and to participate in developing some of the parent-hour tasks might generate more enthusiasm for the program. To incorporate the idea of family-centered care into the "parent hours" concept, programs can survey parents individually about their interests and the ways they would like to do their parent hours, survey the group through a big chart on the bulletin board, or organize a small parent-teacher committee to poll parents and to work on creative parent-hour tasks. Some other ideas for parent hours include planning and organizing a parent event such as a dinner or a meeting; developing curriculum materials; bringing a special activity into the classroom; organizing a parent lending library; creating a family resource binder; setting up a family support system for families in crisis; planning cultural events; or interviewing a teacher, parent, or child for the purpose of writing a newsletter article.

As programs work to breathe life into their parent-hour tasks, it is important to keep in mind the broader purpose of parent hours. As well as providing physical help and support for the program, parent hours are a way of acknowledging the knowledge and expertise of family members. They can help build support networks among families in the program. Under the right circumstances, they can become another way of nurturing two-way communication and sharing power. When families create some of their own choices about how to contribute to the program, the results are greater diversity in the program culture and a deeper, more family-centered program.

SUPPORTING PARENTS AS TEACHERS AT HOME

Partnering with parents as teaching partners means that programs also need to acknowledge the teaching that parents are already naturally doing with children, even when parents themselves haven't identified it as teaching. In order to support parents as children's first and primary teachers, teachers can acknowledge the education parents are providing for their children at home, facilitate parents sharing their ideas with other families, and offer resources for new activities and experiences for parents to do with their children at home. In a parent meeting teachers can ask parents to describe favorite things they like to do with their children. In small groups parents might then identify all the things children are learning in those activities. This can also be an activity done as a graffiti bulletin board, a big piece of butcher paper with a topic or question written at the top, such as "Learning Activities Families Do at Home with Children." More informally, as teachers talk with parents about experiences children have at home, teachers can take time to acknowledge what a child might be learning by walking through the park, helping Dad squeeze oranges for juice, or sorting silverware into the drawer. Parents could be encouraged to contribute ideas to the newsletter about favorite learning activities with children. Any time teachers make a presentation about children's play and learning, they can ask for ideas from family members.

In addition to acknowledging the important ways parents are already supporting their children's learning, programs often provide resources for educational activities for parents to do at home. Some programs provide handouts for parents on learning activities they can do at home with children, and some programs have homework boxes or bags that families can check out. Homework boxes for families encourage families and children to work together on learning activities. For example, a homework box might contain a set of puzzles, a card describing what children learn through working puzzles, a list of vocabulary words associated with the puzzles, and ideas for ways to use the puzzles. Other ideas for a homework box include a bug box and magnifying glass, playdough or clay, blocks, "feely" shape boxes, a set of snap-together blocks, sets of laminated pictures, and matching games. Homework boxes can also contain idea cards with activities like these:

- Find three things in your house that are yellow, three things that are red, three things that are blue, three things that are orange, three things that are green, and three things that are purple.
- Find three things in the kitchen that start with the letter P.
- Find three different kinds of seeds. (Hint: You can look outside or in the kitchen.)
- Find four different kinds of leaves.

To invite two-way communication and to build networks between families, the box can include a note pad or journal and pen for the family to write an observation of the child using the puzzle, some of the child's words about the activity, or something that interested the family about the activity. These notes or journal can be shared with the next child and family who use the box. Making these take-home boxes interactive can encourage parents' initiative and support the teaching partnership. As well as making observations and notes on their child's experience with the activity, parents can participate on the team that designs and assembles these boxes, and they can help set up the checkout system for the boxes.

Some programs also have a lending library for children. One system gives each child an envelope with his name on it and a list recording the book he has checked out (and all the ones previously checked out). When the envelope is at home, the family is reminded they have a book checked out. When it is at school, it stays in the checkout basket and the child is reminded he can check out a book. In one classroom parents and children also take home "book report" forms that have space

for words and pictures. Parents and children are instructed to read the books together and to write some words and draw pictures about the books. When a parent and child bring their book and report to school, the teacher takes a picture of them together with the book and glues it to their book report. All the book reports are posted on the bulletin board.

REFLECTING ON PARENTS AS TEACHERS

What are some of the activities you know that parents do with their children? What is the learning that happens in these activities? What are all the ways you have in your program to acknowledge parents as children's first teachers? How else could you recognize the expertise and knowledge families have about their children? Discuss with coworkers or fellow students.

12

Welcoming Families into the Partnership

Your relationship with a new family begins before their child officially starts attending your program. Every interaction with the family and child before the first day of school sets the tone for your future relationship and lets the family know how they will be treated in your program. These critical early interactions are your first opportunity to introduce families to the concept of family-centered care. In your very first conversation with a family, you can let them know you are interested in two-way communication by listening empathetically to their ideas and their questions. Giving families comprehensive information about your program and listening to their needs and wishes set the stage for sharing power and decision making. Using inclusive language and images in your program literature and making information available in different languages will welcome a diverse group of families. Providing referrals for families to other child care and family resources demonstrates your program's commitment to building networks of support.

The first part of this chapter will look at some possible encounters between program and family before the child starts and consider the message conveyed in each. The second part of the chapter will cover orienting a family to a new pro-

gram, helping families and children begin in the program, and managing a new separation.

THE FIRST CONTACT

The relationship with a new family may begin with a phone call, an ad placed in the paper, a program brochure, or a visit. Many families begin their search for child care by making phone calls. Some programs have full-time staff to answer the phone; however, many do not. If your program doesn't have someone whose job it is to answer phones and talk to the public, it may be better to use an answering machine than to expect teachers to pick up the phone and respond to questions at the same time they are supervising children. One child care program starts its message like this: "Hello, you have reached the Little Horse Children's Center. We can't come to the phone right now, but we are glad you called and look forward to talking with you in the future. If you leave your name, number, and a short message, we will call you back today or tomorrow at the latest." That same program has a receptionist who engages in two-way communication with families and helps them find networks of support. She answers questions, listens empathetically to parents' concerns, sets up meetings and visits, and provides encouragement and referrals to other programs or services, even if her program does not have space available for their child.

Often the first person families talk to is the person who answers the phone. It is useful for this person to have information about the program as well as good listening and communication skills. In some cases this person is the first a parent has talked to outside of the family about her child. It is useful to establish a protocol and provide some training in two-way communication to the people who might answer the phone so that they can be friendly, encouraging, and respectful of parent knowledge and expertise. In addition, make sure everyone responsible for answering the phone has access to written information about the program as well as about available community resources for families.

OFFERING FAMILIES INFORMATION

Some families have lots of resources in learning about their child and about parenting. They have access to books, parent-oriented Web sites, friends and families who already have young children, parent support groups, and resource and referral networks. These parents are likely to have a concept of what quality child care is and to have extensive lists of questions they want to ask about your program. They know what they are looking for and how to look for it. On the other end of the continuum is the parent who doesn't have much information about the variety of child care programs and the factors that create a quality child care program. While each family can be respected for the knowledge they bring, your program will need to provide different kinds of support, introduction, and orientation to families depending on where they are on this continuum. Many programs have useful brochures, booklets, or handouts that help parents learn about different kinds of child care, assess their own needs for child care, identify quality indicators, and formulate questions to ask to determine if a program is the right one for them. It is useful to communi-

cate some of this information orally as well as through written materials, so families know that you are open to their questions. In this way you also meet the needs of families who are more comfortable with spoken than written communication. This can be one of the first steps a program takes toward supporting a mutual partnership in which two-way communication and shared decision making are welcomed and encouraged.

Talking to Families

Given that looking for child care can bring up a variety of feelings for families who may already be stressed or overwhelmed, it is helpful to have some ideas of how to talk to these families. Here are some possible responses to parents who may be experiencing feelings ranging from excitement to ambivalence to anxiety during these initial conversations.

To the parent who seems frantic or worried:

- "It can be challenging to find just the right care for your child, yet when you do, it can be so gratifying."
- "Tell me more about the kind of child care you are looking for."
- "I'm glad you are taking the time to research the right child care for your family. It will benefit both you and your child in the long run."
- "There are some resources in our community to help families find the right child care. Would you like the number or the Web address of the child care resource and referral network in our area?" (Other good resources to have on hand are the local chapter of the Association of the Education of Young Children or the local child care planning council or the family child care home association.)

To the parent who seems distracted or hurried:

◆ "Do you have questions or concerns you would like to share?"

◆ "Is this a good time to talk, or shall we set up another time?"

To the parent who seems ambivalent:

◆ "It can be a big step for a family to put their child in care for the first time."

◆ "Many families feel both excited about looking for child care and a little sad and worried about what it might mean for their family."

To the parent who doesn't seem to have any questions:

◆ "Tell me about your child. What kind of a program do you think would be good for her?"

◆ "Would you like to see a brochure that outlines what to look for in a quality child care program?"

◆ "Maybe you would like to observe the program and see if you have any questions."

To the parent who has questions and concerns beyond what you have the time or resources to answer:

◆ "Those are very important questions. Right now is not a good time for me to give you the kind of thoughtful answers your questions deserve. Can we make an appointment later today or this week to talk further?"

◆ "Those are important questions. I would like you to talk to our director so that she can give you the answers you need. When would be a good time for her to call you?"

◆ "I'm glad you are asking those important questions in looking for child care for your child. We don't have the resources here to help you with those questions. I can refer you to other agencies in the community or some Internet resources that might be helpful to you."

Some programs have lists of child care information resources, family support agencies, or child care funding programs in the community that they can offer families.

PRACTICE TALKING TO NEW FAMILIES

Set up a role play in which people responsible for answering the phone can practice supportive, informative responses. Have one person be the parent making the phone call, and decide which feelings she is having. Assign a person to answer the call. Assign a third person to observe, offer suggestions to the people doing the role play, take notes, and give feedback about helpful responses. After the role play it can be useful for the person taking the call to talk about how it feels to take a call from a parent who is anxious or demanding.

INTRODUCTION TO THE PROGRAM

Most programs have either a formal or an informal program introduction, orientation, and enrollment procedure. It can be helpful to the program staff as well as to prospective families if that procedure is written and accessible. Sharing information in this way empowers families to be partners in decision making and information sharing during the process of their orientation. The statement does not have to be complex to provide a reassuring road map for families. Here is a sample:

WELCOME TO BUILDING BLOCKS CHILD DEVELOPMENT PROGRAM

We understand that choosing a child care program for your child is a very important decision for your family.

Here is a brief outline of our introduction, orientation, and enrollment procedures:

- *Initial contact: This is a phone or in-person conversation to get basic information about the program (hours, cost, availability of care, ages of children, accreditation and licensing status, children's schedule of the day).*

- *Second interview: This is a conversation with the director or head teacher to get more information about the program including program philosophy, curriculum, discipline policy, family partnership policy, and expectations for parents.*

- *Program visit: Parents may want to visit the program alone for the first time, or they may visit with their child. This gives families a chance to experience the program in person to see if it is a good fit.*

- *Program visit with child: This is a chance to see how your child responds to the classroom, children, and teachers. Note that it is not unusual for a child to be reticent on the first few visits, until he or she gets comfortable in the setting. This is not necessarily an indication that the program is not a good fit for the child.*

- *Enrollment: When your family and the program have agreed that this is the right program for you, we will give you the enrollment packet to fill out.*

- *Classroom warming-in visits: Once your child is enrolled in the program, we encourage you to develop a plan with your child's teacher for your child to visit the classroom, first with you and then for increasingly longer periods by himself or herself to help the child adjust to the program and his or her new relationships.*

Program Visit: Before Enrollment

Visits to your center allow families to see and experience your program in action. Many programs ask parents to visit first, without children, so that parents can decide whether they think the program might be a good fit for their child. It can also cut down on lots of visiting for children that may be disruptive for the program and possibly confusing for the prospective child. For some families, visiting more than once at different times of the day can be helpful so that they can see the different types of activities and routines that occur throughout the day. It is important to have someone available to answer questions and to help parents interpret what they are seeing during an observation. You will design your program's approach to visiting depending on the resources you have available to support parent visits. Ideally, a staff person would be available to talk with the parent during the entire visit. Alternately, the parent might have an orientation, including protocol or guidelines (see sample below) for visiting the classroom, and check in with the staff person during and after the observation.

Guidelines for observation can be as simple as these:

WELCOME TO FALLING LEAVES CHILD CARE CENTER

We are glad you came to visit. Here are some simple guidelines for your classroom observation:

- *You may want to leave your purse or bag with the receptionist. That way you won't have to keep it with you all the time in the classroom. It is important that it doesn't get left where children might explore it.*

- *We have small note pads and pens available if you would like to take notes during your visit.*

- *Please sit on the low children's chairs, benches, or couches, or stand out of the way of the children's traffic flow.*

- *Teachers will be glad to answer simple questions if you have them. Please wait until they are not talking with children to ask. If you have more complicated questions, please make a note of them so you can ask the director or teacher when you meet with her after your observation.*

If there is no staff available, it is important to have a more comprehensive written observation guide available and a telephone follow-up to respond to any questions. Some programs arrange to have a few parents visit at a time to start building a sense of community and support network and to maximize the use of the staff's time. One program uses one Saturday a month to meet with prospective families in the center environment for an introduction to the program.

It is useful to remember that the program visit is a crucial time for building the partnership and establishing two-way communication with the family. It provides a relaxed opportunity to have a dialogue about both what the program offers and what the family is looking for. It gives program staff the time to articulate the philosophy behind the practice. Many parents would otherwise not know how the playdough activity is so essential to helping children establish safety and comfort, develop social skills, practice fine motor and language skills, and begin to use symbols to represent thought. Likewise, watching the children dig ditches in the sand area for the water to run through will give the parents a chance to share with you how they feel about messy play.

Once parents have determined that they are seriously considering the program for their child, it is a good time to set up a visit with parent and child. In scheduling this visit, you can give the parent ideas of good times to come (avoiding times like the middle of snack, group, or nap time). It is also important to establish a greeter for the child and parent who is on either the administrative or the teaching staff. This person can check in and interact with the observers as well as to be aware of how the child is doing on his visit. This person can also introduce the child and parent to other children, families, and staff to help them feel welcome and connected. It is useful to give parents a written program description, which is helpful for all families but particularly important to hand out if there is not a staff person available to meet with the parent right away.

Even before a family enrolls in your program, you can start building a relationship. Being thoughtful about introducing the family to the program, about hosting classroom visits, and about sharing program information will help the partnership start off on the right foot. As teachers prepare to meet, greet, and orient families and their children, it is important to reflect on what parents might be feeling and experiencing as they search for the right program for their child. Thinking empathetically about what parents might be feeling helps teachers understand the family's viewpoints and communicate with families more effectively. Most parents feel some ambivalence about their child's first experience being cared for outside the home and are asking themselves questions like these:

- Is it all right for someone outside of the family to care for my child?
- Am I going to lose touch with my child's development while he is in child care?
- What will my child be learning?
- Will my child be safe? What if my child gets hurt in child care? How will they let me know?
- What if my child cries?
- Will my child still know who her family is? Will she still know that I love her?
- What if my child likes his teacher better than me?
- What will the teacher think about our family?
- What will the teacher think about me as a parent?
- Is it bad to feel a sense of relief that I am going back to work?
- Can I afford this?
- How will I get everyone out the door in the morning, drop him off at child care, and still get to work on time?

Parents deal with these questions in their own ways, based on their experience, their ability to be reflective, and their level of skill in understanding and managing their own feelings. Some parents have family and friends they can talk to about their anxiety and will show up to your program ready to build an easy, mutually respectful relationship with staff. Others may arrive to your program with feelings they don't fully understand or know how to express.

It is important to understand that parents may be feeling many, sometimes contradictory feelings including concerned, excited, uncertain, worried, hurried, frustrated, anxious, desperate, afraid, relieved, ambivalent, grateful.

SHARING THE MOST VALUABLE THING

Imagine for a minute your most valuable possession. Think about a stranger coming up to you and saying, "I'll take care of your valuable possession for you every day. I'll take good care of it, but I might change it a little because I'd like to have my own relationship with it. You can pick it up from me at the end of each day, but you'll need to bring it back to me again every morning." Discuss your feelings with a coworker or fellow student. Understanding what a leap of faith it is for parents to entrust us with their children is an important step in building a respectful partnership.

With that in mind, if you had all the resources you wanted, what kind of an orientation would you like every new child and family to have to your program? What kind of an orientation would you like to have to the new family and child? How close is your program's present practice to your ideal? What might be some first steps you could take to improve the orientation component of your program?

(Thanks to WestEd's Program for Infant/Toddler Caregivers for the "Valuable posession" exercise.)

ORIENTATION FOR FAMILIES

Once both the family and the program have made the decision for the child to begin in the program, the partnership begins to develop on a whole different level. It is time for the next steps in getting to know each other. In order to integrate family-centered principles into the process of beginning care, it is important to think about a two-way or a many-way orientation. Families need full orientation to the program, the teachers, the administrative and office staff, and the facility. This kind of orientation invites them to be participants in shared decision making. They will start to get to know the other children and families in the program as a way to begin participating in networks of support. Children will begin to be familiar with the teacher, the other children, and the facility. The program staff will have an opportunity to recognize and respect family knowledge during this time through observation, interaction, conversations, and questionnaires. The program staff can respect diversity among families by adapting their orientation practices to meet the needs of individual families.

Programs have differing procedures about who does the initial meetings with the family. If your program's goal is to build partnerships with families, it is very useful for a family to meet with both the program director or site supervisor and their child's teacher before the child begins in care. This allows both family and program staff to become oriented to each other and the relationship. While this may seem like a time-intensive process, the groundwork that is laid for a successful partnership with the family is invaluable and may very well save time and misunderstanding in the long run.

Here are some things to consider in setting up family orientations:

- Orienting families to both the people and the program
- Helping families get to know other families
- Allowing time for the family to be in the facility
- Supporting two-way communication
- Letting families know what to expect

- Finding accessible times for families to visit
- Creating a family-friendly meeting space
- Providing language support

Orienting Families to Both the People and the Program

It is essential for families to have an orientation to the staff and the program. Some orientation happens the first week, and some can happen a little later. Families need to meet all the strategic people. This includes all the teachers in the classroom as well as everyone who will be providing care and education for their children, the administrative staff, and other parents, whenever possible. Posting pictures and information about all staff will help familiarize family with staff who aren't there when they are touring. Families should be familiarized with all the aspects of the program, including the children's schedule and curriculum, procedures for drop-off and pick-up, and expectations for families in the program.

Helping Families Get to Know Other Families

Another way to implement the principles of family-centered care, particularly building networks and empowering parents, is to support family relationships with other families from the very beginning. As you tour a parent through the program, you can stop to introduce them to parents who are around. Some programs use volunteer parents, and other programs pay parents to provide a friend, guide, and support person to new families as they begin the program. Mentor parents can provide a peer perspective, create a safety net, and offer new parents a place to share the concerns and questions they are not yet comfortable sharing with program staff. Further, a mentor parent program provides a model of parent competence for all parents and provides leadership development and mentoring skills for the mentor parents. Sometimes program staff set up mentor-

ing, and sometimes it happens spontaneously. For example, when Jacqueline noticed that a family with twins was visiting the program, she went right over and introduced herself, pointed out her own twins, told the family what a great program it was, and offered to answer any questions about the program that the visiting family might have.

Allowing Time for the Family to Be in the Facility

It is integral to your partnership with parents that they feel comfortable in your facility. This comfort invites their input and their support and allows for them to communicate a sense of trust to their children. In getting to know the facility, families should know where to sign children in, where they can put their belongings if they are going to stay for a while, where the adult and child bathrooms are, where the family resources are, and where the systems for staff-family communication are. They should know all of the areas children will be, including inside and outside areas, as well as special resource rooms.

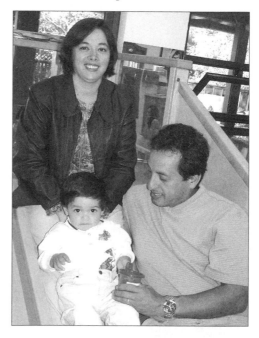

It can be interesting for parents to visit the facility both with children present and without children present. In addition to the visits that parents made before their enrollment decision, it continues to be important for them to have opportunities to visit your program. Some programs have periodic parent meetings in the evening in which parents can explore and play in the children's environment. This is wonderful "hands-on" teaching of how important play is to learning and lets parents really see how the environment is set up. Equally important is for parents to visit when children are present. This can happen when they bring their own children for warming-in visits, during daily drop-off and pick-up times, or whenever they can drop in spontaneously.

Supporting Two-Way Communication

Giving families complete information about your program, philosophy, and policies assures them of your competence, professionalism, and expertise. Giving information and encouraging questions will begin your two-way communication. It is equally important to establish that you expect and look forward to shared decision making, including active family contributions to the relationship, the program, and planning care for the child. This is a wonderful opportunity to ask families questions about their child and family and their goals, interests, skills, and ideas about involvement with the program. If you are meeting with more than one family member, ask each one if he or she has questions.

Letting Families Know What to Expect

Using written and verbal communication you can let families know what they can expect during the orientation, enrollment, and beginning care steps. It is helpful for them to know what the timeline and procedural steps are. In addition, you can let them know about some of the feelings and issues that come up when a child and family are transitioning to child care.

Finding Accessible Times for Families to Visit

Finding a convenient time for families to visit can be a challenging step in the orientation process. Finding a time that works for both the program and the family can take creative scheduling. It is important to remember that for some people, taking time off work is not a possibility. One director schedules occasional Saturdays to orient new families. Some programs hire a substitute teacher for part of the day so the teacher can spend time orienting a family. Early evenings might work for some working families. Lunch hour visits are another possibility. Doing part of the orientation over the phone can work for some parents. Being sensitive to families' needs as well as staff workload and overtime are important when scheduling orientation activities.

Creating a Family-Friendly Meeting Space

Some families may want or need to bring children or other family members with them to orientation meetings. This provides you an opportunity to honor the diverse structures and needs of families. You can ask families who is coming to a meeting and set up the meeting space accordingly with toys or drawing materials for children and enough seating for all the adults. Alternately, you can have these things available to use so you are prepared whenever extended family shows up.

Providing Language Support

Provide language support, whenever possible, if the family speaks a different language from that of the program staff. If you don't have people who can provide translation, it is possible that the family might be able to bring someone, such as a family or community member, to help with translation. When there is a language difference, your respect for diversity is conveyed both by your efforts to arrange for language support and by your interest in learning about a family's culture and language.

ORIENTATION FOR CHILDREN

What is the optimal way for a child to begin a new program? There are different theories. Some teachers believe it is useful to have parents leave as soon as possible, so that the child learns quickly that he has to count on the teachers in the program to help him. Some teachers are concerned that if the parents stay too long, the child will cry. Others don't know what to do if several parents are standing around in the classroom. However, if we are building family-centered care, we are not just enrolling the child; we are enrolling the family. The belief in family-centered care is that both the family and the child make the transition to child care and are essential partners in the process. This chapter offers a number of specific strategies to address the concerns parents bring and the feelings children have about separation. Specifically, it will help teachers think about ways to understand children's and families' ideas about separation, help children and families with separation and good-byes, promote attachment through the separation process, create warming-in activities, and plan for parents and teachers together in the classroom, home visits, and reverse home visits.

Separation: Whose Problem Is It?

Having families involved in the transition to child care can be worrisome for some teachers because they have experienced that parents sometimes have bigger issues with separation than children do. Bernice describes eighteen-month-old Aidan as he was beginning in care: "I remember Aidan bounding up to the door, so excited to be at school, ready to explore everything. But by the time his mom had checked his diaper four times and said good-bye five times, he was crying at the door." Bernice observed that Aidan didn't have the same issues with separation as his mom did but that spending time with his mom during the separation time made him anxious about saying good-bye. In order to avoid this problem, some programs give parents guidelines about saying good-bye quickly and leaving. While this might be helpful to the child in the short run, it does not adequately address the parent's anxiety in leaving. Nor does it help the parent develop the trust necessary for building an effective partnership with the program. Supporting parents through their separation anxiety is as important as supporting children.

To support parents effectively, it is essential to understand the issues they may be facing. As mentioned earlier, parents may feel ambivalent about leaving their child in care, worried about their child's safety, guilty for not taking care of their child themselves, resentful that they have to go to work, or jealous of the relationship that the teacher is building with their child. In addition, a parent may have her own unresolved experiences with separation. Any one of these feelings could make separation hard for the parent.

Acknowledging Parents' Feelings about Separation

There are several things teachers can do to help parents recognize and manage their feelings about separation. Most teachers don't have the time or training to be therapists; however, they do have experience with feelings. Your program can include a few lines in your written materials about typical feelings a parent might have during good-byes. Using your network of support, you might invite several parents to write accounts of their feelings when their child began care and share those in a newsletter, as a handout, or as part of the orientation materials. During a parent orientation meeting with several families, parents can be encouraged to share both sad and happy feelings about their child beginning care. Inviting the family to share decision making with you, you can create a plan with a parent about how the separation might go and ask for ideas about ways you can support both child and parent during the good-bye. You can simply acknowledge during the good-bye that both child and parent might feel sad at first when they say good-bye to each other but that it will get easier later. Some parents who seem to have prolonged feelings of sadness over the transition to child care might benefit from a referral to services, such as counseling.

Promoting Attachment through the Separation Process

The separation process is not just about separating; it is also about attachment between children and their families, between children and their teachers, and between teachers and children's families. One of the teacher's most important jobs is supporting the attachment between a child and his parents. Especially for children who are in a program for many hours a day, this is an essential component. When children spend less time with their families, both child and family need support for nurturing their attachment. Interestingly, secure attachment with his family helps a child make a more comfortable attachment with his teacher.

Here are some ways a teacher can support the attachment between a child and his family:

- Post pictures of the child and his family in the classroom.
- Talk to the child about his family during the day.
- Display familiar items from the child's family and culture in the classroom.
- Care for the child in a way that is reasonably consistent with the way his family does.
- Let the child know that the parent is thinking about him throughout the day.
- Tell the child when it is getting close to pick-up time.
- Listen respectfully and patiently to the child's feelings when he is missing his family.
- Sing songs and tell stories about the child's family.

- Learn about the child's home and family, and make references to it throughout the day.
- Help the child develop a ritual to say good-bye to the parent at drop-off time.

Equally important to supporting the child's attachment to the parent is supporting the parent's attachment to the child. Here are some ways a teacher can support the attachment between a parent and a child.

- Talk to the parent at drop-off time to get an update on the child and her family.
- If child has had a particularly difficult good-bye, call the parent to let him know how the child is doing.
- Let the parent know when the child has spent time looking at her family pictures, mentions her family, or cries about missing her family during the day.
- Offer the parent specific information about the child's day at pick-up time.
- Acknowledge parenting strengths you observe.
- Remind the parent of the importance of saying "good-bye" at drop-off time.
- Help the parent develop a ritual to say good-bye to the child.

Nancy, a teacher of three-year-olds, set up an activity for families and children to do together at drop-off time that helped with the good-bye ritual, promoted attachment, and addressed an important health and safety issue. Outside her classroom door, she set up a small table with a basin, a pitcher of water, and a pile of clean terrycloth towels. There were pictures and instructions to help parents and children wash hands together before entering the classroom. Children and adults alike looked forward to this daily routine as part of the child's transition to school.

Other classrooms have picture cards of children that children can move from one slot to another when they arrive and leave school. Some programs encourage preschoolers to sign themselves in on a clipboard next to the parent clipboard. Many programs have a good-bye window, where children can stand and blow kisses to parents as they leave. Pictures of families displayed at child level also provide a transition ritual for some children.

In addition to the attachment between a child and his family, there is the attachment that builds between a child and his teacher. This is an important topic to discuss with families. Because some families may feel threatened about their child becoming attached with the teacher, it is important that families learn that this relationship doesn't negatively affect their child's attachment with them. Knowing this and learning that teachers are also working to support the child's attachment with the parent will help parents be supportive of the teacher-child relationship.

Helping Parents Understand Separation

Thinking about how separation looks to a child is not always easy for adults. Many adults assume that children understand separation the same way the adults do. As child development professionals, you can help parents understand children's thinking about separation. There are many articles and books on the subject that you can make available to parents. And there are some specific points that you can share with parents when they seem ready for the information. Any time you want to offer

information to parents, it is important to be respectful and responsive.

Important points for both teachers and families to know about children's views of separation:

- ◆ Young children don't understand time the same way adults do.
- ◆ Young babies are still working on the concept of object and parent permanence.
- ◆ Many young children don't fully understand that their families are theirs forever.
- ◆ Usually a child cries for a while at drop-off.
- ◆ Some children have an easy good-bye for the first few days and start crying later.
- ◆ It is important to let a child know when her parent is leaving.
- ◆ It is a gift to be trusted with a child's feelings.

YOUNG CHILDREN DON'T UNDERSTAND TIME THE SAME WAY ADULTS DO

Under the age of two, children are focused primarily on the immediate moment, without much understanding that there was a past or will be a future. For a child who is being left for the first time, this may mean that she is focusing more on her sadness about her parent being gone than she is on the possibility that her parent will come back. Somewhat older children may understand that there is a yesterday, today, and tomorrow, but they still do not understand time well enough to know when they will be picked up today. Even older children may feel worried about a parent coming back. It takes time for children to learn the routine and the schedule, so that they can begin to predict the return of their parent.

YOUNG BABIES ARE STILL WORKING ON THE CONCEPT OF OBJECT AND PARENT PERMANENCE

Most babies don't understand that if a parent is out of sight, he still exists. They may need physical reminders of their parents, such as a T-shirt, a photo, or a familiar song.

Many Young Children Don't Fully Understand that Their Families Are Theirs Forever

Young children don't necessarily know that their parents are their parents, no matter what. Some might believe that their parents have dropped them off to be with their new family. It can take them time, experience, and reassurance to trust that their family will still be there for them.

Usually a Child Cries for a While at Drop-Off

Typically children will cry for a while at drop-off and then become interested in playing. Sometimes they will cry off and on a little throughout the day when they miss their family. This is a normal response and doesn't mean that the child isn't doing well. It is part of how a child demonstrates that he is attached to his family and is thinking about them. After the child begins to understand the drop-off and pick-up pattern, he will probably be able to think about his family without being so sad.

Some Children Have an Easy Good-Bye for the First Few Days and Start Crying Later

At first, some children focus on the exciting new environment and people. They are not thinking about their parents being gone. It takes a few days for them to understand that while they are at this wonderful place, their parents are gone; then the children start to miss them. After a while, they will adjust to parents leaving and coming back.

It Is Important to Let a Child Know When Her Parent Is Leaving

It is tempting for parents to wait until a child is involved in an activity and just slip out. However, when the child discovers the parent is gone, she can feel confused, sad, and betrayed. If this pattern continues, the child may become very clingy in an attempt to keep the parent from sneaking out. Even teachers going out on breaks need to let children know that they are leaving. This way children will come to trust that they will know the comings and goings of their important people, they will feel confident to become absorbed in play, and they will learn that that they are entitled to know the whereabouts of their special people.

It Is a Gift to Be Trusted with a Child's Feelings

When a child shares his sad feelings with you, it is a sign that he trusts you to support him with his important feelings. Sometimes a child will save his feelings for the end of the day when his parent arrives, and he will cry the moment he sees his parent. Sometimes a child will feel comfortable enough with a teacher to share feelings with her. Ultima, a teacher of infants, often tells parents at the end of the day, "I felt honored today. Your child cried and shared her feelings with me."

Knowing how a child perceives and experiences separation will help teachers and families develop a plan that best supports each child's beginning in child care.

Helping Young Children Handle Separation

What is the teacher's role in helping children through separation? Understanding and communicating to families the meaning of separation for children are important parts of a teacher's job. Equally important is communicating to parents how the teachers and program will help children (and families) through this experience.

It can be useful to provide families written information to help them understand the transition to child care and how your program supports children through it. Here is a sample handout.

Welcoming Children to Child Care

Starting child care is a significant event for children. This may be a child's first step into the world, his first experience of having someone take care of him who is not part of his family. This could be a child's first time spending all day in an environment different from her home. A child has much to learn from her first experience in a child development program. Here are some of the messages we hope to convey to children as they begin care in our program.

◆ *You will be safe here.*

We will take care of both your physical needs and your emotional needs. We will make sure that you are well fed, well rested, clean, and safe. Equally importantly, we want you to know that all of your feelings will be respected. Your happiness, excitement, delight, sadness, frustration, and fear are all feelings we value. If you need to cry, we will offer listening, support, and comfort.

◆ *You will be taken care of by a special person whom you will get to know very well.*

Your special person will learn your communication style, and you will learn hers. She will talk to you about your family and will help you when you are missing your family.

◆ *Every day your family will come to pick you up and take you home.*

There will be a predictable schedule that will help you to learn when you can expect to be picked up. Also, your teacher will let you know when pick-up time is getting close. When it is pick-up time, your teacher will let your family know all about your day at school.

◆ *Your family is welcome here too.*

Your family is an important part of this program. They might spend time here talking to your teachers or other families, watching you play, or helping in the program. We plan to have pictures of your family displayed where you can always see them.

◆ *You will also get to know other teachers, children, and families here when you are ready. As well as your special teacher, there are other people you get to meet, play with, watch, and talk to. When you are ready, you will be able to make new friends.*

◆ *There are lots of fun and interesting things to explore here, and you can choose what you want to play with.*

This is a place for you to explore when you are ready. There will be things for you to play and learn with; there will be active and quiet activities for you; and there will be things to do with friends and with teachers and things to do alone. Most of the time, you will get to choose what you want to do.

We look forward to working with you to make your child's transition to child care a wonderful start to his or her time in our program.

Warming In

Some programs have developed a "warming-in" phase as children are beginning care. This time gives the child, caregiver, and family a chance to spend time together getting to know each other—ideally, both at home and in the center setting. There are several things that happen during this getting-to-know-you period. It is a time to establish the practice of two-way communication, respect for one another's knowledge and expertise, and shared decision making. Warming in provides an individualized, personal orientation to all involved. Teachers have the opportunity to see the child and parent together, how they interact, and how they communicate. Teachers can learn the song that the parent sings during diapering; they can see how the child eats and where she sleeps. The child gets to see the parents and teacher together. This is one of the most important relationships in the child's life. From the beginning the child will be watching to see whether these two important people like each other, trust each other, respect each other, and communicate with each other. Children spend a lot of time "social referencing," that is, reading the cues from their important people to tell them about the world. As the child meets the new teacher, she is implicitly asking the parent, "Is this a safe person? Is it all right with you if I like her? Do you think I should trust her? Can she take good care of me while you are gone?" The child's ability to make a successful transition to a program is directly tied to how she perceives the parent-teacher relationship.

Finally, during the warming-in period, the family gets to see the teacher and child together. Actually witnessing someone care for and about your child can be very reassuring to parents, especially parents who haven't had anyone outside the family take care of their child before. All of the observing, the talking, and the sharing of ideas that go on in the warming-in period help to build the relationships that create the secure network of care for children.

The warming-in period can be structured in many different ways. In one infant program that operates during the school year on a college campus, there is time for a week-long warming-in period. The plan involves a primary caregiver making two visits to the infant's home alternated by the infant and parent making three visits to the center. These visits to the center offer a chance for parents and babies to start meeting the other families in the program, as well as the staff. This happens the week before the child begins to stay at the center by himself. In addition, there is a parent meeting for parents to begin to meet each other and be oriented to the program together.

Warming in for older children and for year-round programs may look somewhat different, but the elements are mostly the same. Many programs don't have the staff time and availability to do this kind of intensive warming in, but it is important to think about what warming in can offer and if there are simpler ways to incorporate elements of it into your own program.

One important thing to remember is that not all children's and families' needs are the same around warming in. This can be influenced by temperament, past experience with child care, and family culture. Even if your program has a standard orientation procedure, it is important to discuss it with the new family to see if it will meet their needs. Further, you and the family may discover once you are into the transition that you need to make some changes to your standard procedures.

For example, Lonnie, a toddler teacher, tells the story of twenty-two-month-old Nate and his mother, Cathy.

> We had done the traditional warming in with a home visit and a few center visits in which a family member stayed with Nate. After two program visits, the family began leaving him. He cried for several days. I'm comfortable with children's crying and know that it is an important part of their learning to say good-bye. But Nate's crying was longer and harder than most children I had known. I was talking to Cathy every day, and we were both trying to figure out how to help him feel safe in our program. Finally, we looked at Cathy's schedule and figured out that she could spend some more time with him in the program. After she was in the classroom a few more times, you could see Nate venturing out to play for longer periods of time. Two weeks later, she was able to leave again, this time more successfully.

As part of the transition to child care, parents and families may spend a significant amount of time in the classroom. This provides a chance for families to start developing friendships and networks with other families and children, and it helps families learn how things are done in the program. For some teachers, this is fairly comfortable. For others, there are some issues to address. Some of the issues raised when families act as teachers in the classroom may also come up when families are visiting a lot as part of the warming-in process. See more about this in chapter 11.

IMPROVING OUR ORIENTATIONS, ONE STEP AT A TIME

If you were going to add one element to your program's orientation process to improve a child's transition to care, what would it be? Is this something you can do on your own, or do you need the support of coworkers, administration, or both? What would be a first step you could take?

HOME VISITS

A visit to a family at home provides a special kind of connection to the program. It gives the child a chance to meet with the teacher in the safety of the family home environment. It gives the teacher a chance to see the family in their most comfortable surroundings and gives the family a message that their family and culture are valued by the teacher. Further, it gives the teacher, child, and family a chance to build their shared history. The home provides a wonderful place to acknowledge diversity, respect one another's knowledge, have two-way conversations, and begin to share decision making for the child. Visits to a family's home often give teachers a sense of a family's existing networks.

Children have been known to refer often and with pride to a home visit from their teacher. Three-year-old Raja said to his teacher several months after a visit, "'Member yesterday when you comed to my house?" Teachers find that home visits give them information about children and families that can help them plan curriculum

and provide more responsive care. Bo, a teacher in a four- and five-year-old classroom worked with Mario's grandfather to create a unit on corn after a visit to Mario's home and corn patch. When ten-month-old Laine pointed to the pig on his diaper and said, "Ze-da," his teacher recognized that he was talking about his cat, Zelda, whom she had met on the home visit. When two-year-old Tadashi began loudly hitting all the surfaces in the classroom, teacher Beatriz understood that he was doing Taiko drumming, which she had seen pictures of his father doing at the home visit.

Home visits also offer opportunities to take pictures of children's families. This can provide representation of all families in the classroom, even those who don't have easy access to a camera. One teacher who was sensitive to children living in different kinds of housing took pictures of families by their front doors. Another teacher took pictures of a child and her family at the bus stop, where they waited for the bus to take them to school. Teacher Gabe asks children and families, "What pictures would you like me to take of your home to take back to school?" Children enjoy seeing pictures of themselves and their families displayed in their classrooms. Pictures help children feel that their families are honored and also document the home visit for later discussion.

Depending on the goals of the program and the family, different kinds of home visits may be used. One kind of home visit is part of the orientation to the program; the child and family are able to have one of their first meetings with the teacher in their own home. Often the purpose of this visit is to establish trust and get to know one another better. In this type of visit, the teacher spends time with both the child (meeting the child's favorite toy or reading a special book) and with other family members (seeing the family garden or photo album, tasting a family recipe, watching big sister on her new skates, or hearing a family story). Another type of visit might be for the program to help families fill out forms or give the program enrollment information.

Home visits can also happen after the child has been in the program for a while as a way for the teacher, child, and family to connect and get to know each other better. Some programs schedule home visits when a child is having a hard time adjusting to child care as a way to help the child make the bridge from the safety of her home to child care.

Marleena recalls doing home visits as a new teacher. "I didn't realize until I had done several home visits that I had been making assumptions about the children in my group and what their families and homes were like. I guess I just thought that every family looked like mine and that every home was like mine. But when I started visiting every corner of the county and seeing where people lived, I was really touched, and I slowly started to understand that it isn't the size of a child's house or having his own bed that makes a difference in that child's happiness, well-being, or school success. It's the way the family relates to each other, the way they spend time together, that makes the difference."

Challenges to Home Visits

As well as benefits to home visits, there are multiple challenges. Many families feel uncomfortable or self-conscious about where they live. It may feel embarrassing to have the teacher come to see their home. Families may also feel threatened by someone in a position of authority coming to their home, and they fear being evaluated and/or reported. Some families may not live in a "home of their own." This includes homeless families and those who live in shelters, with friends, or with other family members. Many families have the experience of feeling that their parenting is judged by the way their home looks to the teacher. Knowing some of the possible issues for families in relation to home visits helps teachers approach home visiting more sensitively and responsively.

Teachers may feel some discomfort with home visits as well. Home visits may take them to neighborhoods they aren't familiar with. Some teachers who are temperamentally slow-to-warm or "private" people may feel uncomfortable or out of place in a new person's home. Teachers may feel concerned about their ability to put a family at ease during the visit or may worry that they won't know what to say. Further, if teachers are expected to do home visits but are not adequately compensated for their time, they may feel resentful. Knowing yourself as a teacher can help you design home visiting in ways that increase your own comfort as well as that of the family.

REFLECTING ON YOUR OWN EXPERIENCES AS A CHILD

Do you remember any special visitors to your home as a child? Clergy, family, friends, teachers, the ice cream vendor? How did you feel about these visits? How did your family feel? If a teacher never visited your home, imagine what it might feel like to have one of your favorite teachers come to visit you to see where you sleep and what you play with.

Helping Families Feel Comfortable with Home Visits

Teachers and programs have found many sensitive and creative ways to address the challenges inherent in home visiting. Many programs include a section in the parent handbook about home visits. Some programs write a letter to families before scheduling home visits. Others put up a note on the bulletin board about home visits, along with the sign-up sheet. It is important to include information to families about the purposes of home visits, who will be visiting, and the length of the visit. It is useful to let parents know that home visits are a regular part of the program and that all families are offered one. You can include quotes from children and families who have enjoyed visits in the past. It is also helpful to families to know what to expect on a home visit. You can let them know what you think might happen and also ask them what they would like to happen. You can tell families that home visits are different depending on the child and the family. Some children are very quiet for a few minutes (it can be very different to have the teacher at your house) before warming up and taking charge of the visit. There are children and families who like to tour the teacher all over their home, and there are those who will have the whole visit on the front porch. Some visits may be taken up with reading books to the child the entire time; others may involve talking to the parent while the child sits on her lap for the whole visit. Once you have given parents an idea of what you expect, you can ask them if there is anything that they would like to have happen on the visit. Keeping the tone informal and friendly will help ease some of the anxiety parents may have.

Another alternative that some families appreciate is meeting with the teacher outside of school but not in their home. Local parks, a child-friendly restaurant, or a community center can provide a space to make a special teacher-child-family connection.

One teacher had this story to tell about a home visit:

Demetra's family kept putting off the home visit. "This week's not a good week; I've got cousins visiting. Next week won't work because I'm going to be too busy." I finally figured out that they might be really uncomfortable with the idea of me coming to their home, so I asked if we could meet somewhere else besides their home. We made an appointment for the next Saturday at the park in her neighborhood. It was interesting because at the end of our visit, Eleonora looked at Demetra and said, "Maybe next time Teacher Londa will visit us at our house." I think it took that first step for

Eleonora to feel safe enough to imagine that I could come to her house.

Here is an example of a letter to families to introduce the concept of home visits and ask families to sign up for one.

Dear Families,

It is the time of the year when teachers plan to visit children and families at home. This is a wonderful tradition in our program that gives children the special experience of sharing their home and family with their teacher. Children often remember the visits months and years after they occur. This is not a formal visit, and there is nothing you need to do to prepare for it. We expect children's homes to look "lived in." Visits last between thirty and forty-five minutes. If you would be more comfortable arranging a meeting at a local park with your teacher, that would be fine. Please talk to your child's teacher to arrange a good time for a visit.

Helping Teachers Feel Comfortable with Home Visits

Teachers may also have some discomfort, anxiety, or uncertainty doing home visits. There are several ways these feelings can be addressed. In some programs new teachers accompany experienced teachers on a few home visits before doing their own. It can also be helpful for new teachers to role-play with a coworker some of the conversations for planning and doing home visits. It can also help new teachers to talk to some families who have had home visits about their experiences. Teachers may appreciate an outline of possible activities on a home visit. For instance:

- Talk with the family before the visit to let them know it will be informal and that you are open to whatever they and their child would like to show you.
- Remind the family that you are coming to visit them and not their house. (You don't need

them to clean up especially for you.)

- Agree on a time and a length for the visit. Let the family know how much time you have available, and ask how long they would like the visit to be.

- Ask the parent if there is anything he would like to do on the visit.

- Get directions (from the family or from the Internet).

- Meet and greet all the family members who are present.

- Ask the child if there is anything she would like to show you.

- Accept simple food, if offered.

- Ask permission if you would like to take pictures. Ask for family input about what they would like you to photograph.

- Notice and mention interesting things in the environment, if it seems appropriate. (You might ask questions like these: "There are a lot of people in this picture. Can you tell me about them?" "This is a beautiful piece of cloth. Is it special to your family?")

- Give the child a notice when you have five minutes left, so she can get ready for you to leave.

After the Home Visit

Documenting the visit provides an experience in literacy and memory for children. If you put up pictures and words about the visit, the child can start to recognize symbols and words about his family and also have his memory rekindled about the visit. This kind of documentation may also help reluctant families see what a home visit looks like and feel safer about a visit to their home. You can also write a thank-you note to the family that mentions what happened while you were there and expresses your appreciation of the visit. Additionally, you can cocreate songs, stories, and finger plays with the child about the visit.

Here's an example of a simple song a teacher made up about her home visits. This is a "zipper" song—any child's name and activity can be "zipped" into the song.

I went to Kirtan's house, Kirtan's house, Kirtan's house

I went to Kirtan's house and _____
(saw his kitty, ate some lumpia, played with his ball)

Reverse Home Visits

A few programs also invite children and families to visit the teacher's home. This can be done in an open-house format or by appointment. Young children (who often believe that teachers live at the center) are fascinated to see their teachers' homes, and children's families often feel honored to be included in these reverse home visits. Vicki, a veteran teacher, relates:

It used to be one of my favorite activities, having children visit my home. They said the funniest things. Some would ask where the playdough was, as if it was something I took wherever I went. They always wanted to see my refrigerator, toilet, and bed. They loved my cat. The next day, back at school, I could feel a shift in our relationship. They were excited to talk about my house. Some asked me every day how my cat was. I think it was important for them to see me as a whole person. I could feel a shift in parents, as well. I think they felt closer to me and more trusting.

Index

Other Resources from 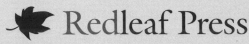 Redleaf Press

THE PARENT NEWSLETTER: A COMPLETE GUIDE FOR EARLY CHILDHOOD PROFESSIONALS

Sylvia Reichel

 Written by a trusted educator with years of experience, this practical how-to guide provides a step-by-step process for creating and implementing a parent newsletter— from advice on writing effective articles, to design and layout suggestions, to scheduling and distribution.

#536501-BR **$24.95**

TRANSITION MAGICIAN FOR FAMILIES: HELPING PARENTS AND CHILDREN WITH EVERYDAY ROUTINES

Ruth Chvojicek, Mary Henthorne & Nola Larson

 Transition Magician for Families includes more than 100 easy-to-make activities for both home and away, as well as reproducible activity handouts and outlines for two transitions workshops for parents.

#532201-BR **$19.95**

SO THIS IS NORMAL TOO? TEACHERS AND PARENTS WORKING OUT DEVELOPMENTAL ISSUES IN YOUNG CHILDREN

Deborah Hewitt

 The best guide for coping with perplexing behavior, *So This Is Normal Too?* includes easy-to-follow reproducible materials for building cooperation between parents and children. Also available in a new version just for parents, *Behavior Matters.*

#153901-BR **$19.95**

PARENT-FRIENDLY EARLY LEARNING: TIPS AND STRATEGIES FOR WORKING WELL WITH PARENTS

Julie Powers

 Parent-Friendly Early Learning shows how to turn parent problems into warm, confident relationships by improving parent-teacher communication, understanding a parent's perspective, addressing a parent's fears, developing and upholding policies, discussing child development, and sharing information with parents.

#535801-BR **$22.95**

USE YOUR WORDS: HOW TEACHER TALK HELPS CHILDREN LEARN

Carol Garhart Mooney

 The connection between the ways we speak and the ways children behave and learn are examined in this humorous and thoughtful guide. Commonly missed opportunities to support cognitive development through meaningful conversation, develop receptive language and expressive language, and avoid and address behavioral issues in the classroom are reviewed.

#155401-BR **$18.95**

ROUTINES AND TRANSITIONS: A GUIDE FOR EARLY CHILDHOOD PROFESSIONALS

Nicole Malenfant

 A complete guide to turning the most routine daily activities, such as hand washing, snacks, and naptime, into nuturing experiences for young children from birth to five. This is an excellent training manual for new staff.

#134101-BR **$34.95**

Product availability and pricing are subject to change without notice.

800-423-8309 • **www.redleafpress.org**